Orby Shipley

Eucharistic meditations for a month

Orby Shipley

Eucharistic meditations for a month

ISBN/EAN: 9783742838261

Manufactured in Europe, USA, Canada, Australia, Japa

Cover: Foto ©Lupo / pixelio.de

Manufactured and distributed by brebook publishing software (www.brebook.com)

Orby Shipley

Eucharistic meditations for a month

Eucharistic Meditations for a Month:

TRANSLATED AND ABRIDGED FROM THE FRENCH OF AVRILLON;

With an Appendix.

Second Thousand.

EDITED BY
THE REV. ORBY SHIPLEY, M.A.

London:
JOSEPH MASTERS, ALDERSGATE STREET,
AND NEW BOND STREET.
1864.

Contents.

MEDITATION	PAGE
I. Of the Benefits & Blessings of the most Holy Communion	1
II. Of the Same	13
III. Of the Same	25
IV. Of the Same	36
V. Of the Adorable FLESH of JESUS CHRIST in the most Holy Communion	46
VI. Of the Precious BLOOD of JESUS CHRIST	56
VII. Of the Same	67
VIII. Of His HEART	78
IX. Of His SPIRIT	90
X. Of His SOUL	101
XI. Of His LIFE	113
XII. Of the Same	124
XIII. Of His DIVINITY	134
XIV. Of the General Preparation before the Blessed Sacrament	142
XV. Of the Preparation of Faith	152
XVI. Of the Preparation of Hope	161
XVII. Of the Preparation of Love	170

Contents.

MEDITATION		PAGE
XVIII.	Of the Preparation of Purity .	180
XIX.	Of the Preparation of Humility .	190
XX.	Of the Preparation of Desire .	200
XXI.	Of the Effects of Reception of this Holy Eucharist . . .	209
XXII.	Of Union with JESUS CHRIST in It	219
XXIII.	Of the Advantages of frequent Reception of It	228
XXIV.	Of neglecting to approach It .	239
XXV.	Of receiving It in trouble . .	247
XXVI.	Of receiving It in barrenness of spirit	258
XXVII.	Of receiving It in lukewarmness of spirit	267
XXVIII.	Of receiving It in Reparation .	277

Appendix.

Acts of Christian Virtues in preparation for the Blessed Sacrament	287
Conferences between the Disciple & the Divine Master, after Holy Communion . .	308
Aspirations after the Blessed Sacrament .	321
Affections on the Sacrament of Love . .	325
Acts of Contrition	333
Eucharistic Prayers	344

EUCHARISTIC MEDITATIONS FOR A MONTH.

Eucharistic Meditations.

First Meditation.

Of the Benefits & Blessings of the most Holy Communion.

I.

SINCE the most Holy Communion is the Sacrament of all Sacraments, the Love of all Love, & the Sweetness of all Sweetness; & since Almighty GOD is Wholly Present therein, both in His HUMANITY, & in His DIVINITY, the Blessed Eucharist can contain nothing but what is Great, Wonderful, & very Blessed. For not only does It contain Him in a Sovereign Degree, but It also communicates Him bountifully to all those who, with hearts duly prepared, worthily draw nigh unto this Holy Sacrament.

The Divine Eucharist is the Sacrament of all Sacraments, because It is the most Holy, the most Noble, the most Sublime, & the most Wonder-working of all the Blessed Sacraments under the

the New Dispensation. It is the Sacrament of all Sacraments, because It communicates to us a CREATOR, a SOVEREIGN, a SAVIOUR, a SPOUSE, a MEDIATOR, a Heavenly PHYSICIAN, & a GOD, with all the glorious Attributes which belong to Him—with His Holiness, His Power, His Mercy, His Goodness, His Spirit, His Sanctity, His Gentleness, His Grace, & all other Heavenly Attributes assumed in His Sacred HUMANITY, or inherent in His DIVINITY, which, in some ineffable manner, are given unto us in this August & Venerable Sacrament. Such are some of the Benefits & Blessings we receive in this Sacrament of all Sacraments, if we hinder not Its Efficacy by our sins or by our lukewarmness; & if we present ourselves before the Altar with a chastened Spirit, & an earnest Desire to be made One with GOD, with profound Humility, & with fervent Charity.

Those who love GOD with all their hearts, & who often approach the Blessed Sacrament, possess a happy experience of these Divine Workings in their Souls. The Effects which result from the Visit of so Holy a HUMANITY, & so Perfect a DIVINITY, influence them, nourish them, & continue with them, purifying, elevating, & sanctifying their Souls, & even transforming them, to such an extent, that they are no longer themselves, but can say, in humble confidence, with the great Apostle—*I live; yet not I, but CHRIST liveth in me.*

Again,

Again, the Blessed Eucharist is the Love of all Love, because It is the Sacrament in which the GOD of Heaven has most completely humbled Himself for the Love of us; in Which He makes the greatest efforts to regain our Love; in Which the creature receives the largest amount of Grace; & by Which she is the most highly exalted. It is the Love of all Love, since, by It, the Soul participates in the Divine Nature, & in all GOD's most precious Treasures; for in It she possesses the GOD from Whom they are all derived. Could the GOD of all Goodness prove more practically the exceeding greatness of His Love, than by coming down from the Throne of His Majesty, to redeem us; to take up His Abode in us, Spiritually & Personally; to place Himself in our hearts; to fill us with Grace, Blessing, & Love; to become our Food & Sustenance; to unite Himself to us, Heart to heart, & if I may venture to say so, Substance to substance, so as to give us certain Pledges of the Eternal Union with which we shall be One with Him in Heaven, provided only we make a worthy use of that Union, in Holy Communion, which we have the happiness to possess in this our earthly pilgrimage?

This Ever-Blessed Sacrament is also the Sweetness of all Sweetness, & the most pure of all Delights; because we derive both Delight & Sweetness from their Fountain Head. From this Perennial Spring, so full & so abundant, we we draw at the Holy Communion. It comes nigh unto us, It washes us, It cleanses us from our sins, It interpenetrates us, It slakes our thirst, & It only asks of us, in return, to realize Its Sacred Presence within our Souls. It is an ineffable Sweetness, because It is a Divine One, because it surpasses all pleasures that earth can bestow.

What deep reverence ought we not to cultivate towards such an All-holy Sacrament? What desires & longings ought we not to feel, when we draw nigh unto it? What return does not that extreme Love deserve, which JESUS CHRIST expresses towards us in the Blessed Eucharist, Which may truly be called the Sacrament of Love? What innocence, again, & purity of heart, should we not possess to be made worthy to taste the Celestial Sweetness, Which makes Itself felt in the hearts of those only which are pure, & free both from earthly attachments, & from all created pleasures? What chaste & holy pleasure is it, to be partakers of a GOD, Who is Sweetness Itself? But, above all, at what a distance should we not keep the poisonous pleasures of the world, the flesh, & the senses, which corrupt the taste of this Heavenly Manna, & which prevent our realizing, at His Sacred Altar, how Sweet the LORD is?

Let us make ourselves worthy, then, to participate in all the Gifts & Graces of this most Blessed Sacrament. Let us bring thither hearts so pure, & so well prepared, that we may lose none of them. Close we carefully the avenues of our hearts to all that is false, flattering, & seductive in the creature; & open we them to receive this GOD of Majesty, Who comes so nigh unto us, & Whose Visit is so blessed unto us. Strive all we can to feel the inestimable Benefits of this Eternal & Incomprehensible Love, which desires only to impart Itself unto us, to purify, & to transform us. Lastly, let us prepare, & purify our hearts for Its reception with all possible diligence, from all the vain & perishable attractions of a seducing world, to make them more worthy of that Super-Substantial Food; being well assured that it is GOD Alone Who is able to fulfil & satisfy them.

II.

Never forget that, in Holy Communion, JESUS CHRIST gives Himself to you unreservedly; that He gives you His FLESH, His BLOOD, His SPIRIT, His SOUL, & His DIVINITY; & remember, that to each one of His Gifts is attached a Virtue, for your benefit. Let us then consider these Gifts in detail, meditating separately upon each of them, that we may lose none of the infinite Treasure that is offered each time we draw near unto the Holy Altar of GOD.

In the Virginal FLESH of JESUS CHRIST is inherent a Spirit of Purity, Innocence, & Sanctification, to consecrate our flesh, to bring it into subjection to the Spirit; to restrain its natural inclinations towards sensual pleasures, & the repugnance it feels towards penitence & mortification; & to efface from it even the slightest tendency to sin. Say we then, to ourselves before Holy Communion—O Divine FLESH, Thou art about to come in contact with my flesh; Thou art about to become enclosed within me, & there to take up Thy Abode with me; & pray earnestly for Benefit from so intimate an Union; that your flesh may be endowed with a portion of His incomparable Purity.

To the Adorable BLOOD of our Blessed LORD is joined a Spirit of Expiation. He satisfies, in our stead, the severity of Almighty Justice; He also makes us meet to withstand the Judgment of His Heavenly FATHER, for all the sins we have committed since our Baptism; & He ever lives to make Intercession for us. This Allholy BLOOD, shed for our sakes, speaks within us, with more energy, & cries more loudly than that of innocent Abel, not to the Throne of Righteousness, for vengeance, but to that of Mercy, for pardon. Nor is it ever refused. Moreover, let us pray, that this Divine & Sacred BLOOD may nourish us, sustain us, & give us strength; that It may effectually arm us against our enemies, & against ourselves; that It may help us, boldly & with success, to enter into the thorny path of penitence; & may keep us steadfast in the same unto the end.

Within

Within the Sacred HEART of JESUS, in this Adorable Sacrifice, which may well be called the Sacrament of His HEART, since He gives It to us Wholly, is found a Spirit of Sanctity & of Love. This Spirit is best shown forth in us, by a lively, burning Faith, which gives us new increase of fervour, to enable us to find pleasure & delight in the severest proofs that Almighty GOD requires of our attachment.

To His Divine SPIRIT, Which we receive in the Blessed Eucharist, is united the Grace of Supernatural Light, which enlightens us, & conducts us in the Way that leads to Everlasting Life; which carries the Torch of Truth into our Spirits, hearts, & Souls, to enlighten our darkness; to heal our blindness; to instruct our ignorance; to clear away all our doubts; to bring us back from our errors, obstinacies, & prejudices; to give us submission & docility to all Christian Virtues; to increase our Faith, & to make it more prompt, & desirous to obey & submit itself to the Commands of GOD; in a word, to give the Soul a more perfect knowledge of GOD, & of itself.

The All-holy SOUL of our Blessed SAVIOUR conveys the Grace of Redemption, which is renewed in us, & on our behalf, as often as we communicate worthily. For this Redemption was fulfilled once on Calvary, when our Adorable SAVIOUR committed His SOUL into the Hands of His Heavenly FATHER, at that precious moment

ment in which His Sacrifice & our Redemption were consummated; & is now extended to us in this most Blessed Sacrament of the Altar.

In the LIFE of JESUS CHRIST, in this Holy Sacrifice, is present the Grace of Life, of an inward & supernatural Life, which is none other than the Life of Grace. United in this LIFE to CHRIST, we live in Him, & He in us; we live with Him, & for Him, according to His Divine Words; all our actions are evidences of that Divine LIFE, which sustains, & strengthens us, & renders us less susceptible to the temptations of the Devil.

By the DIVINITY of our Blessed LORD, in Holy Communion, is effected the Grace of Illumination & Transformation. We come out of our own being, as it were, & enter into the BEING of GOD. We cease, after some sort, to be what we are, so as to participate in the Divine Nature, & to be wondrously transformed into that of GOD. This is the ineffable working of DIVINITY which, when we have worthily prepared our hearts to receive It, comes to us in the Blessed Eucharist.

Lastly, to the Sacrament of the Eucharistic Sacrifice, in Itself, belongs the Grace of Spiritual Nourishment, to make the Spiritual Man arise from the remains of him who is earthly—provided always, that the Heavenly Food meets with nothing corrupt or impure in our hearts; no sin festering there; & no lukewarmness, to
prevent

prevent our digesting & incorporating into ourselves this strong & life-giving Nourishment.

Let all these Graces be profitable unto us. Forfeit none of them by neglect. And since they are offered unto us as often as we communicate, we may continually possess them; & in possessing them, we are enriched by them for time, & for all eternity.

Affections.

Enter into thyself, & search after thy GOD, O my Soul. He is doubtless there, if thou hast had the blessed privilege to communicate worthily. He is there, not by His Power, nor by His Infinity, nor by His Grace; but He is there in Substance, Personally, in thy Soul & in thy body. There is no need for thee to search after the Throne of Almighty GOD in Heaven; to address thy prayers to Him, thy vows, & adorations;* to offer unto Him thy Homage, thy Acts of Love & Gratitude. Go not out of thyself, for He is within thee. Thy heart is at present His Throne; it is the Temple, the Sanctuary, the Altar whereon the Majesty of GOD dwells, the animated Heaven, wherein Angels adore beside thee. Speak to Him thyself, as if He were thyself; but let it be in the accents of the heart which He loves, & hearkens unto far better than those of the lips. Invoke lovingly, & one by one, His FLESH, His BLOOD, His HEART,

Heart, His Spirit, His Soul, & His Divinity, since They are all Present unto thee.

O most Pure Flesh of Jesus, Which art united unto mine, in the Blessed Eucharist; O Flesh, at once Divine & Human, I adore Thee from the bottom of my heart. Purify, sanctify, & consecrate, I beseech Thee, this sinful flesh of mine, that is vivified by Thine; & bring it under subjection for ever.

O Adorable Blood of Jesus, wash me throughly; blot out, & remove far away all my uncleanness; perfect my reconciliation; & be Thou the Sacred Character wherewith my name may be indelibly written in the Book of Life, for admission to that Kingdom of Heaven which Thou didst open by the shedding of Thy Blood on Calvary.

O Divine Heart of Jesus, Fount of purest Love, Object of my deepest desires & affections, unite Thyself to my heart for ever; bestow upon it Thy Divine Fervour; & extinguish in it, for ever, that strange fire which carries it not straight towards Thee.

O Spirit of Jesus, enlighten my darkness, & drive from my spirit all those empty phantoms which the spirit of error has introduced there; & do Thou cause the Spirit of Truth to reign supreme.

O most Holy Soul of the All-Merciful Jesus, save Thou my Soul; & never allow that to be lost, which Thou hast suffered the most cruel of Deaths to save.

O Hid-

O Hidden Divinity of Jesus, with Which I am now fulfilled, strengthen me; nourish me; take me out of myself, to be transformed into Thee; make me worthy to behold Thee, to love, & adore Thee in Spirit & in Truth, for the remainder of my life; & after my death, grant that I may possess Thee eternally in Heaven.

Thanksgiving.

O Sacrament of Sacraments, Love of Love, & Sweetness of all Sweetness, God the All-powerful, God at once both Priest & Victim for love of me, how can I, wretched creature that I am, how can I render unto Thee worthy Acts of Thanksgiving? How can I make them meet for the infinite Benefits I have received from Thy Divine Charity, to which Thou hast placed no bounds; since in giving Thyself Wholly unto me, in Holy Communion, Thou dost give unto me not only all Thou hast, but also all Thou art, as God & Man? The Priest, Thy Servant, invokes Thee; &, notwithstanding Thou art God, Thou hearkenest unto him, Thou comest unto me from Heaven, as if Thou wast born on wings of Love. Thou comest, all Great & Glorious as Thou art. Thou dost voluntarily become enclosed within the habitation of my sinful breast, to visit me, to live in me, to fill me with Thy Grace, to nourish me with Thy Substance,

Substance, & to take up Thy Abode within my Soul.

O LORD JESU, I am now Thy living Temple; &, without going out of myself, can listen unto Thee; can speak unto Thee; can ask of Thee, & beg from Thee, new Blessings; & I can give Thee Thanks for those Graces I have already received at Thy Holy Altar. This I purpose to do at the blessed moment in which I receive Thee, O my GOD. Help me, LORD, to do so as I ought.

O most Blessed Sacrament, what Treasures dost Thou contain. O ineffable Love, what Attractions dost Thou possess. O infinite Sweetness, what Delights Thou dost impart to those that love Thee, to those that worthily & with desire approach unto Thee.

Most Pure FLESH, Most Precious BLOOD, SPIRIT of Truth, All-holy SOUL, Adorable DIVINITY of JESUS, Thou art in me, I possess Thee, Thou art One with me. Strengthen me, I beseech Thee, that I may make more acceptable Acts of Thanksgiving unto Thee, & that my Soul may be interpenetrated with the remembrance of Thy Benefits & Blessings in the most Holy Eucharist.

Second Meditation.

Of the Benefits & Blessings of the most Holy Communion.

I.

The Act of Communion not only includes the Reception of the BODY, BLOOD, SOUL, SPIRIT, & DIVINITY of our Blessed LORD JESUS CHRIST, but also the participation in the most intimate & transcendental manner of His Purity, His Love, & His Mercy, of His Holiness & His Glory, of His Divine Attributes, & of His Adorable PERSON Itself.

Be careful then, that your Communion be a true Communication. In other words, that as, in the world, property may be shared in common by two persons united by the fellowship of love in Holy Matrimony, who mutually & by solemn pledges give each other all that they possess; so, in this Holy Sacrament, Which emphatically may be called an Union between CHRIST & the Faithful Soul, GOD gives to you, & you give to GOD; He gives you Himself; you give to Him all that you have, & all that you are, & you give it to Him for ever.

You never possess CHRIST more perfectly than

than when you give yourself up to Him entirely & unreservedly; & in exchange, He gives you, & gives liberally, all that He has received from His Heavenly FATHER, together with Himself; all that He possesses, & all that He is, as GOD & MAN. Hence, since you possess very little, & the little you do possess comes from Him, & belongs to Him more than to yourself, & since He possesses all things, consider how full of Blessing must be the change, & how unreasonable it is to deprive yourself of so great a Benefit, One Which you can so easily obtain, & Which costs you nothing but the worthy Reception that He requires at your hand—a Reception not above that you are able.

The Grace of this Communion consists, then, in the annihilation of the earthy & physical man, in order to take unto himself the Strength, the Feelings, the Spirit, the Deeds, & the Life of the Heavenly & Supernatural MAN, Who is CHRIST JESUS our LORD. We enter into the Nature of the Nourishment we receive; we are endued with all Its Graces, Virtues, & Benefits; & this Precious Food, Which incorporates us into Itself, & Which makes us One with It, is none other than GOD made MAN, for love of us.

Let us be well assured, that to communicate worthily is something much more than merely to clothe oneself with the LORD JESUS CHRIST; because a garment is only external to oneself, & alters not at all our substance. True it is, that

by

by an Act of Virtue, or of Humility, or of Patience, or of Love, we put on the LORD JESUS, as the Apostle says; but to receive CHRIST in the Blessed Eucharist, is to be nourished by Him, is to be incorporated into Him, is to participate in His Divine Substance, to possess His Rights, to live His Life, & to make Him live ours—in short, to use the words of the same great Apostle, to become *Members of His BODY, of His FLESH, & of His BONES.*

It is thus that S. Paul speaks to the Corinthians—*Ye are the Body of CHRIST, & Members in particular.* And lest they, through false humility, should doubt the many Benefits which the Blessed Eucharist ensures for them, if they receive It worthily & sufficiently often, the Apostle, in order to comfort them, adds these comfortable words—*The Bread Which we break, is It not the Communion of the BODY of CHRIST?* And if you approach GOD's Altar, as did these early Christians; you, as they were, are also Members of the BODY of our Blessed LORD. For, through the Working of this Divine Nourishment, you lay aside the weaknesses & frailty of the creature, & take unto yourselves the Strength & Steadfastness of GOD made MAN, for the love of man. All that you are, as sinful, sensual beings, must perish & come to nought, or must be absorbed into the Divine, by the efficacious & superhuman Influences of this Heavenly Food. The BODY of JESUS has the Power to transform into Itself

those

those who receive It, who are nourished by It, & who know how to benefit by the Gifts & Graces inherent in the FLESH, the BLOOD, the SOUL, the DIVINITY of an Almighty GOD.

Since our great High Priest possesses sufficient Power to consecrate the mere creatures of Bread & Wine, into His Precious BODY & His All-saving BLOOD; & by the Words of Consecration with the Co-operation of His HOLY SPIRIT, to become Present on the Altars of the Church, Himself both GOD & MAN; how much more is He not able to change you into Himself—you who are reasonable & responsible beings, made in GOD's Own Image, & created after His Likeness, who have a mind to know Him, & a heart to love Him, & in whom He already dwells by the Power of His Grace. Surely this Bread of Angels, our daily Super-substantial Food, so oftentimes Incarnate, so to speak, within your very selves, cannot fail to produce, in your substance, a new Creature differing from the old, new instincts, new feelings, new desires, new aspirations, & a new life.

Ask yourselves then, the reason why, after so many Communions, you have failed to realise these blessed Effects of Sacramental Union with your Divine MASTER? And be not ashamed to make answer to the question thus—Because I have not approached His Altar with sufficient Faith, & Purity, & Love. Yes, O my GOD, I well know that, through lukewarmness, I have

hindered

hindered the reception of those Graces, Which Thou hast prepared for them that love Thee, in the most Holy Communion. May all that I inherit from the old Adam be buried within me; may all carnal desires die; all human & interested inclinations die; all lukewarmness, & indolence die; & all excessive care for myself, & inordinate love for the creature die, come to nought, & utterly perish.

I am nourished by the very Substance of my GOD, Which transforms me into Itself, Which destroys whatever I am by myself, & whatever I have become by sin. O LORD of all Goodness, what purity, what illumination should not I have possessed, had I but prepared myself, each time I ventured to approach Thy Holy Altar, with greater carefulness to communicate in Thy BODY, Thy BLOOD, Thy SOUL, & Thy DIVINITY?

II.

Keep well in mind that he who communicates, & receives worthily, becomes One with the BODY & the SOUL of JESUS CHRIST. This one truth, together with the thoughts to which it gives rise, is sufficient to make you realise the preparation it behoves you to make before you venture to approach the Altar of your GOD. If you become incorporated into the BODY & SOUL of our Blessed LORD, by Holy Communion, the outward, as well as the inner man experience the effects of this Heavenly & wonder working Influ-

Influence, by which they are both transformed into GOD.

Examine we, then, what are, & what ought to be the results of this change. Thus—If I am transformed into JESUS CHRIST, by Holy Communion, & if It makes me participate not only in His Divine NATURE, but also in His Sacred HUMANITY, I ought no longer to think, nor to desire, nor to love, nor to act, but as my Blessed LORD acts, & loves, & desires, & thinks. I have within me His DIVINITY. I must, therefore, act as GOD acts. I must conform myself, as far as I can, to this surpassing & Heavenly Pattern, Whom I ought ever to keep before my eyes, that He may become the Ruler of all my thoughts & my desires, my feelings, & my deeds.

The All-holy SOUL of JESUS has entered into mine. Hence I ought to act through It, & to copy all Its Actions, so that I may be made worthy to participate in Its Illuminations, Its Graces, & Its Merits, all of which are infinite. And since His Sacred BODY has chosen mine for Its living Temple, I must do all in my power to become a sharer of His spotless Innocence, & of His more than perfect Purity.

The BODY of my LORD & SAVIOUR is mine. It is within me; It has come to me; It has become my Nourishment. It is, therefore, only meet & right that my body should be unreservedly dedicated to Him, in the Blessed Sacrament.

From henceforth I must only hear through the Ears of JESUS CHRIST; & mine own must be closed, from this time forward, to all useless & worldly conversation, to which my Adorable SAVIOUR is unwilling to listen. I must only see through the Eyes of JESUS CHRIST, which have become mine own; & I must prevent them from opening upon dangerous & seducing objects, which convey the love of vanity or wickedness to my heart. I must only speak with the Lips of JESUS CHRIST; or rather He must only speak through mine; in other words, I must only speak as I believe my Divine MASTER would speak, if He still conversed amongst men; & I must make Him the Medium of all my communications. In short, I must see nothing, I must hear nothing, I must think nothing, & I must do nothing but what I firmly believe my Blessed SAVIOUR would do, or think, or hear, or see, were He still dwelling upon earth; & this is what, GOD helping me, I will endeavour to perform.

Respect, therefore, your own selves. When you possess within yourselves, by Holy Communion, the Adorable BODY of JESUS CHRIST, do nothing to violate or profane the living Sanctuary wherein your GOD is pleased to dwell; be careful to retain Him there as long as possible; & act so as never to drive Him thence. Respect yourselves in JESUS CHRIST, because you are His Temple; & reverence JESUS CHRIST within your-

yourselves. He dwells in you, & you ought, on your part, to dwell with Him by Love; for Love is the means whereby this mutual indwelling is begun & continued & perfected, until you are blessed in possessing Him, without danger of being separated from Him, when you shall see Him Face to face in the Beatific Vision.

Do nothing to defile the Temple of GOD, Whose Temple you are. This you have had the privilege to be made; but you are something more. A Temple does not become what it contains; but you can become That which you contain within yourselves, because you are nourished by It, & because this Divine Food has the power to incorporate you into Itself. Bear about in your bodies, then, the LORD JESUS CHRIST, with honour; & glorify Him in your whole person, which enjoys the blessing of being filled, nourished, sustained, & strengthened by the very Substance of GOD made MAN.

The Blessed Eucharist, in truth, is the commencement of DIVINITY. Begin then to become really That which you receive; for it is within your power so to be. To attain this, you must resolve to lose what you are; such is an essential element in the conversion. First of all, cast aside all love of self; & in its stead, embrace the Love of GOD, Who dwells in the Sacred HUMANITY Which you have within you. Next, cast away all earthly thoughts, in order to welcome His, which are Heavenly. Cast yourself into, lose your-

yourself in, be absorbed by the boundless Ocean of DIVINITY; & you will find yourself blessed in the possession of It, for you will cease to be yourself. Succeed in pleasing Almighty GOD, & He will make you satisfied with yourself. He only wishes to raise you to participate in His Divine Attributes. He is a BEING, All-powerful, & the Source of all Existence; you must therefore be filled with love towards Him, you must offer no resistance, you must be undivided in attachment, you must be quite unreserved, you must be influenced by no rival, unworthy of GOD; & above all things, you must be perfectly passive in His Hands. Labour ceaselessly, & at once, with all possible diligence, for this Union with JESUS CHRIST; & for your encouragement, be assured that He will effectually work with you.

Affections.

Canst thou think too often, O my Soul, of the inestimable Benefits thou dost receive in the Blessed Eucharist? Hadst thou been elected, from all Eternity, to communicate but once during thy life, would thy whole life, be it never so long, suffice thee to meditate profitably upon this single Communion? & didst thou pass thy life entirely in Eucharistic Thanksgivings, would that be sufficient to remember worthily so great a Blessing? Say then to thyself, in thinking over thy past Communions—Is it really true that

that I am incorporated into the Adorable BODY of JESUS CHRIST, as often as I receive It at the Holy Altar; & has His Virginal FLESH purified & ennobled mine? Alas, my body has still the same tendency to self-pleasing & sensual delights, the same shrinking from the practice of penitence & mortification, as if she had neither received, nor been nourished by the BODY of her Blessed LORD.

Whilst His Sacred HEART, consumed with Heavenly Fervour, was in contact with my heart, did mine participate in His Divine Love? did she learn to love only those like unto Him, & for love of Him, & only to love those whom He loves? Alas, she has felt none of His loving Feelings; or, if at all, has only experienced them in a transitory manner, because old attachments have not been uprooted, nor expelled, & because she has straightway returned to the same creatures she formerly loved, to the detriment of duty, & the single-hearted love which Almighty GOD requires.

This All-precious & All-saving BLOOD, wherewith I have been so often cleansed, pervaded, & nourished, in the Holy Communion, has It overcome my ruling passion, against which I have only, up to the present time, fought most feebly; & has It washed away all stains of sin? Alas, I feel deeply, to my sorrow, that I have again fallen into sin, after having been washed & purified so often in the Adorable BLOOD of JESUS,
Which

Which is the Fountain opened for sin & for all uncleanness.

Has the Holy Soul of Christ effectually healed all the wounds, & bruises, & putrefying sores of my Soul? Has It curbed my temper? Has It cured my pride, or chastened my desires, or purified my thoughts? Ah, Lord Jesu, what cause have I to complain of myself, to mourn over the past, to anticipate the future, if I would henceforth realise all the Power, & all the Depth of this Mighty Sacrament of Thy Love.

Thanksgiving.

With what confusion of face, do I feel, O my Adorable Lord, my unworthiness, my faithlessness, & my want of purpose. It is meet & right, & Thou dost will it, that I should render Thee Thanks for having come down from Heaven on my behalf, for having taken up Thy Abode within me, & for having nourished me with the precious Food of Thy Body & Blood. If I were unthankful for these Blessings, I should be guilty of the most base ingratitude, which would richly deserve eternal punishment. But, O my God, how can I ever perform this needful duty? The Benefit is infinite, because Divinity gives Himself Wholly unto me; & my gratitude is finite, because I am a weak creature, having only poverty for my portion. This thought over-
powers

powers me, & covers me with shame & confusion. Ah, Lord Jesu, wouldest Thou make me powerless to do that which Thou dost expect at my hands? Thy Justice, & Thy Goodness forbids it. Hence, O my God, I take courage when I consider that I have received Thee, that Thou art within me, that I am incorporated into Thy Person, & that Thy Merits are mine, because Thou hast made them over unto me in the Blessed Eucharist; because Thou thinkest, & lovest, & speakest in me; & because, if Thou art the Living Word of the Eternal Father, I have been made, in some sort, a Word of Thine. Accept then, O God of Love & Mercy, this my Thanksgiving as Thine Own, since all I have is Thine; & since, if I may venture to say so, Thou dost possess nothing in which I have not a share. Do Thou, Who dost accept Thine Own Gifts in accepting my service, since Thou art both the Author & Finisher of them, do Thou receive my Acts of grateful Thanksgiving as if they came forth from Thy Spirit, from Thy Lips, & from Thy most Sacred Heart.

Third Meditation.

Of the Benefits & Blessings of the most Holy Communion.

I.

REMEMBER that when our Adorable SAVIOUR instituted the most Holy Sacrament of the Eucharist, He began, says the Beloved Disciple, by reminding His Apostles of the many & great Gifts of which His Heavenly FATHER had put Him in possession; & that He made these reflections with the intention of teaching them that He inclosed all these Gifts in the Blessed Sacrament of His BODY & BLOOD, which He was then about to institute, & to leave with the Faithful, until the end of time.

But observe, that afterwards, to prepare the minds of His Apostles for this great Act, & to take them as it were, at their weakest point, for they were still but ignorant men, that is to say by Love & Affection for the greatest & most lasting of all Gifts, He gave them, & us in their persons, an assurance of such extraordinary devotion, & of a Love so perfect, that nothing could exceed the loving & gracious expressions of which He made use. Even as a good father, who, when about to die, makes a last effort of affection to bid farewell to his children; so did our Blessed LORD, in order to bestow the great things He promised, & was about to give them at that very moment, without their expecting it. And this He did, in order to certify to them, & to all the Faithful, that His infinite Love for man was to be the principle, the rule, & the measure of His Divine Generosity in this most Blessed Sacrament.

After such generous & tender assurances of Love, our Adorable LORD took both the Bread & the Wine into His Sacred Hands. And to draw down the Attention of His Heavenly FATHER on what He was about to do, He gave thanks unto Him, as He was wont before performing any great Act, & with Divine Voice pronounced the Words of Consecration. He brake the Bread He held in His holy Hands, & said—*THIS IS MY BODY, Which is given for you;* Which then became His Own Very BODY, & Which He gave in Communion to His Apostles. He did the same likewise with the Wine, Which then became His most Precious BLOOD; & He gave It them to drink, saying—*THIS IS MY BLOOD, Which is shed for many,* that is to say, for all mankind.

He then ordained the Disciples to be the first Priests of the New Dispensation, by giving them Authority—*Do this in remembrance of Me.* He thus communicated to them both His Priesthood & His Power; & also promised that He would be with them always, even unto the end

of

of the world; by which He made them understand, that He did not give them Himself for once, nor for any stated time, but that He would daily renew these precious Gifts, until the end of the world.

It was to perpetuate this Sacrament of Love & Generosity that He consecrated them Priests, & associated them in His Priesthood by thus endowing them with Authority over His BODY, with the right to consecrate the Sacred Elements, the power to make Him Present on His Altar, & of distributing Him to the Faithful, as our Blessed SAVIOUR had done to them.

It is astonishing, says a Holy Father, that the Love of GOD for men here exhausts, as it were, three of His great Attributes, His Power, His Wisdom, & His Plenitude. For though He is All-powerful, I will venture to say that He can give us nothing greater, since He has given us Himself; though He is infinitely Wise, He is unable to find anything more fit to perpetuate His Love; & though He is infinitely Rich, & possesses all Treasures in Heaven & in earth, He had nothing more precious, more Divine to give us; for in giving us His FLESH, His BLOOD, His SOUL, & His DIVINITY, He gives us, at the same time, both the Source, & the Use of the greatest of Treasures.

The best parents in the world, though affectionate to their children, can only give them perishable possessions, of which accident may at any

any moment deprive them. Oftentimes they only give them these possessions, because they are not able to take them with them when they die. They cannot give themselves to their children for ever, because they too are mortal, & their bodies are subject to corruption; & even if they could give themselves, it would be no great gift, considering that they are but weak & perishing creatures. But JESUS CHRIST, Whose Love infinitely surpasses that of the most loving father, gives us Himself, & All that He possesses both as GOD, & MAN, & that unreservedly. He gives us Himself for ever; He gives us an All-powerful CREATOR, a SAVIOUR, a FATHER, a SPOUSE, & a REWARD, all in One.

Therefore, after you have received the most Holy Communion, look upon yourself, not merely as inheritor, & legitimate possessor of the Treasures of GOD,—of His SPIRIT, His Virtue, His Mercy, & His Kingdom,—but also as possessor of Him, Who possesses all these Treasures, even of GOD Himself. What an infinite Happiness; what an unspeakable Honour. Use every means then you can to obtain Him, & when you have the happiness to possess Him, keep Him with much faithfulness & take care that you never lose Him.

II.

You cannot possess JESUS CHRIST worthily, except you possess Him entirely; He cannot give
Himself

Himself to a true believer in the Blessed Sacrament, without at the same time giving all that He has that is most Precious, most Great, most Glorious. To give us Himself is a great proof of His Love; but to give Himself, with all His Possessions & in lawful Claims to an Eternal Kingdom; to make us a Deed of Gift, the most binding ever made, in the face of Heaven & earth; & to sign it with His Own BLOOD, is indeed an excess of affection, for which we cannot be too grateful, that can only belong to an All-powerful, All-loving GOD. And all this is what our Divine LORD gives us in this Venerable Sacrament, whenever we receive It worthily.

What is it that forms the most precious part of the Treasures of our Blessed LORD, besides His Divine PERSON, & His Sacred HUMANITY? What but His Graces, His Mercies, His Illumination, His Labours, His Sufferings, His infinite Merits, the Rewards due to Him from His Heavenly FATHER, & yet He gives us all these gratuitously whenever we communicate worthily. This Adorable SAVIOUR has loved us so deeply, that not content with asking for our hearts, & giving us His Sacred HEART in return, in spite of the difference between an All-powerful GOD, & mortal man, in spite of His having consummated this Love at the cost of His very Life; He willed, out of His exceeding Love, to give us the Reward which He has purchased, & which He has a right to receive from His Heavenly FA-

THER, for all the Actions He performed on earth, & especially for the Sorrows of His Passion, & the cruel Death which He endured.

Consider then, on the one hand, the Labours of our Adorable REDEEMER from the moment of His holy Incarnation, until the time of His precious Death. What can be greater or more deserving of reward than the persecutions which began even from His sacred Infancy; His hurried Flight, & Poverty during His abode in Egypt; the long duration of His Exile amongst an idolatrous people; His Journeyings, His Fatigues, His Preaching, His Conversions, His Fasts, His Solitude, His Prayers, & Devotions to GOD His FATHER, His Acts of Charity towards the sick, the afflicted, & the sinful, His external & His internal Sorrow, His Agony & Bloody Sweat, His Cross & Passion, & His most precious Death, & Burial?

Consider, on the other hand, of what value & weight these Actions were in One Who was both GOD & MAN, Who did nothing that was not infinitely Meritorious, in virtue of His Hypostatic Union with GOD the FATHER. Moreover, consider what JESUS CHRIST gives you. These are the Privileges He yields & transfers to you, in the most Blessed Sacrament of the Eucharist; it is thus that He has the goodness to substitute you in His Place, & to put Himself in yours; taking your sorrows, & giving you His Comforts; taking your poverty, giving you

you His Riches; unburthening you of your sins, to bear the weight of them upon Himself; abasing Himself to you, that you may be drawn up to Him. It is thus you enter into all His Rights, all His Claims; & that you are made partakers in the Rewards He has inherited, during the course of His mortal Life.

After the reception of the most Holy Communion, you are in a position not only to ask for them, but absolutely to demand them, as a debt due from our Heavenly FATHER, & to put yourselves in the place of this Adorable SAVIOUR, Whom you have received, asking for them even as He would have asked for them. Speak then with unshaken confidence, & even with a holy intrepidity in the PERSON of the SON, for He is within you, & has given Himself to you. Remember that then you are something more than mere mortals; speak, pray, ask, not in your own name, for of yourself you are nothing, but in the Name of a SON Co-equal with His FATHER, Who like Him is GOD, All-powerful, Who has given Himself wholly unto you. Be then assured, that if you love Him, He will also love you; that He speaks in you & for you; & that the Voice of His most Precious BLOOD reaches to His FATHER'S Throne. Unite then your voice to His; you will be heard, & will obtain assuredly all that you ask for in His Name; for if you ask not, it is because you are wanting in faith.

Be not afraid; you cannot be refused; for you
possess

possess within you an Almighty MEDIATOR, to Whom everything is given, & nothing can be refused, not out of favour, but in Justice. For in Him you have an incontestable Title to obtain all that you ask; & the Power of the MEDIATOR is equal to that of the FATHER, to Whom, through His Name, you address yourself. Profit therefore, by the inestimable Treasure you have within you, when you possess Him.

In truth, you may well be afraid when you possess Him not, & then are forced to ask for favours; because you deserve nothing but through Him. But when you have received Him, be of good cheer, & let your Union with Him justify your confidence, & boldness; for then you are filled with the Grace of the Only SON of GOD. Ask then for great things, & they will be granted you. Lose none of the rich Treasure you possess, after having received the Ever-blessed Sacrament; but preserve It entire, & for as long as possible, making good use of the precious moments of CHRIST'S Abode within you, for they are of inestimable value.

Affections.

Inexhaustible Fount of Riches & Mercy, O most Blessed JESU, my SAVIOUR, I adore Thee as GOD with my whole heart, I adore Thee as my Benefactor, in the most wondrous Sacrament of the Eucharist, which is the Sacrament, the Triumph of Thy Love, Wherein Thou showest forth

forth to us the excess of Thy Love, by Thine infinite Munificence. I adore Thee within my Soul, after I have had the happiness of receiving Thee in the most Blessed Sacrament. I adore Thee with all possible feelings of reverence & gratitude, because I am assured that in possessing Thee, I also possess all Thy Riches.

O infinite Fulness of most precious Treasure, Thou art so much the more to be adored, because Thou art only Rich that Thou mayest bestow Thy Riches, without measure, & without price. Thou art only Full, that Thou mayest bountifully distribute the great Treasure, of which Thy Heavenly FATHER has put Thee in possession. Not satisfied with giving me Thy BODY, Thy BLOOD, Thy SOUL, & Thy DIVINITY, Thou offerest me Thy Divine Mercy, Thy Favour, & Thy Love; & Thou offerest them gratuitously, without my having deserved them. Nay, I say more, Thou dost yield to me Thy Merits, to enrich my poverty; Thou makest over unto me all that Thou hast purchased on earth; Thou dost put me in Thy stead, as if I myself had suffered all that Thy Love had made Thee suffer for me, by bestowing upon me all that Thou hast a right to demand, from Thy Heavenly FATHER.

O most Blessed JESUS, what hast Thou not deserved, by Thy Prayers, by Thy long Endurances, by Thy Sufferings, by the Shedding of Thy Precious BLOOD, & by Thy most cruel Death?

Death? But these Treasures are mine. I can make use of them, as of a possession which belongs to me, to attain Heaven. If I make a holy use of them, they cannot be denied me, & all these Treasures I present to Thee.

Thanksgiving.

What can I render unto Thee, O my GOD, for the infinite Benefits Thy Divine Bounty has given me, in the most Holy Communion; & what can I give Thee in exchange for these most precious Treasures? Shall I offer unto Thee my deserts? Alas, I have none, I can have none, but through Thee. Shall I offer Thee my works? Alas, till now, what have I done to promote Thy greater Glory, & to advance in the path of Perfection? Have I even tried to make what amends I may, for the innumerable sins I have been guilty of? Shall I offer Thee my desires, or my love? Alas, can I flatter myself with having loved Thee till now? Shall I give Thee my life, & my blood? Oh, this I would willingly do; but alas, in offering Thee all that I have, all that I am, can I offer Thee anything but what Thou hast given me? Does not all come from Thee; & all I have, ought it not to return to Thee?

What then shall I do in this state of helplessness? O my GOD, my Benefactor, Thou dost inspire me with the words of Thy Holy Psalmist, & I

& I will say with him—*I will receive the Cup of Salvation, & call upon the Name of the* LORD. I can only discharge my debts, by contracting new ones; therefore I will approach Thy Holy Altar with Zeal; I will receive Thee there with lively Faith, profound Humility, & burning Love; & thus shall I find means to pay my debts. I will strengthen myself with Thy most Pure FLESH; I will drink of Thy Precious BLOOD; & thus my hunger being satisfied, & my thirst quenched, I will offer Thee Thyself, in childlike confidence, with Thy Labours, Thy Sufferings, Thy Merits, Thy Love for man, & Thy Love for me. I cannot say too often to myself that It is my possession, since Thine exceeding Charity has given it to me. I have therefore the right to present Thee with all these Treasures in Acts of Thanksgiving, without their ceasing to belong to me; & Thou wilt not refuse them, because they come from Thee.

Make me worthy, O most Blessed SAVIOUR, to receive Thee often, that I may be enabled to offer Thee something meet for Thine Acceptance, in offering Thee Thyself.

Fourth Meditation.

Of the Benefits & Blessings of the most Holy Communion.

I.

To be conscious of the Benefits & Blessings of the most Holy Communion, you must humbly meditate on What you receive therein from the Bounty of GOD; on What you have the honour to present unto Him; & on what Almighty GOD does for you, as well as on what you do, or at least what you ought to do, for love of Him, & in return for His infinite Goodness.

Consider as attentively as you can, the marks of Love & Affection which JESUS CHRIST shows you, until the Sacred ELEMENTS, which contain His most Precious BODY & BLOOD, are consumed. You need only follow, & examine them with the attention they deserve, to be filled with love, respect, & gratitude; for the proofs of Love are all great, & noble, & worthy of the HEART of a GOD of Love, Who always delights in giving Himself bountifully to us, when He desires to show us His Love, & to ask for ours in return. A GOD of Majesty, an All-powerful GOD comes down from His Heavenly Throne, All-sovereign as He is, because
He

He loves us without our having deserved it. This Eternal PRIEST obeys the voice of a human Priest, who is His creature & His subject; & obeys him so entirely, that as soon as the sacred Words of Consecration are pronounced, He becomes Present under the Humble FORMS of BREAD & WINE.

Behold then, how much the Divine SAVIOUR does in the most Blessed Eucharist, to shew forth His Love to us. For an Almighty GOD to obey the voice of His creature, more readily than any mortal has ever obeyed his GOD, is indeed a marvel. For an Incomprehensible GOD, Whom Heaven & earth cannot contain, to enclose Himself under the FORM of BREAD, in the narrow limits of our heart, thus uniting Himself to us by the closest & most intimate of Unions, & to become our Food & Nourishment, is indeed a Miracle of Love. What a prodigy of wonder is this, to shew us the longing Desire He has to take up His Abode with us; to draw near, truly & in PERSON, to our hearts; & to contract, & cement an Alliance, an indissoluble Union between His Sacred HEART & ours. Try to realise that you would be very unjust, ungrateful, & utterly unworthy of this Favour, were you not to respond to the Desire of so Good & Gracious a GOD.

Not content, says a Holy Father, with having once taken upon Himself our nature, by His Incarnation & Birth in time, it is His Will that, in the most Blessed Sacrament of the Altar, we should take upon us His NATURE, & enter into all His Rights. And this He desires to such an extent, that He willingly grants unto us all the Benefits of this Divine Union, which alone is the Source of our glory & happiness, & which has cost Him such an infinity of Sorrow; whilst if Love were not the principal of this Union, it might appear to take somewhat from His Greatness, for it seems as if all the advantages of this Union were on our side, & as if He could not do without us.

Besides, it is in the most Holy Communion that the SON of GOD makes, on our behalf, a miraculous Extension of the Incarnation; & this in favour of as many people as there are Christians in the world, who worthily receive this Blessed Sacrament. And this Extension is repeated & renewed, as often as they receive Him at the Holy Altar. For, not content with having once espoused human nature itself, in taking upon Himself a BODY like unto ours, in the Womb of His Ever-blessed Mother, His ineffable & unbounded Love extends still further in this most Adorable Ordinance; He espouses in It each one of His members in particular. And this is what He adds to the Mystery of the Incarnation. Not satisfied with endowing His members with His Grace, to make them more worthy of Him, He gives Himself wholly to each one of them, & He gives Himself, as He is now in Heaven.

Nor

Nor does one sole Donation of Himself exhaust His Love. He contracts, reiterates, & ratifies again this Divine & Heavenly Marriage, at each of our worthy Communions; He not only espouses our Souls, which He unites intimately to His Own, but He incarnates Himself in our bodies, He lives there in Substance, He brings us His FLESH to purify & to consecrate ours, He allows Himself to be consumed there in His ELEMENTS, & to lose there His Sacramental BEING.

Yes, let us say more; it is His gracious Will that this Union should be continual & eternal; He gives us Himself BODILY, & in PERSON, as a Token, & an Assurance that we shall be eternally united with Him in Heaven. There possession & enjoyment shall succeed to our exile; there songs of joy shall give place to our sighs; & there an eternity of Happiness shall repay our tears & temporal sorrow.

Behold, O my Soul, what CHRIST gives in the Holy Sacrament of the Blessed Eucharist. This is what His Love does for you, when you there bring Him the preparation He requires at your hands, which is not above your strength. Think then, what you ought to give Him, & what you ought to do for Him, in acts of Thanksgiving, & Gratitude, for so many, & so undeserved Benefits & Blessings.

II.

It is a great & crying ingratitude always to receive

receive gifts from the fame PERSON, & to give back nothing in return. Especially is this true when our BENEFACTOR places us in a condition, & gives us the power to acknowledge the Favours He has bestowed upon us, & only asks in return a small portion of that which He has so bountifully given unto us; & when He is willing to pay back to us a hundred fold, that which He begs at our hands. What a cause of confusion, & sorrow would it be to a well-disposed heart, to feel always burthened with gratitude unacknowledged, & overwhelmed by continued & infinite Benefits, & yet to be powerless to repay the BENEFACTOR, in return for unceasing Favours bestowed.

Before the Institution of this most Blessed Sacrament of the Altar, mankind could not but deeply feel their poverty & weakness. They could only offer to GOD a feeble, barren gratitude, which produced nothing worthy of being presented to GOD. They were obliged to confine themselves to simple desires & longings to possess Him, in order that they might have something to give Him back. We are far happier, under the Law of Grace, since our SAVIOUR & our GOD has called us to His Table, to give us His BODY as FOOD, & His BLOOD as DRINK. We are thus delivered from this disgrace, because in the Divine FOOD He gives us, we are able to give back to GOD That which we have received from Him.

When you have the Blessing to receive JESUS CHRIST in the most Holy Communion, He grants you the absolute Gift of Himself; & in virtue of this Gift, He belongs to you, & you have the right to dispose of Him, as of a Possession belonging to yourself. And this, because you have a Contract, & a legitimate Title of possession. It is true, that by this Contract you give up yourselves entirely & irrevocably to Him; but the Gift is reciprocal, He gives Himself to you, belongs to you, & can be applied by you to all your needs. You can moreover make use of all His Possessions on your own behalf; you can appropriate to yourself not only His BLOOD, His SOUL, & His DIVINITY, but also His Attributes, & those Qualities which are inseparable from Him, such as His Strength, His Purity, His Light, His Merits, His Mercy, His Love, & even His Kingdom.

As He has given Himself to you so entirely, & unreservedly, with the sole condition that you must in like manner give up yourselves to Him —a condition more profitable, & full of honour, than difficult & burdensome to you—you can offer Him as your own Possession to the Eternal FATHER, in Satisfaction for your sins, & in Gratitude for all the Favours & Graces you have received from His Divine Goodness. What honour, & advantage far beyond that of our brethren of the Old Dispensation, to be able to offer to our GOD, a Gift worthy of GOD, & of a

Son Equal to Him, in Authority, Greatneſs, Power, Goodneſs, & Majeſty; & to be perſuaded that this Gift is infinitely pleaſing to Him, that It does Him honour, & that He cannot & will not refuſe It.

A Holy Prophet, full of fervent gratitude for the Favours Almighty GOD had beſtowed upon him, & not knowing how to repay them, on account of his poverty & weakneſs, ſpeaks thus to himſelf—*Wherewith ſhall I come before the* LORD, *& bow myſelf before the High* GOD? *Shall I come before Him with Burnt-Offerings, with calves of a year old? Will the* LORD *be pleaſed with thouſands of rams, or with ten thouſands of rivers of oil? Shall I give my firſt born, for my tranſgreſſion, the fruit of my body for the ſin of my Soul.* But his difficulty would ſoon have been removed, had he been as rich as we are; if he had had in himſelf, as we have after the moſt Bleſſed Sacrament, the moſt Precious of all VICTIMS to offer up to the Eternal FATHER. We have this Unbloody VICTIM—even JESUS CHRIST—let us then profit by this Advantage, & by It appeaſe the Juſtice of GOD. Let us, by Its Aid, change the dreaded Tribunal, into one of Divine Mercy. Let us redeem ourſelves, with this Precious RANSOM, from the captivity, into which our ſins have brought us; & let us preſent It, each time that we receive It, to Him, in Acts of Thankſgiving for having given It to us.

In truth, the reception of the moſt Bleſſed Eucha-

Fourth Meditation.

Eucharist gives us not only GOD for our Nourishment, but also an entrance into a portion of His Priesthood. It gives us the right to offer It up for our sins, & for those of the people, in gratitude for the temporal & spiritual Gifts we have received from GOD. We offer then to the Heavenly FATHER, a VICTIM Who is GOD like Himself. We present Him with What is most Divine, & the Object of His Affection, & with What He loves as much as Himself, with an eternal & infinite Love. What glory, what happiness, what an advantage is this, for a creature to possess.

Affections.

To receive & to give: to receive all from GOD, even GOD Himself, with all that is Great & Precious, what exceeding happiness is this; to give Him all that He esteems, all that He loves as Himself, all that He has loved, all that He will love through all Eternity, what glory.

Behold, O my Soul, the holy intercourse thou hast with thy GOD, in this most Blessed Sacrament. Meditate upon it seriously; value thy happiness; & make thyself worthy of it. Receive with desire this precious Treasure, Which is even GOD Himself; give Him the reception He deserves, or at least the best thou canst; preserve Him with all possible care, lest He be taken from thee; & make use of Him, as of Something
given

given thee by GOD, which confequently is thine own, by the juftest title of all thou doft poffefs. Divest thyfelf of all earthly affections. Leave not in thine heart the leaft attachment for a creature, which might be difpleafing to Him; but give Him unreferdly all that thou haft received from Him, & give it in fuch a manner that thou always remaineft fulfilled of GOD. In prefenting JESUS CHRIST to GOD, His FATHER, thou haft the advantage of being able to give All, & yet to keep All for thyfelf. When thou giveft to creatures, things perifhable as themfelves, thou doft lofe them in the giving, & haft no longer any right to them, but in giving them to GOD, in giving GOD to GOD, in this Divine Sacrament, the more perfect is the Gift, & the more doft thou poffefs It even after having given It.

Give me then Thyfelf, O moft Bleffed SAVIOUR; give Thyfelf to my Soul, & to all her faculties, that I may take poffeffion of Thy moft Precious BODY & BLOOD, & that I may feel Thy Heart clofe to mine, with all the Graces & Bleffings which accompany It; fo that in poffeffing Thee, I may inceffantly offer Thee myfelf, without lofing Thee.

Thanksgiving.

O Almighty GOD, Supreme BEING, Divine REDEEMER, & GLORIFIER, Thou Who haft abafed abased Thyself, through infinite Love, to become my Food & Sustenance, Thou art now within me, with all Thy Treasures of Love, Wisdom, Grace, & Knowledge. Thou comest to me that all these Treasures may enter into me. Thou art there in Substance, as Thou art in Heaven. Thine infinite Love has brought Thee down, to come & abide with me. Speak then, LORD JESU, to my Soul; enlighten & instruct her; & enkindle her with Thy Love. Make her to bring forth such Acts of Thanksgiving as are worthy of Thee. Warm them with the Divine Fire of Thy Charity, which will raise them even unto the Throne of Thy Majesty; & that they may be favourably received, do Thou, by Thine Infinite Goodness, supply what is wanting to their incapacity & weakness.

In order that I may be able to render Thee what I owe unto Thee, I must know & feel the value of what I receive in the most Holy Communion; so that my Acts of Thanksgiving may at least attempt to equal the Benefit received. But alas, how can my Spirit, which is only darkness, understand the extent of the Favour Thou grantest me, in giving me Thyself? How can my heart, which is colder than ice, feel how weak a creature I am, with only misery & poverty for my portion? How can I repay Thee what I owe Thee, for the Infinite Treasure which I now possess within me?

O LORD JESU, Thou that art the only True Light,

Light, enlighten my Spirit, that I may know the value of What Thou haſt given me, in giving me Thyſelf. O Divine SAVIOUR, Thou that art a conſuming Fire, inflame my heart to love Thee, as Thou wouldeſt be loved, that it may realiſe that Thou art near unto it. O infinite Treaſure, unquenchable Fount of all Good, Who art preſent unto me, both as my SAVIOUR & my GOD, my Food & my Benefactor, put Thyſelf in my place; & do Thou, I pray Thee, make Acts of Thankſgiving to Thyſelf, ſince it is only Thou Who canſt do ſo worthily; & grant that as Thou art mine, I may perform all that Thou doeſt, & ſayeſt in me, out of Thy great Love for me.

Fifth Meditation.

Of the Adorable FLESH of JESUS CHRIST, in the moſt Holy Communion.

I.

YOU muſt firſt conſider, that when you receive the moſt Bleſſed Sacrament, you have the happineſs of receiving the Precious FLESH of JESUS CHRIST. This FLESH, is at once Divine & Human, becauſe having been formed in the Womb of Ever-bleſſed Mary, of her ſubſtance,

by

by the ineffable Working of the HOLY SPIRIT, It was united hypoſtatically to the Eternal WORD, at the moment of the Incarnation. This was & is the cloſeſt & moſt intimate Union ever made, which ſhall exiſt as long as GOD is GOD; conſequently this Divine FLESH muſt be infinitely Pure, infinitely Adorable.

This FLESH ſo Precious, ſo Venerated, ſo Holy, hid beneath the VEILS & FORMS of BREAD & WINE is about to dwell with you, & to act as your Spiritual Food & Suſtenance. That you may prepare yourſelf worthily for Its Reception, you muſt meditate that this Divine FLESH was formed by the Overſhadowing of the HOLY SPIRIT, in the ſubſtance of a ſpotleſs Virgin; that It grew little by little in her holy Womb, & thence came forth with perfect Purity, by an unheard of Miracle of Almighty GOD, Who joined, in this Holy Virgin, the wondrous Union of Virginity & Maternity; that it was nouriſhed with Her ſuſtenance, paſſed through all the ſtages of Infancy, & only acquired Its true Perfection after a lapſe of years; & that It became the Inſtrumental Cauſe of our Salvation, by making Itſelf a VICTIM for our ſins on Calvary, & the Nouriſhment of our Souls in Holy Communion. You are about to receive this Same FLESH of JESUS CHRIST, Which was ſo Small & Hidden in the Womb of His Virgin Mother, Which was ſo Bright & Luminous on Tabor, ſo Sorrowful & torn with ſtripes in the Prætorium;

torium; so Disfigured & Bloody on Calvary; & Which is now so Glorious, & Resplendent with Light in Heaven. This Divine FLESH is about to unite & incorporate Itself in your mortal flesh, that It may communicate to it Its Own Purity, Innocence, & Immortality. This Adorable FLESH is so Pure, that to become well acquainted with it, you must banish all coarse & carnal thoughts; for the Spirit, purified by Faith & Love, is alone capable of knowing in part, Its admirable Qualities & inestimable Value.

Consider Its origin; & you will know that there is nothing Greater, or more Noble. Enter into the detail of these Prerogatives; and you will agree that there is nothing more worthy of your veneration. Look upon It with reference to the wonderful effects It produces in a Soul that receives It with purity; & you will see that It is clothed with the Power of GOD Himself. What is the Origin of this Adorable FLESH, which you receive in the Ever-blessed Sacrament of the Altar? It was formed, by the HOLY SPIRIT, of the Substance of a Holy Virgin, GOD is Its FATHER, & Virginity Its Mother. It is the chaste Production of a Pure Virgin, who by the greatest of all Miracles gave birth to It, without losing her Virginity. It is a FLESH formed only that it might be borne by a GOD, to be raised to the hypostatic Union, & to become the glorious Instrument for the Salvation of man. DIVINITY is then Its glorious lot. Innocence,
Purity

Purity, & singular Beauty form Its Attributes. It carries & communicates them everywhere. It impresses these precious Qualities on all who receive It worthily. It purifies & beautifies their Souls, & sanctifies & sustains them against the weakness & frailty of their own flesh.

Lose none of these Gifts & Graces. They are all inherent in the Precious FLESH of JESUS CHRIST; they reside there, as in their Source, from whence they flow abundantly, when you make yourself worthy of them; nay, let us say more, that this FLESH becomes yours, or rather you become the FLESH of CHRIST, as often as you receive It with Faith, Purity, & Love. Enjoy this Precious FOOD, says a Holy Father, purify & cleanse the palace of your Souls from all sins & pleasures, which would prevent your realising Its Sweetness. Purify your Spirit from all worldly thoughts, & your imagination from all that is contrary to the infinite Purity of this FLESH, at once Virgin & Divine. Purify your memory from all that could hurt this sensitive Virtue. Purify your heart from all attachments, which have not GOD for their object; since that which is able to enervate you, may also be able to take away from you the Love of GOD. Purify your flesh from all the dangerous imaginations, which pleasure may have left there. In a word, extirpate with carefulness all these sad remains of our evil nature; & remember that the least stain, known & neglected, may deprive you of this Heavenly

Heavenly Food, & of the Gifts & Graces of Purity which accompany It.

The Precious FLESH of CHRIST, says a Holy Man of old, can only be the delight of Saints, or of those who try effectually to become Saints. When It is received into a pure flesh & a burning heart, perfection is soon attained. You must then begin, says an Ancient Father, by partaking rightly of this Adorable FLESH; & by Its Aid, you can attain to the practice of Holiness; for the one is the reward of the other.

II.

It is important that you should consider attentively, that the flesh which was formerly man's most deadly enemy, & which is one even now when licence is given to its wishes & pleasures, is now become the most Sovereign Antidote against the evil & corruption of which it is the cause. And this it has become, because the Divine WORD clothed Himself with Mortal FLESH, raised It to dignity, bore It for the space of three & thirty years, & offered It by His Passion & Death as a Sacrifice to His Eternal FATHER; & especially has it become so, since He has vouchsafed to give us His Sacred FLESH for our Sustenance in the most Blessed Sacrament of the Altar. But our flesh participates only in the Advantages, Graces, & incomparable Purity of the FLESH of CHRIST, when it approaches often, & with the preparation necessary for so intimate a Union with Him. In truth,

truth, our Flesh is ever a dangerous enemy, & is the more to be dreaded because it is domesticated with, & makes a part of ourselves. It is a flesh rebelling against the Spirit; it is susceptible of evil impressions; it flatters us, & we flatter it; it leads us to pleasure, & does not restrain us from it; it corrupts us, & prevents our rising towards Heaven; it even continually weighs us down to earth, which is its origin, its centre, & its end. This is what ought to alarm us; this is what gives us material for unnumbered conflicts; this is what makes the greatest of Saints tremble. It is by applying this Divine FLESH to our sinful flesh, in the Blessed Sacrament of the Altar, that we moderate & extinguish those fires which devour it; that we soften the strife to which it excites us; that we appease its rebellions, which become less frequent, & less difficult to resist; that we restrain its leanings towards pleasure; & finally, that we are able to purify it from all its stains.

By contact with this All-pure FLESH, the desire of our flesh for what is even lawful is diminished; & it becomes less susceptible to sensual pleasure. The impression of the FLESH of GOD, Which has touched it, remains insensibly & protects it. Hence, patience & mortification of the senses are less disagreeable, & flattery no longer so strongly influences us. Its weakness is imperceptibly healed by the Sacred Union it contracted in the most Holy Sacrament of the Eucharist. It obeys the

the SPIRIT with less resistance & trouble. It becomes peaceful & victorious in all its strifes, through the Strength & Purity which it has acquired by frequently partaking of the Blessed FLESH of its GOD & SAVIOUR, by which it is preserved & sustained.

If CHRIST felt a secret Virtue go out of Him to heal the sick woman, who touched & pressed upon Him in the crowd, how much more reason must there be for our flesh to be cured by the most Blessed Sacrament of all the most incurable & obstinate diseases? We not only come in contact with this Adorable FLESH through our raiment, & those of our Divine LORD, but we receive It into our very selves, & It passes into our system, like any other food which sustains our body; we incarnate & incorporate It, so to say, in our flesh. What remains, becomes part of our substance; & we become, in a measure, & after a transcendental manner the FLESH of JESUS CHRIST. It is therefore much more Powerful & full of Virtue than His mere Raiment; & provided we draw nigh unto It with lively Faith, sustained by ardent Charity, we shall find that this Divine FLESH, united to ours, according to a Holy Father, like two pieces of wax melted together, make an impression of Purity, Strength, Innocence, & Grace, which will sanctify & cure ours from all evil desires; & will elevate it, in order that it may participate in all the Gifts & Graces of the SPIRIT.

It

It is true that this Adorable FLESH is hidden in the Bleſſed Sacrament of the Altar, under ELEMENTS Which conceal It from our bodily eyes. We behold It only with the eye of Faith; but It is always the FLESH of a SAVIOUR, of a GOD made MAN for love of us. There is not leſs Virtue in It, than if we ſaw It with our very eyes, & touched It with our hands in the FORM It bore, whilſt JESUS CHRIST was upon earth, & converſed viſibly amongſt men.

Let us then, approach with true Faith, & perfect Confidence, aſſured that this Living FLESH not only ſuſtains our fleſh againſt the various enemies which attack its purity; but that It nouriſhes & ſanctifies our Spirit, heart, & Soul, & infallibly procures for us an increaſe of Grace & Purity.

Affections.

Divine FLESH of my SAVIOUR, & my GOD; chaſte Production of a Spotleſs Virgin, Fount of Life, of Grace, of Strength & of Purity, I adore Thee in the moſt Auguſt Sacrament of the Altar, where Thou art Preſent to receive my homage & reſpect, though Thou art concealed beneath the Sacred Euchariſtic ELEMENTS. I adore Thee within me, where Thou comeſt in the moſt Holy Communion to nouriſh, & to fill me with Grace; to purify me; to incarnate Thyſelf in me, & to unite Thyſelf to me, SUBstance to substance; & to transform me in Thyself.

My flesh has but frailty & weakness for its portion; it has a desire only for pleasure, & is ever ready to fall, if it be not sustained & strengthened by Thy Virtue. My flesh inclines only to delicacy & corruption; cleanse it therefore, Lord Jesu, sanctify it with the incomparable Purity of Thine Own, which Thou didst take, O most Blessed Lord, from the Womb of the Ever-Virgin Mary. My flesh shrinks from the least thought of penitence, or mortification; deliver it, I pray Thee, from this lukewarmness, & weakness; & give it strength to bear the temporal sorrow it has deserved in this world, that it may be spared from enduring griefs, which are eternal, in the Life to come. My flesh is mortal, because it is sinful; give it then, Good Lord, a life of Grace & Glory, through Thine Own Immortality.

All-pure, All-holy FLESH, come Thou unto mine which is so frail, & so corrupt; cleanse it from all its infirmities, from all its stains; & make it a Sanctuary worthy of Thyself. O Adorable FLESH, now Glorious in Heaven, I hope so to receive Thee during this mortal life, that I may have the happiness of seeing Thee Face to face, Unveiled through a happy Eternity.

Thanksgiving.

Eternal & Living WORD of the Everlasting FATHER,

ther, Who hast made Thyself FLESH for love of me, in the Womb of Blessed Mary, & Who givest me this same FLESH in the most Holy Communion, I offer unto Thee many Acts of Thanksgiving for this inestimable Benefit, & I will not cease to make them till the last moment of my life.

Possessing this Adorable FLESH, I ought to dwell in Thee, as Thou livest in me. My weak & sinful flesh ought to be fortified & sanctified by Thine; & to rest entirely on Thee, hoping to enjoy Thy Divine Presence for ever in Heaven. Being *planted in the House of the* LORD, it ought, according to the Psalmist, *to flourish in the Courts of the House of our* GOD, when it participates in the incomparable Purity of Thy Divine FLESH, & enjoy the supreme satisfaction of being united to Thee, by the bonds of a tender & indissoluble Love. Thy All-pure FLESH having so often united Itself to mine in the Ever-blessed Sacrament, I ought to say with the Psalmist, Henceforth, *I will not fear what flesh can do unto me;* since having been nourished by the FLESH of my SAVIOUR, nothing can make me afraid.

In a word, I ought never more to be separated from Thee, my GOD; & according to Thine Own Words, my flesh & Thine ought henceforth to be but One FLESH; for this great Sacrament of Thy Love is a Celestial Marriage by which I may become one with Thee, for time &
for

for all Eternity. This, O Heavenly SPOUSE, is the end of all my hope, the object of all my desire; nor will I have any other desires, but those which draw me to Thee. Do Thou, I humbly beseech Thee, grant me their happy fulfilment.

Sixth Meditation.

Of the Precious BLOOD of JESUS CHRIST, in the most Holy Communion. Part I.

I.

REMEMBER that when CHRIST instituted the most Blessed Sacrament of the Eucharist, & at the moment He gave the Cup containing His BLOOD to His Apostles, He said these wondrous Words—*This Cup is the New Testament of My* BLOOD, *Which is shed for you.* Therefore, whenever you receive It worthily, you make a new Contract with JESUS CHRIST; & His most Precious BLOOD, Which you drink, gives you, in your person a solemn Promise & an infallible Token of the Eternal Life, which is promised by Him, Who alone has the right to give & to promise.

Preserve then, with sacred fidelity, so great a Gift, which assures you of safety, of happiness, & of peace; & which sustains your hope against any fear or alarm, which might seek to overcome you.

you. It assures to you the possession of GOD, & of an Eternal Kingdom; what can you ask for more? By this possession, all desires which your Soul can form, either for pleasure or greatness, shall be perfectly fulfilled; & you will have nothing more to wish for, since you have, & shall possess for ever all that GOD possesses. These are the Treasures which the Precious BLOOD of CHRIST obtains for you, in the most Holy Communion; but you must not forget with what exactness & faithfulness you must fulfil the conditions of so solemn & august a Contract, made in the sight of Heaven & earth, lest you should be deprived of all that It conveys in your favour; of a Contract authorised by the Precious BLOOD of CHRIST, from Which He derives all His Strength, & which contains so many Gifts & Graces. For there is no Power in Heaven or earth that can oppose It; or can dispute the possession of that to which by Its Virtue, He gives you a right to lay claim.

By virtue of this Contract, which you make at the Foot of the Altar, CHRIST gives you His HUMANITY, His DIVINITY, His PERSON, His Riches, His Eternal Kingdom, through the medium of His most Precious BLOOD, Which He gives you as a Pledge of all that He has promised you; & you, on the other hand, give yourself entirely to Him. This Contract is too advantageous for you to annul It, too binding for you to break It. It is the most Precious BLOOD of
GOD

GOD & MAN; & the Sacred INK with which it is signed. This Holy BLOOD is its Promise, its Sign, & its Token; what can be more infallible, what can be more able to sustain your confidence? To enter into contract with GOD; what can be more glorious? To be made, by so solemn a Testament, the inheritor of His BLOOD, for a certain Token of the eternal Happiness which that BLOOD has procured for us on the Cross; what can be more advantageous?

Reflect, that after this Contract & Testament made at the Last Supper, when He instituted the Holy Eucharist, & gave the Apostles His BLOOD to drink, He went out into the Mount of Olives, where, without any enemy but His own Love, He began to shed His most Precious BLOOD in Agony. Then He was delivered up into the hands of His persecutors, who, by unheard of tortures, drew from His Sacred BODY whatever BLOOD He had remaining. The Hall of Judgment was more covered than watered by It; & whilst It issued forth from the sacred Wounds, which His Love & His enemies had inflicted upon Him, It had a secret but eloquent Voice, which cried to Heaven with more virtue & energy than did that of Abel. The blood of Abel demanded Justice against a brother, & a murderer; but the Precious BLOOD of JESUS asks for Mercy. He pleads on our behalf, at the Tribunal of His Heavenly FATHER, in order to obtain for us the pardon of our sins, which deserved

served eternal punishment; & He asked for us the opening of Heaven, the doors of which had, till then, been closed against us.

By this most Adorable BLOOD was then inscribed in the Book of Life the merciful Decree of our perfect Reconciliation; & at the same time was revoked the sentence of our death, which we had incurred. It promised to obtain, & did obtain for us both the life of Grace, & the life of Glory, on condition that we never profane It.

Our Adorable REDEEMER, Who ever delights to fulfil His designs of Love & Tenderness for man, not satisfied with having shed His Precious BLOOD upon the Cross, wills to sprinkle It every day where the Daily Sacrifice is offered upon the Altars of the Christian World; & will continue to do so in the hearts of men, at the Ever-blessed Sacrament, until the end of time. It sufficed not the Love of the LORD JESUS to have given It to us once on the Cross, & to have shed It there unto the last Drop; He gives It us again at the most Holy Communion, & this Blessed Sacrament is Its prize of possession, & Its investiture, wherein the application of It is made in our favour.

In the Passion of our most Blessed SAVIOUR, this Precious BLOOD was only shed upon the ground, & in the midst of His enemies & executioners; but in Holy Communion, It is poured into our hearts. On the Cross It acted from afar, for distant

distant times or places; but here It is present, & comes very nigh unto us. It cleanses us, It purifies us, It nourishes us, It quenches our thirst, It saves us, & unites us to Itself for time, & for Eternity, & It obtains for us numberless Blessings; & we not only have the use of It, but also possess It in entirety with all Its Treasures.

II.

That we may lose nothing of the precious Treasure, which is given us in the most Adorable BLOOD of CHRIST, whenever we approach the Blessed Sacrament, it is well that we should meditate upon It under three different aspects. The first is, that, in which this All-holy BLOOD sustained the mortal Life of GOD made MAN for love of us, from the time of His Incarnation to that of His Passion. The second is, that of His Passion & His Death, when It was shed in the Hall of Judgment & on Calvary, for the Salvation of man. The third, is at the time of the most Holy Communion, where we really receive It, for our strengthening.

Say then secretly to yourself, after having communicated, I now possess within me, & very near my heart, that Same BLOOD, Which the HOLY GHOST drew from the Womb of a spotless Virgin, at the time of the Incarnation, to make of It, One, both GOD & MAN. I possess this Same BLOOD, Which flowed through the Veins of my SAVIOUR,

Saviour, while He was hidden in the Womb of His Virgin Mother, & Which increased little by little during His Infancy until His perfect Growth, to be shed one day on the Cross, with the more abundance, that my Redemption might be the more perfect. I possess within me the Same Blood, Which sustained the mortal Life of my Saviour for three & thirty years. This Adorable Blood acts as my Nourishment; & if I receive It with the preparation It requires, It will unite with my blood to purify & sanctify it from all stain, which after a transcendental manner will become, by this most Blessed Sacrament, the Blood of Christ Himself.

I have then obtained, by the Holy Communion, not only an intimate & spiritual Union with my Saviour, but also a new degree of relationship with the Sovereign Lord of Heaven & earth; because His Blood is mine; & because His Blood, as powerful as God, Whose Life It sustains, gives me a new birth unto Grace, as often as I worthily receive It. This is at present my blessed condition, which from henceforth forbids me to commit any action that is unworthy of such August & Noble Blood, Which is so often renewed within me, at the most Holy Communion. I should be very guilty & unworthy, were I now to form any attachment, the shame & infamy of which would reach even to the All-holy Blood of Jesus. What cause of tears & sorrow is it, to see in the Church some persons who are less

less Christian than worldly; who boast of their human descent & make it a false cause of boasting, in order to draw down contempt on others; while they are blind enough to forget the more august Nobility, which they derive from the Precious BLOOD of JESUS CHRIST.

Consider again, this Adorable BLOOD, at the time of our Divine Redeemer's Passion; reflect that you possess within yourself the Price of the Salvation of all men, & consequently of your own; a BLOOD, Which alone made a perfect Sacrifice & whose sweet-smelling Savour ascended to the Throne of His Heavenly FATHER, to appease His most just Anger, to disarm His Justice, & to draw down His Divine Mercy; a BLOOD, which a Saint of old calls the Key which effectually opens for us the Gates of Heaven, & procures us an entrance into Celestial Habitations. You still possess within you that Same BLOOD Which issued from the BODY of our Blessed SAVIOUR, during His Agony in the Garden, & Who, in His desire to be sacrificed for love of us, & to hasten our Redemption, opened all His sacred Pores to bear us more quickly to Glory.

Consider that your heart acts as a vessel to contain this Divine & most Precious BLOOD, Which issued forth from the Head of the most Blessed JESUS & flowed over His Eyes & His Sacred Face, when He was crowned with Thorns; from His All-holy BODY, after His cruel Scourging; from His Hands & His Feet,
when

when He was being fastened to the Cross; & from His Side, when It was pierced with a lance. This is what you truly, really, & substantially receive at the most Holy Communion. Draw from thence the same meditations as did a Holy Saint of old, & say with him—My Soul must be very precious in the Eyes of Him Who created her in His Own Image; since she required no less than the BLOOD of GOD to redeem her, & this Same BLOOD is given every day to nourish, & renew in her the traces of the Redemption, when her sins have unhappily effaced them. But, alas, the fall of a Soul into mortal sin must be very dreadful, very grievous to GOD, since she can only rise again by the Assistance of the Same BLOOD which redeemed her.

Affections.

Dost thou realise within thee, O my Soul, this Divine & Sacred BLOOD, with Which thou hast been cleansed & purified in the most Holy Communion? Be assured that if thou hast approached It worthily, It has most certainly produced Its Effect upon thee, so that thou oughtest to be not thyself, but another person, & if I may dare to say so, another JESUS CHRIST. It is into Him, that this most Adorable BLOOD has transformed thee; & consequently thou oughtest to have passed from the weakness of a creature, to the Strength & Virtue of a God. Thou art now signed

signed with the BLOOD of the LAMB without spot, & thou haft in this BLOOD a sure & certain Promise which assures thee of Eternal Happiness. Preserve carefully its impressions & characters; & never efface them, as they are too precious & blessed for thee to neglect.

If blood is the principle of natural life, That of JESUS CHRIST is the Principle of the Life of Grace & of Glory. Live then this Life of GOD, since thou art nourished, & vivified by His most Precious BLOOD; & be careful, that the world, the flesh, & the Devil, or thy evil passions, never efface this Character, the impression of which cost JESUS CHRIST so much.

Constantly remember then, that the BLOOD of thy GOD, with Which thou art interpenetrated & filled, has the Power of purifying, of cleansing, & of strengthening thee. Are thy stains washed in this health-giving Purification? Has this precious BLOOD purified thy Spirit, thy Soul, thy heart from all their secret sins? Dost thou feel the blessed Effects of this Precious Food, Which for many years sustained the natural Life of thy GOD? Art thou fully satiated with earthly pleasures? dost thou feel strengthened by this Divine Sustenance? Art thou ready to undertake all for the Love & Glory of Him, Who sacrificed Himself for the Love of thee? Has He kindled thee with His Divine Fervour? Has He inflamed thy heart? Does it now burn for Him? Would it be ready to give back blood for BLOOD,

if

if an occasion offered itself? In a word, art thou holy now, after having so deeply & often drunk from the Source of all Holiness?

O most Adorable BLOOD of my SAVIOUR, produce in me all these blessed Effects, I beseech Thee; purify, cleanse, nourish, & sanctify me for ever.

Thanksgiving.

If I owe Thee, O my GOD & my CREATOR, Thanksgivings for having given me the blood which flows through my veins & sustains my natural life; what do I not owe Thee for Thy most Adorable BLOOD, Which Thou dost give me at Thy Holy Altar, since It is the Principle of that Life of Grace, which sustains my Soul, & the Precious Token of that Life of Glory, which It has purchased for me. This Same BLOOD which is now within me, began to flow through Thy Veins when the HOLY GHOST formed Thy Sacred BODY, of the Substance of the Spotless Virgin, whom Thou hadst chosen from all Eternity to be Thy Mother. It sustained Thy Mortal LIFE, from the first moment of Thy Incarnation, until the time of Thy Death upon the Cross. But Its most important & most glorious destination, was the Salvation & Redemption of man. This it was which cost the entire effusion of It; although one Drop would have been enough to redeem a thousand worlds.

O Blessed Lord Jesu, what Thanksgivings ought I not to render Thee, for so great a Blessing. My sins have indeed separated me from Thee, & I should have been separated from Thee for Eternity, had not a Miracle of Love performed by God, lessened the distance which divided me from Thee. But now I am drawn near to Thee by Thy most Precious Blood, the Instrument, & the Price of my Redemption. It is then, through this most Adorable Blood that I hope to be near Thee, & to enjoy Thy Presence, both during this life, & during an endless Eternity.

O most Adorable Blood, Thou art now mine own, for I possess Thee. Grant that I may know, that I may realise, that I may love, & esteem as I ought, the inestimable Treasure which Thou hast given me in the most Blessed Sacrament. Thou, Who art Strength Itself, sustain my weakness. Thou, Who art Holiness Itself, consecrate & sanctify me. Thou, Who art a Divine Fire, enkindle in me Thy Heavenly Desires, & effect in me a renewal of that which Thou didst do for Love of me in Thy Precious Blood-shedding on the Cross of Calvary.

Seventh Meditation.

Of the Precious BLOOD *of* JESUS CHRIST *in the moſt Holy Communion.   Part II.*

I.

THE Adorable BLOOD of our SAVIOUR JESUS CHRIST poſſeſſes the ſame Attributes as GOD Himſelf; ſince It forms an eſſential part of His Sacred Human Nature & is inſeparably united to Him. It is then, moſt deſirable, before receiving It in the moſt Holy Communion, to conſider carefully all the holy Qualities which It poſſeſſes, & the wonderful Effects It produces in a Soul worthily prepared to know, to value, & to love, as It ought to be loved, What It contains, after having received It; to preſerve It, as in Itſelf the moſt Precious of all Treaſures ; to make a holy uſe of It ; & to awaken in the heart, an ardent longing to approach It frequently. The Holy Fathers call the Precious BLOOD of JESUS CHRIST ſometimes a Divine RANSOM, which has releaſed us from the threefold captivity of ſin, death, & Hell ; ſometimes a Sovereign REMEDY, which not only cures us of paſt evils, but preſerves us from thoſe we have reaſon to fear, from the Devil, the world, or our own corrupt nature ;

sometimes a Healing & Invigorating FOUNTAIN, Which cleanses us from all defilements, & makes us clean; sometimes a Heavenly FOOD, Which supports & strengthens the Spiritual Life within us, making us grow more meet for Bliss; now a Divine & Refreshing DRAUGHT, Which quenches our thirst, & frees us from the dangerous longing after sensual pleasures, leaving us only a thirst for what is holy & just & good; now again, a Sweet & Pleasant MILK, which is the Life, the Nourishment & the Delight of the children of GOD; now a Boundless & infinitely Precious TREASURE, Which enriches us, & procures for us all that we may lawfully desire; & now, a Heavenly FIRE, Which thaws the icy coldness of our hearts & fills us with Divine Heat; sometimes an ORNAMENT, to adorn & make us pleasing in the Sight of GOD; sometimes the IMPRESSION & SEAL of the SPOUSE, which imprints upon us the marks of those predestined to Glory; & sometimes the Master KEY, Which opens the Gates of Heaven, that we may enter in & dwell there; & all these different Qualities, which show the inestimable value of the Blessed Sacrament of the Altar are so many subjects, upon which we should devoutly meditate; as well as so many motives to induce us to approach unto It with all the Faith, the Purity, & the Fervour of which we are capable.

Let us then consider these Divine Attributes one by one; & let us admire the order, the arrange-

Seventh Meditation. 69

arrangement, & the charitable work which our LORD JESUS CHRIST undertook from His Love towards men, that they might pafs through the efficacy of His BLOOD, from cruel bondage to an Eternal Kingdom.

Let us look upon this Bleffed SAVIOUR as a Generous KING, full of Kindnefs, Who, touched with compaffion at the fight of a poor flave, covered with wounds, & treated with harfhnefs by his cruel mafter, at once fets him free by paying his ranfom. Human Nature is this miferable flave; the mercilefs mafter, who keeps him in bondage, is the Devil. The Charitable KING, Who comes to break his chains, & to fet him at liberty, is our Bleffed SAVIOUR JESUS CHRIST, Whofe BLOOD is the precious Gold which pays the ranfom of the flave. This Adorable BLOOD, fays a great Saint, is the Price of the Redemption of mankind, which refcues them from fin, & death, & Hell; & left they fhould fall back into that cruel captivity, He daily repeats upon the Altars of His Church His moft Precious BLOOD-fhedding. He gives It to them, that they may always have fomething Wherewith to guard themfelves from the danger of again falling into this difgraceful flavery; or by Which to redeem themfelves, if they do lofe their liberty afrefh, after having once recovered it. This wretched flave has been ill-treated by his mafter; he is weak & faint; & as foon as he is fet at liberty, his wounds muft be dreffed, that he may be reftored stored to health. The sinner, who has as many tyrants, as he has passions to which he is the slave, is sick, & full of sores. He must have his wounds dressed & cured. The BLOOD of JESUS CHRIST is the Means. In short, says a holy Bishop, the BLOOD of the Heavenly PHYSICIAN has been shed, & It is become the Sovereign REMEDY for the distressed & for the sinner.

We have received countless wounds in our captivity; our liberty is weakened; our understanding is darkened; the love of pleasure is in our hearts; & all our senses have rebelled. Let us then frequently apply to the BLOOD of our REDEEMER. There is no spiritual disease, however deeply rooted & obstinate it may be, that It cannot cure; & that, so effectually, that it will never return, if we sincerely desire it not.

This slave again set free, is still unclean, & an object only of disgust. He must be cleansed with care, before he is fit to appear in the presence of his KING. We are all defiled by the love of this world & of earthly things; but we have, says an ancient Father, a FOUNTAIN opened for sin & for uncleanness, in the BLOOD of JESUS CHRIST. From this FOUNTAIN flows the purest Stream; & as It flows incessantly, It carries away with It all the stains & the defilements which we have contracted by our sins. It brings back the original Beauty which we had when we came from the Hands of the CREATOR. It restores our lost Innocence, & It gives back
all

all the purity & cleanliness which are needful, in order to enter into the Kingdom of Heaven.

This is what the Elder in the Revelation said, in one of the Visions of the Beloved Disciple, when he was carried up to Heaven, when speaking of the Elect, who entered into this Heavenly Dwelling—*These are they which came out of great tribulation, & have washed their robes, & made them white in the BLOOD of the LAMB.* Let us then, wash often, not our robes only, but also our whole body, in this Health-giving FOUNT, that we may be counted worthy of a like happiness.

II.

Let us continue, O my Soul, to admire the kind & loving labours of thy Sovereign LIBERATOR, Who is thy GOD; the cruel bondage out of which He has delivered thee, & the Eternal Kingdom of which He would put thee in possession, by the Efficacy & All-powerful Virtue of that Precious BLOOD, Which He shed for love of thee, & in Which He would have thee wash & purify thyself in the most Holy Communion.

Put thyself in the place of this wretched slave, released from servitude & bondage, cured of all his wounds, washed & purified from all his uncleanness. But be assured also, that the great work is not yet accomplished, & that it will still cost thy Generous BENEFACTOR much, to supply all that is wanting towards the consummation of thy Eternal Happiness.

Truly,

Truly, this poor slave, though he has received so many favours, is still weak, because he has been overtasked with labour. His strength has been over tried; & he has been ill-cared for, & half-starved. His Charitable LORD must then procure for him better food, & more abundant, to restore his wasted energies, & to support Him in the labours & more glorious combats to which he must now be exposed, in order that he may be found worthy to obtain the Immortal Crown which is prepared for him.

What is the nourishment of sinners? Alas, nothing less than poisoned food, which the Devil, the world, & the flesh offer to them, to destroy the spiritual life in their Souls, & to draw them on insensibly to eternal Death. But what food can be more strengthening, & more wholesome than the BLOOD of CHRIST? It is at once the most nourishing of all Food, & the most powerful of all Antidotes. It is as suitable for the weak as for the strong. It gives Itself to both; & is of infinite Value to either. It supports the strong, lest they should fall. It helps the weak to rise again, after they have fallen; & gives them courage & zeal to enter into the path of penitence, & to endure its hardness. And It gives to both Strength to run swiftly, not only in the Way of GOD's Commandments, but also in that of the Counsels of Perfection.

This slave is still athirst; since in all the time that he has borne his chains he has drunk nothing

thing but unwholesome water, which neither quenched his thirst, nor refreshed him. The sinner, a still greater slave than he is, has only drunk stagnant water, drawn, in the words of the Prophet, from broken cisterns which could not hold that which was pure. He has drunk iniquity as water, out of the cup of wickedness; & though he ran with eagerness after that poisoned draught, he has never succeeded in quenching his thirst, even after guilty & sensual gratifications.

Our Blessed SAVIOUR, in the Holy Eucharist, gives us His BLOOD to drink. We taste there pure & innocent Pleasures, which we cannot find elsewhere; & after tasting these we feel no longer a thirst for anything but Holiness. This Compassionate LORD, of His great Goodness, offers to us a Cup filled with His most Precious BLOOD, Which like old wine, strengthens us, & produces in us a grateful & innocent inebriation; Which, far from stupefying us, enlightens our minds; Which sanctifies our Souls, instead of making them guilty; & Which consecrates & sustains the body, instead of defiling it & making it unseemly. And this Adorable BLOOD is not only a strengthening Wine, It is also, for children reconciled with GOD, Nourishing MILK, Which serves to these beginners as Sustenance, & as a sweet DRAUGHT, Which suits Itself to their taste & their weakness.

If the slave is poor, because the tyrant has

taken away all that he possessed, the DELIVERER, Who will not let the charitable work be only half finished, gives him abundantly the means to live, & to supply all his wants. The wretched sinner has let himself be despoiled of all the Gifts of Nature, of Grace, & of Glory, & is reduced by his faults to a deplorable state of poverty. JESUS CHRIST his SAVIOUR restores them to him in His BLOOD, Which is the most abundant & precious of all Treasures, since It procures & multiplies the Gifts of Grace, & is also a sure Pledge of Glory.

But as this slave just ransomed, still bears upon his raiment, & upon his person the shameful marks of slavery; his Divine REDEEMER must cleanse him of these, & clothe him with the more precious & honourable garments of the free man. We are delivered from the most cruel state of bondage, & our Blessed LORD, not content with having purchased our liberty at the price of His Own most Precious LIFE, changes our condition from slaves, to that of GOD'S Children. It is this BLOOD of our Dearest LORD, says a Holy Man, with Which He would clothe us, & Which is the greatest ornament we can possess. We read of a Virgin Saint, as beautiful as she was good, who once affirmed that the comeliness of her person was only caused by the BLOOD of her Blessed LORD. And a true Christian, who has had the blessedness of being ransomed, as she had been, & nourished
with

with this BLOOD, in the moſt Bleſſed Sacrament of the Altar, is able to ſay with her, that It forms the only ORNAMENT of his Soul; & at the ſame time he may reſt aſſured, that this BLOOD, as a Saint expreſſes it, ſo worthy of Adoration & ſo Efficacious, is a SIGN & SEAL Which imprints upon both his Soul & body the Image of the PERSON of the LORD JESUS, & the character of His Elect.

Affections.

Wilt thou return then, O my Soul, to the ſhameful ſlavery of the Devil? Wilt thou be once more the ſervant of vanity, of riches, of the world, & of impurity, after having been delivered & bought with the price of the BLOOD of the Only SON of GOD? O LORD, Thou haſt caſt off my bonds; Thou haſt broken my chains; & Thy Adorable BLOOD has reſtored me to the liberty I had loſt. It has coſt Thee ſo much; & ſhall I not make a holy uſe of it? I will henceforth occupy myſelf ſolely in offering Thee the Sacrifice of Praiſe, & in calling upon Thy Holy Name. Thou haſt made me one of Thy Children; & Thou haſt done me the honour to receive me at Thy Holy Altar. I will then return no more to be a ſlave of the world, the fleſh, & the Devil; neither will I have any dealings with them.

The Heavenly Antidote of Thy BLOOD has cured

cured me, upon Calvary, where It was once shed for love of me; & at the Altar, where It has many times & oft restored me to liberty. It has been applied to my wounds, like a healing Balm, I will not then expose myself to fresh wounds, which might have still more disastrous consequences than the former. I have washed my robes white in the BLOOD of the LAMB without spot; & I will not soil them any more. I have washed my feet; how shall I again defile them? Thou hast given me this Precious BLOOD, Beloved REDEEMER of my Soul, as Grateful MILK to help me to grow in Grace; as Nourishing FOOD, to strengthen me; & as a Delicious DRAUGHT, to allay my thirst after sensual gratifications. I have tasted Its wondrous Sweetness, & am convinced that this Which I receive, is nothing less than the BLOOD of my SAVIOUR & my GOD; that It is no common draught, which only refreshes & quenches natural thirst. Woe be to me, if I return & again taste the insipid & poisonous sweetness of worldly pleasures, which now appear so intensely bitter to me. Finish then, O All-healing BLOOD, I beseech Thee, the work Thou hast begun in me. Support me, & imprint on my Soul, those characters which will give me a title to possess Thee eternally in Heaven.

Thanksgiving.

O Adorable BLOOD of my SAVIOUR & my GOD, is it possible that I possess Thee; & that This is the Same BLOOD Which flowed in Thy Sacred Veins, when concealed in the Womb of Thy Blessed Mother; Which sustained Thy mortal Life, during the time of Thy Sojourn here upon earth; & Which Thou didst shed upon Calvary, as the Price of my Redemption? Yes, LORD JESU, It is indeed the very same. Thou hast positively said so, when Thou didst institute the most Holy Sacrament of the Altar; & I am ready to shed the last drop of my blood in defence of this sure & certain Truth.

But, O Precious BLOOD, a thousand times more valuable than all the treasures of the earth, is it possible that Thou canst be within me, & I not conscious of It, nor of Thy Worth & Power? Should I not feel in my inmost heart what I owe Thee for so many Benefits, how lovely Thou art, & what Wonders Thou workest in a Soul, prepared to receive Thee worthily?

It is nevertheless, O my SAVIOUR, by this Union of Thy BLOOD with mine, that I have contracted so close & so glorious a relationship with Thee. This Union elevates me to a height to which no mortal can aspire, if Thou, of Thine infinite Goodness didst not Thyself invite it. This Relationship inseparably unites me to Thee by the closest ties which can exist; & raises me, from a low estate, in which I have nothing, to a Dignity above all belief, since It makes me a sharer in Thy Divine NATURE. And this It effects, if I have sufficient fervour to prepare myself worthily for It, enough faith to preserve It when I receive It, & am careful & zealous enough to support Its claims.

My blood, so often united with Thine, should no longer be the blood of a creature, however pure, but the BLOOD of CHRIST Himself. It no longer rests with Thee, O Blessed SAVIOUR, whether I will contract this glorious Union with Thee, & be transformed into Thee; since Thou hast already offered It to me. In acknowledgment of this inestimable Favour, I offer to Thee in humble Acts of Thanksgiving, all my life's blood. I consecrate it to Thy Service; & I am ready to shed the last drop of it, for the love of Thee.

Eighth Meditation.

Of the HEART *of* JESUS CHRIST *in the most Holy Communion.*

I.

THE most Holy Communion may truly be called the great Sacrament of the Adorable HEART of our Blessed LORD. It is certainly
the

the Sacrament in which His intense Love & fervent Charity are more conspicuous than in any of the others, since our Divine SAVIOUR in instituting It, only followed the tender yearnings of His Loving HEART, Which has no bounds, when there is the opportunity of giving us any marks of His Love. In this All-holy Sacrament He has, as it were, enclosed His Own HEART, Which is the most precious Portion of His Sacred Human Nature.

But if the Adorable HEART of JESUS CHRIST, Which burns with Love for all men, is given to us, whole & entire, in this Blessed Sacrament, we must not be surprised if He asks in return for our hearts; if He demands them of us at the same time that He presents to us His Own. And this He asks, in order that we may be united to Him by the sacred Bonds of a fervent Charity, as well as by the closest Union; since His Sacred HEART dwells in ours in the most Holy Communion. Would it not then be most ungrateful in us to refuse Him His loving wish?

In short, says a holy Doctor, the most Blessed Eucharist demands our whole hearts; & if we give them, It makes us the keepers & the masters of the Divine HEART of JESUS. It asks them; & when we give them, It cures them of all their weaknesses. It asks for them, continues the Father, & purifies them of all their defilements; It disperses the darkness, & restores them to the light; in a word, It kindles in them
the

the Flame of Divine Love, & drives away all mortal & sensual affections. Prepare yourself then to give it to Him at once & unreservedly. It cannot be better placed than close to the Sacred HEART of our Dearest LORD & SAVIOUR. But take care that you do not leave within it any unworthy attachment, or earthly feeling, which can be displeasing to Him Who is Purity Itself, & Who will not share a divided heart, or one in which remains any stain of sin.

Think then seriously of What you receive, when in the most Holy Eucharist the HEART of JESUS gives Itself to you; when It places Itself in your breast, nigh unto your own heart. You receive the Object of the Joys & Delights of the Eternal FATHER; the Dwelling-place, the Throne, & the most Sacred Sanctuary of the HOLY SPIRIT. You receive the Principle & the Centre of the purest & most intense Love; the precious Source of the temporal Life of Him Who was both GOD & MAN; the Fount of His Sentiments & Affections; & the Cause of His Divine Actions.

Remember then, that you are become the possessor of a HEART Wherein has resided, & Where still resides, the Fulness of the GODHEAD, as well as the Perfection of Love & fervent Charity; & from the depths of Which flow all the Graces, with which mankind ever has been, or can be endued.

From whence then comes it that, you do not
benefit

benefit by the precious Outpouring? Why do you not share in this Divine Favour? Endeavour to profit by this Holy & Blessed Connection, as you should. This Sacred HEART is within you, when you have worthily communicated; & you are united to It at the Fountain-head. Draw then from this Well with holy courage. It is always full; & though It is ever flowing with a superabundance of Graces, It is never exhausted; &, what should above all increase your confidence is this, that this Sacred HEART has no greater pleasure than in giving, & that always in the greatest possible profusion.

Reflect again, that, in the most Holy Eucharist, you receive a HEART, from Which have proceeded all the Praises, the Adorations, & the continual Acts of infinite Love which honoured the Almighty FATHER, as He is worthy of being honoured. One of these Acts of Adoration, one single Act of Its Love, surpasses immeasurably in worth & value all that GOD has received from man, since the beginning of the world; & all that He can receive, until the consummation of all things; & even of those which He shall receive throughout Eternity, from the Holy Saints & Angels themselves. Notwithstanding this, the Divine HEART of JESUS, Which gives Itself to you in the Sacrament of the Altar, has so much Love for you, that It resigns, on your account, & applies to your needs in the most Holy Communion, all this infinite

infinite Merit; & that in proportion to the zeal you bring there.

You receive a HEART, Which, during Its mortal career was never a single instant free from burning with the most fervent Love towards GOD & man; & Which showed that Love, by the most certain of proofs. A HEART, Which softens towards all sinners, who draw near to It with faith, & Which never failed to assist them in their need; & Which was always ready to shew Mercy towards them, when they asked it with a humble & contrite heart, however grievous the crimes they had committed. A HEART, Which was moved with compassion towards the Samaritan woman, & took the first steps to induce her to turn from her wanderings, great as they had been. And One, Which rescued the woman taken in adultery, from the punishment with which she was threatened; Which stooped to the ground to write, in her favour, the words of Life; & Which bent Its Shoulders, like a good Shepherd, as says a Holy Father, to bring back that lost sheep to the fold of penitence.

Again, you are about to receive a HEART Which pardoned the Magdalene; & drew tears from Its Own Eyes, & a Miracle from Its Own Hands, to bring to life again her brother Lazarus, when he had been dead four days. A HEART, Which is the Storehouse of Divine Mercy, the Asylum for the wretched, & the sure

sure Refuge for the moſt abandoned ſinner. A HEART, Which permitted Itſelf to be opened, & pierced with a ſpear upon the Croſs, for love of us, & to ſhew us that there is always in that Sacred HEART a Door of Reconciliation opened unto us. Think then, what you ought to do to reſpond to the call of this Divine HEART. Love It with all your hearts; for this is all It aſks.

II.

Pay then, with the utmoſt reverence, your homage to the Adorable HEART of your Bleſſed SAVIOUR, in the moſt Holy Euchariſt, in which He has encloſed It, for Love of you. But above all, do not forget that this worſhip ſhould be accompanied by the moſt ardent, the moſt ſincere, the moſt faithful & conſtant Love; & be well aſſured, that it will never reach the Divine HEART, unleſs it proceeds from your own, unleſs it is kindled & borne upwards on the flames of perfect Love. Adore then, this Holy HEART, not only in the Bleſſed Euchariſt, Where He has placed It, but in yourſelf alſo, if you have had the happineſs to receive It at the Holy Altar. It is within you in Subſtance, with all Its Love, & the precious Qualities which make it ſo unſpeakably lovely in the ſight of GOD, of Angels, & of men. Thus you poſſeſs within you that Which ſhould be the delight, & is the moſt worthy object of the love &

adora-

adoration of all created beings, in Heaven & in earth.

The Sacred HEART of JESUS CHRIST is then at this moment above, within, & around your heart. It is above it, by Its Power. It leads & protects you, & covers you with Its Wings. Submit then willingly to this Power. It is mild & benignant. It has nothing about It which is stern or severe. Obey It then, in all things; rule yourself according to Its Holy Will; & follow, with a willing obedience, all Its Heavenly Inspirations.

This Adorable HEART is also around you, by a wonderful Providence. It is, at the same time, the HEART of a FATHER, MOTHER, BROTHER, SISTER, FRIEND, SAVIOUR, LOVER, & SPOUSE. It defends you against your enemies. It leads you carefully. It is ever on the watch to procure for you all good things. Trust then entirely to Its care. It is Good, & Wise, & Just; Generous & fertile in Its Resources. You will want nothing; & you will always have abundance of those Gifts, which are necessary for you, whilst you cast all your care upon It, putting your whole trust in It, & taking care to strengthen that trust by Good Works.

Again, It is within your heart, by Love. Not content with protecting you from your enemies, with surrounding you, & placing Itself close to you, It would also enter into the most secret recesses of your heart. It would fill it entirely,
provided

provided your heart were free from the love of any creature. It would rest there, as upon a nuptial couch, because It is your SPOUSE; as upon a Throne, since It is your KING; & as in the Sanctuary & upon the Altar, because It is your GOD. It only asks to shed on you those Gifts & Graces which are inseparable from It, & which It bounteously bestows on those who wish & ask for them. It will inflame you with the same Fervour with which It burns, if you do not offer any opposition to It; for It is a Flame, the heat of which is neither sharp nor painful, resembling as It does the burning Bush of Moses, which burnt without being consumed; or if sometimes It consumes, it is to purify your heart, & to change the objects of its love.

When you have the Sacred HEART of JESUS within your own, you are in the Furnace of Divine Love. Let this fire burn & stir within you, since It is GOD Himself. Strive to share in Its Fervour which It will impart to whoever desires It, with all his heart. The Flames which proceed from It are so searching, that they are felt by all who seek them with hearts purified from mortal attachments. If you are well prepared for It, It will consume & reduce to ashes the slightest stains upon your heart; & you will come cleansed & purified out of the fire. It is thus you should profit by this close & intimate visitation which It pays you in the most Holy Communion. Beseech this Adorable HEART, with

with all possible earnestness, to make you a new creature, or rather to make you part of Itself. Give your heart to It without reserve; & It will fill the place of your own heart. It has Power enough in the Blessed Sacrament to work this change, provided you co-operate with all Its Actions by your docility & fervour. Love It; wish for It; listen to It; & speak to It. Do not lose one Word which this Divine HEART would speak to you. Profit by the feelings which It inspires within you; & then It will dwell with you, & in you for ever.

Rest assured that the HEART of your Divine SAVIOUR & your own, are formed for each other. They are two depths, of Heaven & of earth. These two deeps call one to another, that they may be inseparably united by the bonds of Charity, not only for time, but also for Eternity. In the words of the Holy Psalmist, one Deep calls to another; but the HEART of JESUS, Which is the Depth of Heaven, is not contented with calling to you, It descends from Its Throne to find you out. Your heart then, should respond to this Work of Love, so disinterested & so un-sought; & it should feel assured that it will never find true Peace, until it is closely united to the Sacred Heart of the Blessed SAVIOUR. But in order to attain more surely to that glorious & blessed Union, you must conform in all things unto Him. You must love what He loves; hate what He hates; desire, live, think, & act like

like Him, with Him, by Him, & for Him; & then your Union with your Dearest LORD will be a perfect one.

Affections.

O Adorable HEART of my Beloved REDEEMER, the bright & glorious Throne of the purest Love; the resting Place of all hearts capable of truly loving; the inestimable Treasure of Holiness, of Grace, of Light, & of Purity; the inexhaustible Source of Goodness, of Clemency, & of Mercy; the sure Refuge of all unhappy Souls who invoke Thee, reign Thou as a KING, over all the hearts which Thou dost nourish with Thy FLESH at the Holy Altar, & fulfil them with Thy Light, Thy Grace, & Thy most perfect Love.

Above all, reign Thou for ever over my heart, over its desires, its wishes, its attachments, & its will; & grant that it may never break the blessed Bonds which bind it to Thy Sacred Heart. Suppress in it all that is not pleasing in Thy sight. Light there a holy Flame, which shall never be extinguished; & which may proceed from, & be the reflection of, that which burns incessantly within Thine. Be for ever the only Object of all its thoughts, & all its affections. Be Thou the single Motive of all its actions, & wishes; the Centre of its rest & happiness; & the blessed End of all its hopes & confidence in this life, as well as in that which is to come.

What happiness for me to have possession of, & to feel the Adorable HEART of my SAVIOUR so near unto mine own; to be able to live for Him, to love with His Love, to know by His Knowledge, & to burn with His Heavenly Fervour. Why do I not say in the words of the Sacred Canticle—*I hold Him Whom my Soul loveth, I will not let Him go, until I have brought Him into the secret recesses of my Soul?*

If the FORMS under which the FLESH of this Divine HEART are contained, consume away within me, & so It ceases to be there in Substance; I will, by Acts of Spiritual Communion, use every effort to preserve the affections & the impression of It until my death. It is mine own; & I would keep possession of It until I am made a partaker of It in all Its Fulness, Whole & Entire, in Heaven.

Thanksgiving.

What Goodness, O my Well-beloved SAVIOUR, only to ask of me that my heart should be in all the Acts of Thanksgiving which I pay unto Thee, in return for the precious GIFT of Thine, in the most Holy Communion; what Generosity, to require no more after giving me the most Priceless GIFT in Heaven & in earth. Shall I then be ungrateful enough to despise this GIFT, & not to give Thee my heart? Not so, O my GOD; I offer it to Thee wholly, without division, without

without reserve, at once, entirely, without self-interest, & for ever. I owe it to Thee, LORD JESU, not only because Thou hast made it, but because Thou hast willingly descended from Heaven to make it Thy Dwelling-place. Receive it, then, I pray Thee; accept it; & make it worthy of being presented to Thee. Infuse into it the qualities which will make it pleasing in Thy Sight. It is Thine, & will be Thine even unto death; & I trust, through Thy great Goodness & Mercy, that it will be Thine throughout Eternity.

Now, whilst my heart has the blessedness of being near to Thy Sacred HEART, do Thou, I pray Thee, inflame it with Thine own Fervour. Teach it to profit by such a glorious position; so that, henceforth, it may have a true sense of Thy Divine Love; that it may never turn away from Thee; that it may have no other office than loving Thee; & that it may repay its deepest & most reverent Acts of Thanksgiving, for the infinite Mercies which Thou hast bestowed upon it, in giving it Thyself. It is true, LORD JESU, that the Act of Thanksgiving does not equal the Benefits received; in the stead of that, I can only give Thee a heart of flesh, subject to a thousand weaknesses, & guilty, since its creation, of an innumerable number of sins, in return for a Divine HEART, Which is Purity Itself, & the Source of the purest Love. But Thou hast asked it of me, with so much desire & with so much affection, that Thou wilt have the Goodness to accept it as it is. Nevertheless, O my LORD, purify it, I pray Thee; shed upon it the Light of Thy Love, & stamp the impression of Thy Divine HEART upon it, that it may become more worthy of being presented unto Thee.

Ninth Meditation.

Of the SPIRIT *of* JESUS CHRIST *in the most Holy Communion.*

I.

THE Adorable Sacrifice of the Eucharist is an infinitely precious & inexhaustible Treasure, Which procures many others for us, to sanctify & enrich our Souls. It makes us share in the Holy SPIRIT of JESUS CHRIST, as well as in His Sacred FLESH & BLOOD. But it is important to remember, that this glorious Participation is twofold, & that it may be understood in two ways; & we may derive much Grace from it, when we consider it attentively, & unite our Spirits to That of our Blessed SAVIOUR, at the time of the Celebration of Holy Communion.

If by the SPIRIT of JESUS CHRIST be understood one of the Powers of His Sacred SOUL, that is to say, the Natural SPIRIT which performs

forms in His Holy Humanity the same functions which our spirit works in us, when we think, meditate, & reason; we have the happiness to share in this as often as we draw near to His Holy Altar, since we receive there, not only Perfect GOD, but also Perfect MAN, composed of BODY, SOUL, & SPIRIT, with all their Powers, Whole & Entire.

If, on the other hand, we understand by the SPIRIT of JESUS, the Qualities & the Graces, inseparably in Union with His Sacred PERSON, that is to say, His Illumination, His Wisdom, His Knowledge, His Dignity, His Sanctification, His Purity, & in a word, His Divine SPIRIT, Which gives us knowledge & insight into Heavenly things, & Which makes our actions tend towards Him, we receive this also in the most Blessed Sacrament. But with this difference, that the Natural SPIRIT of our Adorable SAVIOUR is given indifferently to all who receive worthily, because they are inseparable from His Holy Human Nature; & it is one of the greatest Powers of the Incarnate WORD, Who in the Holy Eucharist is GOD as well as a MAN. Whereas His Heavenly SPIRIT is only given by measure, & always in proportion to the faith, the purity, the love, & the other dispositions, we bring to GOD's Sacred Altar.

We receive then, in the most Holy Communion, not only a Portion of, but the Entire SPIRIT of JESUS CHRIST, with all Its wonder-working Qualities.

Qualities. We receive that SPIRIT in Which resides Wisdom, Light, & Knowledge in all their fulness. The Same SPIRIT Which directed all the actions of the WORD made FLESH, whilst He was Visible upon the earth; the SPIRIT Which can penetrate the most secret motives of the closest & most hypocritical of hearts; Which knows the past, & the future, as well as the present; Which had such perfect & sublime thoughts, & conversed so familiarly & intimately with GOD; Which could realize His Greatness, & Which paid Him such pure Homage, & a Worship so perfect & worthy of His Majesty: this is the SPIRIT of JESUS, Which we receive in the Ever-blessed Sacrament.

Again, you receive in the most Holy Eucharist that SPIRIT of our Divine SAVIOUR, Which found so readily the means & the resources to feed that great multitude, which followed Him into the desert to listen to His gracious Words; the Same SPIRIT, in Which is contained all the secrets & causes of that adorable Providence which procures for us, so abundantly, all the Gifts of Nature, of Grace, & of Glory; the Same SPIRIT, Which foresaw in the Cradle all the sufferings to which He should be exposed, in the Judgment Hall & upon Calvary; & Which had them ever before His very Eyes, & by their mournful & vivid image made Him the MAN of Sorrows throughout His mortal Life.

Think again, that you receive in the Blessed Sacrament

Sacrament of the Altar the Same SPIRIT, Which sustained with so much endurance in Gethsemane the most intense Agony that ever was endured; Which thought so sorrowfully upon all the humiliating & mournful circumstances of His Passion & Death; & Which grieved more for the little use which godless Christians would make of the excessive Sorrows which He was about to endure, the BLOOD which He was about to shed, & the LIFE He was about to Sacrifice for Love of them, than for His Own Personal Sufferings. You receive that SPIRIT Which, at the moment when JESUS entered for the last time into the Holy City, knew & distinguished, in that triumphal entry, the judges who should condemn Him, with so much injustice, to the cruel & shameful Death of the Cross; Which saw, with prophetic Vision, the Hall of Judgment to which He should be led as a criminal, & the executioners who should crucify Him; & Which, after having suffered this dreadful punishment, left the Sacred BODY upon the Cross, to commend Itself into the Hands of His Heavenly FATHER.

This then is one portion of the Attributes & Powers of the Natural SPIRIT of the LORD JESUS, which you receive in the most Holy Communion. Do not be satisfied, as others are, with only a mere reception of the Sacrament; but draw near with all your heart to this Adorable SPIRIT, in order that It may instil into you more fully all Its Heavenly Qualities. Profit by all of them; & do not
lose

lose any. Everything that belongs to It is great, & of infinite value. Unite your Spirit closely to That of your GOD & SAVIOUR. Think seriously before approaching this Ever-blessed Sacrament. Enter with all your power, & with all your faith & reverence into the designs of the SPIRIT of JESUS CHRIST towards you. Perform with readiness & faithfulness all that It dictates to you, that It may conduct you in the path of Perfection, & may assure you of your ultimate Salvation.

II.

Consider carefully the wondrous Graces which belong to the SPIRIT of JESUS CHRIST in the most Holy Communion. Do not approach It without a deep feeling of reverence, for the Adorable SPIRIT of GOD made MAN. Cast away your own Spirit, in order to be clothed again with His Sacred SPIRIT. Renounce a worldly Spirit, the Spirit of self-interest, a carnal Spirit, & the Spirit of vanity, with all its views & its worldly wisdom. You will then be more meet to receive all the Influences of His Blessed SPIRIT. You will receive them more abundantly, & the impression, which that SPIRIT of Light & Truth will make upon you, will last for ever.

We are not now speaking of the Natural SPIRIT of JESUS CHRIST, but of His Heavenly SPIRIT, Which will make us think, will, love, & act as our Blessed SAVIOUR thought, willed, loved, spoke, & acted; of that SPIRIT in short
of

of Which the Apostle spoke to the early Christians—*Whoever has not the SPIRIT of CHRIST, he is none of His.* From which we may conclude, that those who follow the direction of His SPIRIT, & who possess It, are in Him. It remains, then, for you to prepare yourself for the most Holy Eucharist in the same way in which the SON of GOD prepared Himself, when He instituted this Divine Sacrament—to wish for It, to ask for It, & to resolve to undertake all for the love of It, & you will obtain It. For it is certain that whatever pleasure you may have in receiving the Graces which you ask, in a worthy Reception, He has much more pleasure in granting them, & He will give His HOLY SPIRIT to all those who humbly ask for It.

Again, the SPIRIT of JESUS CHRIST is the SPIRIT of Wisdom, of Counsel, of Purity, of Sweetness, of Humility, of Charity, & of Prudence; & this is the perfect Model upon which you should form your own. Copy then carefully this Heavenly Pattern. It is what He requires of you. It is the purpose for which He gives Himself to you. Follow it, then, with all possible faithfulness.

Be fully persuaded that a worthy Reception begins this good work within you. It is by this that the SPIRIT of our Blessed SAVIOUR makes the first impression of Light, of Wisdom, & of Love within you; but it is only many good Communions that complete the work. Fulfilled with

with the SPIRIT of JESUS CHRIST, It sustains & directs you in all your undertakings; & conducts you safely in the way of Salvation.

It is indeed in the adorable Mystery of the Eucharist, that the Promise of GOD to the Prophet of old is accomplished, when He said—*I will pour out My SPIRIT upon all flesh*, & It will indeed produce wonderful Effects in you. Here the SPIRIT of CHRIST is shed upon all Christians who worthily approach His BODY & His BLOOD, since they are quickened & animated by the Virtue of the Sacrament. This Heavenly SPIRIT is shed upon us; It enlightens our ignorance; It corrects our false opinions; It clears up our doubts; It cures us of our prejudices; & It makes us to know & to love the Truth.

We read in Holy Scripture, that when Jonathan, fatigued with the battle against the Philistines had tasted a morsel of honey, his eyes were opened; & this slight sustenance gave him fresh strength. But the most Holy Eucharist produces still more wondrous Effects, & is far sweeter than honey to the taste; since Its Effects are produced in our Souls & hearts, & It opens the eyes of our Spirits, who worthily receive It, far more than the honey opened those of the son of Saul; for, in receiving the Adorable SPIRIT of JESUS CHRIST, with His FLESH & BLOOD, we consume, as did the Prophet, a Living Roll of Divine WISDOM. This Roll becomes to our Souls as *Honey for sweetness*, a holy Light, & a soft & genial

nial Flame, which is easier to feel than to describe.

That Spirit, full of Light & Heavenly Grace, ingratiates Itself with our spirit. Amongst other effects, It purifies our thoughts, & cures them of all distractions & of their continual wanderings; & makes it easy for them to apply to Heavenly things; It gives them a readiness & a taste for prayer, for praise, & for the service of God. It draws us towards the hidden Life; It teaches us to think as It thinks; It convinces us of sin; It gives us a hatred of falsehood & a love for the Truth; It weans us from earthly things; & It elevates us to reach unto those which are Heavenly.

Remember also, that the Cup of our Redeemer is a Chalice which inebriates with holy Joy, in which our human spirit perishes, & we lose all that is earthly & sensual. It makes a wondrous & happy change in our affections, in which, far from losing, we gain much; since we grow more disposed & more able to comprehend Divine Truth. This blessed change is wrought in us by the Strength of the Spirit of Jesus Christ, Which we receive in the most Holy Communion; & the complete influence which this superior & Heavenly Spirit gains over us, detaches us from earthly things, enlightens us, transforms us, & makes us embrace the qualities of that Spirit to which we are so closely united, in this Blessed Sacrament. Oh, what a happy Joy is this,

this, so holy, & so spiritual; which destroys & changes all that is earthly & sensual in us; which makes us think, & meditate, & reason, & pray, & speak, & act by the SPIRIT of JESUS CHRIST. Communicate then often; but do so worthily, with Fervour, with lively Faith & true Purity of spirit, of heart, & of body, & you will realise the working of this Heavenly Power within you.

Affections.

Come then unto me, O Adorable SPIRIT of my SAVIOUR & my GOD. Thou True BREAD of the Soul, quicken me, & unite me to Thyself. Enlighten me with those Heavenly Illuminations which Thou hast drawn from the Bosom of the DEITY. Reclaim me from my wanderings, Thou Who art the Way, the Truth, & the Life. Deliver me from my distractions; steady my fickleness by the weight of Thy Divine Words; & make me hear, read, mark, learn, & inwardly digest them. Correct me, by Holy Communion, of my inconsistencies, of my listlessness, of my distastes, & of my useless thoughts. Give me an eagerness & longing after Heavenly things, & for the holy thoughts with which Thou dost inspire me, & which can only come from Thee.

Give me the intelligence & the penetration of an understanding heart, of which I stand in need; not that I may become skilful in worldly science, which only puffs up the heart with vanity, & can

never

never make us holy; but that I may know Thy Greatness & the important Truths which lead me to Thy Love & the sanctification of my Soul. Give me the Wisdom of the Saints; since that is the only knowledge of which we stand in need, to arrive at a happy End; & since, by Thine infinite Goodness, Thou hast given Thyself to be my FOOD in the most Holy Eucharist, be Thou also, I pray Thee, my LIGHT, my GUIDE, my MODEL, my MASTER, & my Divine TEACHER.

I have reason to tremble, O my GOD, for having received Thee so often in the Blessed Sacrament of the Altar, Which is a Sacrament of Light as well as of Love & of Happiness, without being more fully instructed in the ways of Salvation & Perfection, in the knowledge of myself, & of GOD. In the midst of Light I have remained in darkness, & in ignorance of the ways which would lead me to true Happiness. United once to the SUN of Righteousness, I have lingered miserably in the obscurity of night. Nourished so often by the SPIRIT of Truth, I have let myself be led away & seduced by the Spirit of error & falsehood. O Divine SPIRIT of my Adorable SAVIOUR, Which is within me, I show Thee all my wounds, & Thou dost see them; cure them, I beseech Thee; & give unto me the Light of which I stand in need to know Thee & to love Thee, that I may know & hate myself.

Thanks=

Thanksgiving.

O Adorable SPIRIT of my Dearest LORD, the Source of Light & Purity, I worship Thee under the FORMS in Which Thou art concealed, in the most Blessed Eucharist. I adore Thee in myself, since Thou art Present there also. All my Spirit is consecrated to Thee, in Thanksgivings for the infinite Mercies Thou art ready to bestow upon me, in the Holy Communion Which I have received.

Oh, that my Spirit may rejoice in Thee, my Beloved REDEEMER, since I possess that SPIRIT Which animated Thee for the space of three & thirty years. Yes, I possess the SPIRIT Which spoke by Thy Sacred Mouth those Words of Life & Truth which enlightened all men; that SPIRIT, Which led Thee into the desert to teach me the practice of solitude & mortification, & to show me how to fight & overcome the temptations of the Devil, by Thine Own Example; that SPIRIT, Which groaned mysteriously, & was troubled at the death & resurrection of Lazarus, when Thou didst call him from the tomb; & the Same SPIRIT, Which Thou didst commend upon the Cross into the Hands of Thy Heavenly FATHER, to plead my cause, & to transfer me from the Tribunal of Justice to that of Mercy. This Wonder-working SPIRIT then is within me; It belongs to me, since It is given to me in

this

this All-holy Sacrament. I belong to CHRIST, since in the language of the great Apostle, those who have the SPIRIT of JESUS CHRIST are His; as those who have not this SPIRIT, are none of His. Yes, my Adorable SAVIOUR, I belong to Thee; & I will never belong to any other.

O SPIRIT of my JESUS, Which is within me, as in Thy FLESH & BLOOD; O Divine SPIRIT, Which bloweth where It listeth, revive my Soul with Thy Holy Inspiration, & fulfil all who receive Thee in Faith, with Thy Grace & Thy Love. SPIRIT of my SAVIOUR, Which is the Source of Life, animate & quicken me. SPIRIT of Adoption, take me for Thy child; do not abandon me, but make me walk in newness of life, that the old man may be destroyed within me, & that my spirit may never rejoice but in Thee, throughout this mortal life; so that I may see Thee Face to face, may know Thee, & may possess Thee eternally in Heaven.

Tenth Meditation.

Of the SOUL *of* JESUS CHRIST *in the most Holy Communion.*

I.

BEFORE approaching the Altar of GOD, consider seriously, that the Noblest, the most Perfect, the most Sublime, the Purest, & the most Excellent of all the Works which have ever proceeded from the Almighty Hands of GOD, since the beginning of the world, is the SOUL of our LORD JESUS CHRIST; & that it is this SOUL Which you are about to receive in the most Holy Communion.

It is the noblest Part of the Sacred Humanity of the REDEEMER; It is the most perfect Image & that Which bears the closest resemblance to the GODHEAD; It is the purest Breath of His adorable Mouth, the most Divine & tenderest Aspiration of His Heart, & the most worthy Object, throughout all space, of His Affection, His Kindness, & His Love. And this Holy SOUL, so Glorious & so Heavenly, after having left the Sacred BODY of JESUS CHRIST, to commend Itself into the Hands of His Heavenly FATHER, & having been united to It again by His glorious Resurrection, becomes Present together with the BODY of the LORD, in the Holy Sacrament of the Eucharist. It unites Itself to you in reception, to nourish your Soul, to communicate to you abundantly Its Gifts & Graces, Its Merits, Its Love, & Its very Life. See, therefore, what you must be prepared to receive in the most Holy Communion.

Consider then earnestly, the inestimable Treasure you possess, in receiving within you the SOUL of CHRIST. Remember that It has been, for the space of three & thirty years, the Source & Support of the Natural Life of that Adored SAVIOUR;

Saviour; the Sanctuary, in Which dwelt all His Virtues, His Knowledge, & His Graces. How is it then, that you do not share in all these priceless Treasures, in receiving this Holy Soul in which they ever dwell; for It only asks to shed them & communicate them on those who fervently ask for them, & who prepare themselves worthily to receive what they ask?

It is important to remember, that we are not less indebted for our Redemption to the Holy Soul of our Divine Lord, than to His Sacred Body & Blood. His Soul accepted the dreadful Sacrifice of the Cross, & accepted it for love of us; & the troubles & secret sorrows which It endured on Olivet, in the Judgment Hall, & on Calvary, were at the least, as severe & as much felt by His Soul, as those which His Body endured at the hands of the executioners.

From whence indeed proceeded that cruel & Bloody Sweat, if not from the awful conflict which that Agonised Soul sustained? It was so intense, that the contemplation of the humiliation, the outrages, & the shameful punishment to which His Body would be exposed, He could not prevent that bitter Cry escaping from His Sacred Lips—*My Soul is exceeding Sorrowful, even unto death*. What grief must It not have felt, when all His Disciples forsook Him & fled, leaving Him alone in the midst of His enemies; & in what a sad situation was It not placed. Abandoned of Its Father, deserted by Its friends,

friends, betrayed in the moſt cruel manner by a Diſciple, & ready to be delivered up to thoſe who only ſought after Its BLOOD; what ſorrowful Thoughts muſt It not have had; what fierce Conflicts; what internal Struggles, whilſt It prayed to Its Heavenly FATHER, & was not heard; & when foreſeeing all the humiliations It ſhould have to endure, the ſhame, & the cruelty It ſuffered in the Agonies of Death.

We may here conſider three different occaſions on which this Holy SOUL has laboured for our Salvation. The firſt was, when the HOLY SPIRIT united It to the BODY of the SAVIOUR, in the chaſte Womb of the Bleſſed Virgin. The ſecond was, when It was as it were torn from the BODY of the SON of GOD by the violence of Its Sufferings upon the Croſs, & when It was reſtored to the Hands of the Eternal FATHER. The third is, in the moſt Holy Communion, when that Glorious SOUL, reunited to the BODY of JESUS, joins us to Itſelf in this Bleſſed Sacrament in ſuch a myſterious manner; when It comes to take poſſeſſion of our bodies, our hearts, & our Souls, to give us an overwhelming proof of Its Love, & a ſure pledge of Eternal Happineſs.

We may notice then, in the SOUL of CHRIST, Its Union in the Womb of Bleſſed Mary; Its Separation on the Croſs; & Its Re-union with us in the Holy Euchariſt. This SOUL, at once Divine & Human, began the Work of our Redemption by Its firſt Union, when It animated

the

the Body of our Divine Saviour, at the moment in which It was Incarnate, through the Operation of the Holy Spirit. It obtained our Redemption effectually at the time of Its Separation upon the Cross. But It continues it still, day by day, in the most Holy Sacrament of the Altar, where It applies to each individual Soul, the Merits of Its Sufferings & Its Death. How precious then, should that moment be to us; & how eagerly should we approach a Sacrament, so Holy, & so Efficacious, Which is the Source of all our Happiness.

Think moreover, that the Soul of Jesus brings with It in the Blessed Sacrament, the Seal, the Pledge, & the sure Promise of our Eternal Bliss; & that It smooths the way for us to arrive at the blessed end of our predestination, which is everlasting Glory. And this it does by giving us a share in, & an impression of, the Virtues which It practised whilst It was united to the Mortal Body of our Saviour. We are thus enabled to exercise those Virtues with more readiness, & to resist temptation with more success; & these are some of the Fruits which we should draw from the Union of the Soul of the Son of God with our own, in the most Holy Eucharist.

II.

Be assured, for your comfort, that the All-holy Soul of Jesus, Which sustains & animates the Adorable Body of Christ, in the Sacrament

ment of the Altar, will not only enter into your person with His FLESH & BLOOD; but It will also penetrate into your Soul & all your powers, to make Itself mistress of them; to refine & purify them; to guide them safely, & to direct them in their different functions; to consecrate all their actions, & to shed upon them abundantly all the Virtues with which It is Itself filled.

Remember however, that though the SOUL of our REDEEMER in the Holy Communion is so Noble, Holy, & Divine, It will profit nothing to those who receive It only in Its outward Sacramental FORM. The SOUL of the Divine SAVIOUR, Which is so Glorious & Spiritual, much more demands our Souls than our bodies; since they are mortal & corruptible, & should only serve as channels by which It may enter into a more spiritual Sanctuary, more worthy of Itself. We receive It only Sacramentally, when we come to the Holy Sacrifice without due preparation, without faith or love, without fruits, & without devotion; or when we come like those slothful & careless Christians, who draw near too often, as if they were about to receive common food, which only nourishes the body.

To prepare ourselves worthily to receive a SOUL so Holy, so Pure, & so Powerful in Its Divine Operations, it is well to observe that It is composed of three Faculties, like our own—the Memory, the Understanding, & the Will. The Memory of JESUS CHRIST, was a Sanctuary only filled

Tenth Meditation. 107

filled with GOD. His Understanding was occupied only in thinking of Him, & in paying Him continual Homage, for the Salvation & Sanctification of men. His Will was inseparably united to that of His Heavenly FATHER.

The most Holy Sacrament is, without doubt, the best Remedy, & the surest Safeguard that can be found against all the sins which we ordinarily commit, by these three powers of the Soul. We have in the SOUL of our Blessed SAVIOUR, Which we receive there, a perfect Model upon which to mould ourselves; & a most gracious & powerful Assistance in enabling us to practise what GOD requires at our hands, in the use of these three powers of the Soul.

As our memory is too often filled with nothing but dangerous recollections; sometimes of injuries, either fancied or real; sometimes of past pleasures; sometimes of conversations we have heard, & which too often leave impressions which we must fight against, if we would preserve the purity of our minds, which, like a fire concealed under ashes, too often throws out sparks & kindles within us a flame hard to be extinguished; so JESUS CHRIST gives us at the Holy Altar that Which will preserve us from these things. He instituted the Sacrament indeed, in part, as a precious Memorial of the surprising Wonders that He wrought during His stay upon earth, for the greater Glory of GOD the FATHER, for the Salvation of guilty & sin-sick souls, who implore His Aid, & for

love

love of us; & also for a Memorial of His Mercies, which are numberless, & above all, of the excessive Sorrows which He endured, of the BLOOD which He shed in the course of His Passion, & of the Death which He suffered upon the Cross, to obtain for us a Life of Grace & of Glory.

The GOD of Mercy has left a Memorial of His Wonders, in the Precious FOOD Which He has given to those who live in His Faith & Fear. And He ever bears in mind this Covenant so advantageous to us, by Which, till the end of all things, He willingly gives Himself to us. And this wholesome Remembrance of it, which He has left us in the Holy Eucharist, should take the place, in our memories, of those unhallowed recollections which will not fail to carry corruption into our hearts, & all our senses.

Therefore our memory should be entirely occupied with GOD in that Holy Sacrament, & we should prepare ourselves for It thus. Before the Holy Communion we should call to mind the sad list of our sins, that we may lament them bitterly; & we should begin our preparation by a sincere Act of Contrition, that GOD may pardon us, & that the Soul thus purified, by the tears of penitence, may receive all the fulness of Grace which belongs to this Blessed Sacrament. During the time of Celebration, we should employ ourselves in meditating upon the Passion & Death of our REDEEMER, that we may be filled

with

with pity, & be found worthy of a more perfect application of It to ourselves, that we may show forth & make It known, according to the command of the Apostle. But, after Reception, we should be filled with a vivid recollection of His Wonders, His Goodness, & His Mercies, that we may be grateful for them, & render continual Thanksgivings, & engrave them deeply upon our hearts.

The Spirit of Jesus Christ then, should stamp upon us the impression of Its Merits. It should humble & cure our pride; should teach us not to despise others; & should curb our vain curiosity. The Will of Christ is united to our will, in order that It may repress its rebellious thoughts, regulate its desires, control all its movements, suppress its wrong feelings, purify its love, conquer its wilfulness, & inspire it with a perfect conformity to the Will of God. In short, the whole Soul of our Blessed Lord should purify our Souls; sanctify & fill them with Its Graces; & give them desire & zeal for the practice of Holiness.

Affections.

Praise the Lord, *O my Soul, & all that is within me praise His Holy Name*, are the words of the Psalmist; that is to say, all the powers of my Soul should bless & praise God, & glorify Him, with body & spirit, according to the command

mand of the Blessed Apostle. But if the Adorable BODY of GOD, Who gives Himself to you in the most Holy Eucharist deserves your gratitude & love, because It is an actual Portion of the GODHEAD, what do you not owe to His Holy SOUL, Which was Mistress of that BODY, & Which sustained Its very Life? If the BODY of JESUS CHRIST suffered Itself to be torn with scourgings, & to be covered with wounds; Its BLOOD to be shed, to deliver you from sin, death, & Hell, & to open Heaven for you; it is because His Blessed SOUL voluntarily submitted to this Sacrifice, for the love of you.

Entertain then with the most profound respect that Divine SOUL, not only in your body, wherein It is verily & indeed taken & received, in the most Holy Communion, but also in the powers of your Soul, that the Impression & Image of It may remain there. Keep that Holy & Sanctifying SOUL in your memory, with all love & veneration. Implore It fervently to fill & consecrate this Sanctuary, that It may root out for ever all that can cause the slightest stain; & that nothing may remain there but the remembrance of Its Mercies, which are infinite. Keep it also in your understanding, & take It for the Director of your life, of all your thoughts, your knowledge, your undertakings, & your actions. That Holy SOUL would unite Its WILL to yours, by this Great Sacrament; do not then place obstacles in the way; but rather long for this Divine Union

with

with much desire. Let the WILL of JESUS CHRIST reign in the place of your own will, with an absolute & sovereign sway. Learn to do GOD's Holy WILL in all things, & It will become your own.

Thanksgiving.

O most Blessed SAVIOUR, I ought now to love Thee more than ever, & to love Thee not only with all my heart, but also with all my Soul, according to Thy command, since Thou dost give unto me Thy SOUL in the most Holy Eucharist. Not content with having exposed It, for love of me, to the most cruel of agonies in Gethsemane, where It cried out, by Thy Lips, that It was *exceeding sorrowful even unto Death;* where It showed Its bitter anguish by the Bloody Sweat, which proceeded from that Sacred FRAME Which It so soon abandoned; not satisfied with having given Itself upon the Cross to die, for the Redemption of mankind, when, after the most exceeding sufferings, It departed from Thy BODY, & commended Itself into the Hands of Its Heavenly FATHER; Thou dost also give It unto me here, Whole & Entire, since It animates that Divine BODY, Which at Thy Altar I receive. As I have the unspeakable honour of possessing within me the PERSON of the Same SAVIOUR, the Same GOD, the Same FLESH & BLOOD, & the Same SOUL, Which was born of Thy Virgin Mother,

Mother, may I not humbly say, in the words of her own inspired Canticle of Thanksgiving— *My Soul doth magnify the* LORD, *& my Spirit hath rejoiced in* GOD *my* SAVIOUR, Who *hath regarded the lowliness of His Handmaiden.* He has not only given me His FLESH & BLOOD, His HEART, His BODY in the Holy Sacrament of the Eucharist, but He has also given me His SOUL, to sanctify me, to consecrate me, & to save my Soul alive.

All-powerful as He is, He is good enough to descend from His Heavenly Throne, & to lower Himself to me, who am but dust & ashes, that He may take up His abode within me, to fulfil me with happiness, if I only know how to appreciate It. It rests with me then, whether this SOUL, All-holy & All-powerful as It is, should work great things within me, & endue me with endless Gifts.

O LORD JESU, what Thanksgiving should I not pay to that Blessed SOUL of Which I am now the possessor? Let It quicken all the powers of my Soul; that my memory may remember nothing but Thee; that my Spirit may only think of Thee; & that my will may love nothing but Thee, through time, & through all Eternity.

Eleventh Meditation.

Of the LIFE *of* JESUS CHRIST *in the most Holy Communion.* Part I.

I.

THE LIFE of GOD, Which forms the support, & causes the happiness of the Saints & Angels in Heaven, is also the Nourishment & Life of the just upon earth, who receive the BODY & BLOOD of CHRIST worthily, in the most Holy Communion. What wonderful Goodness in Almighty GOD, Whom we adore, to give to each one of us His OWN LIFE, for our food. There is however this difference, that those Blessed Ones, who enjoy the visible Presence of GOD in Heaven, & who have arrived at the long desired end of their labours, receive that LIFE of GOD as It is in GOD Himself, in all the Brightness of His Glory, without being consumed by It; that is to say, they receive It openly, unveiled, without any reservation, or being in any way subdued, because being glorified & freed from all encumbrance of the senses, GOD has made them capable of receiving & digesting that Heavenly FOOD. They are strong in the Strength of GOD Himself, Who works within them, & makes them strong enough to sustain all the radiancy of His Glory, without having occasion to cover their face, as Moses did, from the sight of the children of Israel. They live then actually the LIFE of GOD, since they are made One with Him by an intimate & mutual Indwelling, & by a perfect Union of SUBSTANCE with substance, without anything intervening. They are in GOD, & GOD is in them; thus they have the Strength of GOD to entertain the LIFE of GOD.

But the holy, who are still travellers upon earth, really receive the same FOOD of the LIFE of GOD, in the Blessed Sacrament of the Altar, which forms their greatest pleasure & consolation in their exile; but this LIFE of GOD is veiled & hidden under the Sacred Eucharistic FORMS, which soften down the rays of Its Glory. It is, as it were, subdued under a favouring shadow, as when the HOLY SPIRIT worked the Mystery of the Incarnation of the WORD, in the Womb of the Blessed Virgin; & to make use of an expression of the Holy Fathers, that LIFE of GOD becomes Milk, suited to the weakness of human nature. In short, that Adorable SAVIOUR looks upon us as children, whose powers are not equal to digest substantial food, until it has been properly prepared to suit their weakness. To lower Himself to our position, He gives us, in the Holy Eucharist, this Heavenly Sustenance, Which is the same BREAD with which the Holy Saints & Angels are nourished & refreshed in their Glorified State.

It is thus that GOD, Whom we receive as it were

were concealed, at the Holy Altar, is the Same GOD Whom we shall enjoy, when He shall be revealed to us in Heaven; if indeed we make a holy use of the Eucharistic BREAD which conveys to us the LIFE of GOD, & GOD Himself. The Saints, elevated & strengthened by the Light of Glory, see Face to face, without veil or cloud, the Living GOD, Who feeds them with His Own FLESH, & quickens them with His Own LIFE. We see Him now, with the eye of Faith, veiled under the FORMS Which conceal Him from our eyes. They feel the unspeakable Sweetness & the wonderful Strength of that LIFE of GOD, Which sustains them. The same of which the Angel spoke to Tobit, when he said—*All these days I did appear unto you, but I did neither eat nor drink; but ye saw a vision.* This was the LIFE of GOD, & the blessed Vision of which he spake, & to which he was inseparably united, & even when he was upon the earth.

These blessed Spirits are swallowed up & drowned in the Ocean of the GODHEAD, & in an overwhelming Torrent of pleasure, whilst we only receive a small Stream of these pure Delights, though we possess the Source of them as they do. We have need of laborious preparations, we draw with difficulty from a deep Well, that Living Water which springeth up unto Eternal Life; but in Heaven, that Divine LIFE is a Shower Which falls upon all, with a wonderful softness & abundance. With them this LIFE is permanent;

nent; with us It is only passing. Yet we feel, what Faith assures us of, when we draw nigh with fervour to the Altar, that here is something more than common Bread. We gain a Strength, & a Supernatural Life which invigorates our Souls, & fulfils us with a spiritual & real Joy, which we cannot express; & we feel awakened within us a new & precious Existence, which can be no other than the LIFE of GOD, imperceptibly penetrating, through the Holy Communion, into our Souls, & all our powers.

This unearthly & grateful feeling, which we cannot describe, is one in which our bodily powers have no share. This pure & spiritual joy which is shed upon us in such a mysterious manner; this inward warning, like that which the Disciples felt upon their way to Emmaus, when our Blessed SAVIOUR Himself was with them; these fervent desires after perfection; these generous resolutions to live only to GOD; this disgust towards the flesh; this readiness to prayer & the practice of virtue; this new strength against the different temptations to which we are exposed, & which we oftentimes feel more than ever after a worthy Reception; all these things show us that there is within us a Hidden LIFE which animates us; & this LIFE cannot proceed from the common food, which only serves to support the body, but from the LIFE of GOD, Which is communicated to us when we receive at the Holy Altar.

II.

II.

Remember that a half-hearted & lukewarm Christian, who neglects to frequent this All-holy Sacrament, as often as he has the opportunity, because he will not strive to change his heart; or because the preparations he must make before coming to the Altar of the Lord appear to him too laborious; or who only approaches It out of custom, & without any feeling of the Presence of God, can only be considered as an unhealthy tree, drooping & almost dead, or like a wild & barren stem, which only bears leaves & is not capable of bearing good fruit worthy of Life Eternal.

The lukewarm & careless Christian, then, is an unfruitful tree, which hardly escapes being cast into the fire; since he occupies in the Church a place which another might better fill than he. He only possesses an animal & imperfect life; none of his actions are animated by the Spirit of God; all his views are low & earthly; & there is nothing generous or elevated about his feelings; & he produces no good fruit, until he has been grafted upon the Life of God, which can only be done by a worthy Reception of the Blessed Eucharist.

This Holy Communion, indeed, may be considered as a Spiritual & Heavenly Grafting. By It, Jesus Christ, in His Fulness, is engrafted upon us. He takes from our nature all that is unfruitful, alien, & wild. He corrects all that is imperfect in us. He raises our natural life & leads us to a higher state of spiritual existence. He gives us purer views; more elevated & perfect motives. He enables us to bear fruit that is more nourishing, & more agreeable to His taste, & to our own.

As this Divine SAVIOUR is the Principle of our life, & of the spiritual Life within us, He animates all our actions; He quickens us by His HOLY SPIRIT; He purifies our feelings; He directs them towards Himself; & oftentimes He places His Own in their stead. Of our moral virtues, which only gain temporal recompense, He makes, by this Heavenly Grafting, Christian Virtues, which, by the Grace which we receive in the Blessed Sacrament, make us meet to inherit Eternal Rewards. In a word, the wild olive tree, being grafted on the true Stock, can only live the LIFE of GOD. If it grows up from the earth towards Heaven; if it takes fresh strength & new growth; if it puts out new branches, & beautiful leaves; if it produces finer fruit, & more of it, & of improved flavour & quality than when it was a simple wild olive, all comes from the Sap which, drawn from that Divine Graft, spreads itself into all the powers of the Soul. It purifies the memory from all dangerous recollections of earthly pleasures; & It imprints in their place, the remembrance of all His Mercies, of His precious Death & Passion.

It

It makes it easier for the mind to be occupied with Divine Truth. It furnishes it with holy thoughts. It enlarges the understanding, that it may understand mysteries. It implants the purest feelings, & the most perfect & fervent affections in the heart & will; & makes them ever watchful to fight against the carnal desires of the flesh, which may rise up within them. To say all in one word, It is CHRIST Himself, Who quickens them, Who thinks, Who loves, Who acts, & Who lives within them.

It is true that this wild olive tree, which, by a holy use of the Blessed Sacrament, has become a fruitful tree, in the mysterious field of the Church, & in the garden which the Heavenly SPOUSE takes delight in, is still held down to earth, by the necessities of its mortal nature. It is true that it is obliged to draw from earth, the material food, which supports the body, food which can only be earthly; but the Holy Communion, Which It receives with all love, is the Nourishment & the Graft of spiritual Life which supports & strengthens the Soul, & gives it new life & a new nature, infinitely more perfect than the first. And by This it grows insensibly in light & wisdom, in piety & love, in fervour, & in all holy virtues & affections.

That mysterious Tree, planted, grafted & watered by the Hand of GOD, grows by degrees; & in proportion to its being strengthened by Divine Nourishment, it mounts up towards Heaven.
It

It is no longer what it used to be. It has passed from the weakness & infirmity of the creature, to the strength of the LIFE of GOD; & that, because it has the unspeakable blessing of being supported by His Own SUBSTANCE. It ought, consequently, to have changed its manner of life & action. Its thoughts should be purer; its affections should be more free from earthly things; & its actions should be holier & more worthy of the adorable Principle which sets them in motion. And all these should be transformed into Him, Who dwells within them, & Who animates them by His SPIRIT, by His Grace, by His Love, & by His Divine LIFE.

The most natural & the strongest desire of mortal man is for life. There is nothing he will not endure to prolong & to save it. If you love the true Life, draw near unto the Blessed Sacrament of the Altar. It is there you will find the Source, not of the natural life, which only gives you a few more years to live upon earth, but of the Supernatural & Divine LIFE, Which will give you Immortality. This BREAD of Angels will be in you the Fountain of Living Water, springing up unto Everlasting Life. Receive then with meekness, according to the command of the Apostle, the Engrafted WORD, Which is able to save your Soul alive, & to grant it both the Life of Grace, & the Life of Glory.

Affections.

The holy Psalmist has said, that his *heart* & his *flesh rejoice in the Living* GOD; but, O LORD, would not that exclamation have been more lively & fervent, if the lips which uttered it had served as a channel for the Adorable BODY of his SAVIOUR; & if his heart had had the happiness of forming a Temple & a Sanctuary for the FLESH, the BLOOD, the HEART, the SOUL, & the Divine NATURE of that Living GOD, in Whom he rejoiced? This Saint, O my GOD, only possessed Thee in type & figure; but I have the advantage & the blessing of possessing Thee in Reality. Notwithstanding, he was filled with zeal, his expressions were warm & fervent; but I am lukewarm & indifferent. His penitence was excessive, & his constant & generous love had been rewarded by that Grace, which is the precious Outpouring of Divine LIFE. I possess, in the most Holy Communion, the Source of that Grace, & the Principle of that LIFE; & yet I am always fainthearted & cold.

Live then the LIFE of GOD, O my Soul. Droop no more, nor die by fresh contempt of Divine Grace. Let your works be no longer dead works, since you possess within you by the Holy Eucharist, the DESTROYER of Death, & the AUTHOR of Life. Be no longer a wild & unfruitful tree, cumbering the ground in which it is planted; & only bearing leaves, that have no value, & bitter fruits that are good for nothing.

Now that you have taken root, & the AUTHOR of Life is engrafted upon you, bring forth abundantly the sweet Fruits of Grace. Rear also beforehand those of Glory, of which you have so often received the precious Seed, Which only asks for the opportunity of producing them. Be no longer a lifeless corpse, without feeling or action; but live, think, & act in GOD, with GOD, for GOD.

Eat the LIFE Itself, cries a Holy Father. Drink the LIFE, & you shall have the LIFE of GOD. That LIFE is One. It is Health-giving; It is Holy; It is exempt from death; & it is by communicating often, & worthily, that you will share in the LIFE of the BODY, the SOUL, & the Divine NATURE of your LORD & SAVIOUR JESUS CHRIST.

Thanksgiving.

Without Thee, O my SAVIOUR, Who art the Living GOD, & the AUTHOR of Life, I should be dead. I was condemned to die, & I have fully deserved death. My unhappy state was that of a criminal, upon whom the sentence of death has been passed without being informed of the day of execution. But, O Heavenly DELIVERER, Thou art come to bring back to me

Grace

Grace & Life. I cannot indeed enter into Grace, nor hope for Life, but by Thee Alone. Thou art my only Hope. That LIFE is hid with Thee in GOD, & Thou couldeſt not have given It to me without loſing the LIFE Which Thou hadſt as MAN, & without ſuffering Death, which Thou haſt done.

Thou haſt alſo declared, by the mouth of the Beloved Diſciple, that Thou art come to give me LIFE; & Thou haſt fulfilled Thy Divine Word, by taking upon Thee our Fleſh, & in ſuffering the moſt cruel & ſhameful death for love of me. But Thou haſt been pleaſed again to add to thoſe Words of Life, that Thou art come to give me Life abundantly; & it is this Heavenly LIFE, in ſuch abundance, that Thou haſt encloſed in the Sacred FOOD upon our Altars; & in this Divine BREAD, called above all other, the BREAD of Angels, & the BREAD of Life, which I receive, whenever I come to the moſt Bleſſed Sacrament.

I will live then, O my SAVIOUR, & I will live the Life of Grace; ſince I have the Precious SEED within me, in my very heart. I will confidently affirm that I will live the Life of Glory, becauſe I have the happineſs to poſſeſs the Pledge & the Aſſurance of it; & Thou haſt Thyſelf declared, that thoſe who eat this BREAD of Life will live for ever. O LORD JESU, is it too much to give my whole life, as I ought, in return for ſuch an ineſtimable Benefit? Alas, I

feel

feel my gratitude so burdened, & as it were overwhelmed with so much Mercy, & so many & great Favours, that I can make no return; none, at least, unless Thou art pleased Thyself to teach me what I ought to say, & to put feelings within my heart, & words upon my lips, which may be worthy of Thee.

Twelfth Meditation.

Of the Life *of* Jesus Christ *in the most Holy Communion.   Part II.*

I.

The Adorable Saviour, Whom we receive in the most Holy Communion, is not only Living God, but as Himself saith, Very Life. For, being God, Self-existent & Eternal, He subsists by His Own Power; all that is in Him is Life, & none can live but by Him. His Flesh is Life; His Blood is Life; His Soul is Life; & so is His Divinity. All His Sacred Person; all Its component Parts; & All that we receive at the Holy Altar is Life, & is enabled to bestow the same upon us. Yea, His very *Words*,—as He Himself tells us—*are Spirit & they are Life*, because they destroy the Empire of Death within us, & produce the Life of Grace.

There-

Therefore, in communicating worthily, Life is ours with all its Blessings, because we receive the Living GOD Himself, the AUTHOR of Life; & the Divine LIFE, Which He communicates in the Venerable Sacrament is lasting, sweet, & holy, in proportion to the faith, & purity, & fervour wherewith we approach It. How marvellous is the blindness of those, whose love of life, & fear of death is so excessive, & who yet draw near so rarely to this Adorable SOURCE of Life. And here, we do not speak of that lower life, which is the effect of the mere union of Soul & body, & which only produces natural actions & such as are conformable to the principle which gives them birth; but of a Life infinitely more sublime, because Spiritual & Divine, which causes Supernatural Acts, & results from the intimate Union of the Soul with the Living & True GOD, contracted in the Adorable Sacrifice of the Altar, whereby man rises to the glorious participation of the Divine NATURE.

It is indeed in the most Holy Communion that the Living GOD takes entire possession of our whole being; of our memory, & mind, & will, & heart, & Soul, & body. All become peculiarly His Own; & He watches over us with an Owner's care; if only we will receive Him in the Spirit of Humility, of Faith, of Purity, & of Love.

Then, as the Soul acts on the body, in a simply natural way; so, but in a very high & holy manner,

ner, does this Adorable SAVIOUR act upon the Soul, because He is its Soul & its Life. Entirely Present, in all its nature, & in all its faculties, He works by & in it; & thus makes all its actions worthy of Eternal Life, because He now no more regards them as the acts of a mere creature, but as His Own Actions. He rewards them in a manner proportioned to the Principle which inspires them, & to the Life which quickens them—namely, His Own. And when He crowns them, He crowns them as the Gifts of His Own Goodness.

Let us suppose that we bring to this Divine Sacrament the life of Grace, either carefully preserved by the avoidance of all that destroys it, or repaired & restored by the Sacrament of Penitence. Without such a precaution, It were rather a Sacrament of death than of Life; & yet such Grace & Life are weak, because they are not yet perfectly united with the adorable PRINCIPLE whence they proceed, nor supported by the Precious FOOD which nourishes them, & endues them with all strength. With this common Grace, we act too much according to the dictates of nature; & if we practise Holiness, it is in a human & imperfect manner.

But, in Holy Communion, CHRIST, Who is Himself our FOOD, strengthens that Grace, & supports that Life by His Own, which passes into us, & takes the place of ours. Before Communicating, we acted by our own will, & our

works

works were only those of human beings; but, after one worthy & profitable Reception of the Blessed Sacrament, & still more, after many, it is CHRIST Who thinks, it is CHRIST Who desires, Who loves, & speaks, & acts within us. As the Apostle says—it is no longer we that live, but CHRIST That liveth in us; we become His instruments, & our actions, & our virtues have nobler & higher aims, & purer & more perfect motives.

Hence, we must needs conclude, that if CHRIST is the Life of the Soul, as the Soul is the life of the body, we ought with all possible frequency to draw near to the Divine Eucharist, wherein this Life is hid with CHRIST in GOD—& that, worthily & with fervour. Because, as the Soul, though it be the life of the body, cannot animate it without the aid of material nourishment; so CHRIST does not vivify the Soul, without the Spiritual FOOD of His most Precious BODY & BLOOD.

A worthy Communicant, says a Holy Doctor, becomes like unto the SON of GOD. He is transformed into Him, & partakes of His Divine Life, though he seems to act but as a man. Besides the Grace which is the Life of the Soul, he bears about within himself the precious Germ of Life Immortal. That most fertile Plant will speedily bring forth its Fruit; if the tree be well tended, strengthened by that Divine LIFE, enriched by that Quickening FLESH, & plentifully
watered

watered by the BLOOD of CHRIST. So shall it grow & flourish, till it reach the heights of Eternity itself.

Now, think over your past Communions. Consider how you have, & how you ought to have, profited by them. And if you do not yet feel the effects of the Supernatural Life, then, surely, your heart has not been duly prepared; it has not been garnished with Faith, Desire, Purity, & Love; & you will have to render a fearful account of Grace misused. Oh, let your future preparations be more careful; & do you strive to live as if each day were the day of your last Communion.

II.

Consider the awful engagements you enter into, by participating in the LIFE of GOD, in Holy Communion. They are contained in those Words of CHRIST, recorded by the Beloved Disciple— *He that eateth Me, the same shall live by Me:* that is, according to an Ancient Father, he who desires to receive Life, must change his life, & do all things which may conform it to the LIFE of GOD Incarnate, of Whom he partakes in the most Blessed Eucharist. And this the rather, because he cannot participate in that Divine LIFE, without labouring with all his might to become worthy of It, by leading a new life; for the Blessed Sacrament only works Life in us proportionately to our own dispositions. Powerful as It is, It absolutely demands our co-operation, &
never

never acts without it. O admirable Sign of Unity, continues that holy Doctor; O precious Bond of Charity, who shall not long for Thee, seek Thee, love Thee, & hasten to Thee? Would ye live, not the earthly & carnal life of man, but a Life, blessed & sublime, the LIFE of GOD? Draw near to this All-holy Sacrament with burning hearts; cling to the Living BODY of CHRIST; be One with Him; & never part from Him. Yea, live to Him, by Him, in Him, & for Him; since yours is the joy of possessing, through Holy Communion, the Life of GOD Himself.

He who lives to GOD, makes Him the final End of every thought, intent, act, hope, & feeling. He ever looks to Him, loves Him Alone, desiring none beside Him. Towards Him, he aspires; to Him, he tends as the Beginning, the Centre, & the End of every action; & such a life should be the effect of Holy Communion, if we have prepared ourselves to receive It worthily; & if, after Its Reception, we are careful to preserve the Grace It brings, & to keep Its memory & impression in our hearts.

He who lives by GOD, seeks no other stay. He relies on no human help, & trusts in Him for all things, with no apprehension concerning any matter, however grievous, except it affect Eternal Salvation. He preserves with religious care & faithfulness the Grace, & Spirit, & Impression of the LIFE of GOD, received at the Holy Altar;

so

so that, as the body derives natural power only from its material food, so the Soul draws Strength, Courage, & spiritual Life from this Heavenly BREAD Alone. He acts indeed, in all things, as one supported & nourished by the LIFE of GOD. But of what glorious deeds is he not capable, whose Soul lives but in GOD; of what Devotion, of what Good Works, of what Love of GOD?

He who lives in GOD, is never drawn from that dear Home, by voluntary distraction; & far less by undue attachments to any created thing. In Him Alone he seeks to rest; with Him are his delights; to Him he hastens back with loving impatience, if by any chance he be parted from Him. He bears GOD ever in his memory, in his mind, & in his heart, with tender, faithful, & reverent care. He never forgets the Divine Mercies vouchsafed in the Adorable Sacrifice. He calls them frequently to mind, with hearty gratitude. He deeply feels the Infinite Goodness which has made Itself One with our flesh, by Incarnation; with our Souls, by daily Grace; & with both, by the Blessed Eucharist, wherein He makes us partakers of His Very LIFE, by giving us the Heavenly FOOD of His BODY, & BLOOD, & SOUL, & DIVINITY, together with sure Pledges of a Life far more precious & unending, in which our glorified Spirits shall live in Peace Eternal, in & by the LIFE of GOD.

He who lives for GOD, gives Him his whole life,

life, in love & gratitude for the precious LIFE once given on Calvary for our Salvation, & many times in Holy Communion for our prefent Grace, & future Glory; he is in an habitual ftate of readinefs to make an entire furrender of life for the Love or Glory of GOD; & to Him he devotes his mind & talents, his memory & heart, all he has & all he is.

Think on thefe things before you draw near GOD's Holy Altar. Ponder them after you have received the BREAD of Life. Prove your own felves. Live to GOD, by Him, in Him, & for Him; & then you will be fit for daily Communion.

Affections.

When, O LORD, fhall I dare utter thofe words of the Apoftle—*I live; yet not I, but* CHRIST *liveth in me?* As often as I have received the Living GOD; fo often have I been nourifhed by His FLESH & by His DIVINITY; & fo often has His HEART, the Source of very Life, refted near my own; & yet, have I lived a Divine Life, unfhackled by tepidity & lukewarmnefs?

Inftead, alas, of living to my GOD, I have lived wholly to myfelf; divers times refifting His Commands, defpifing His Infpirations, & cafting off His Yoke, as if I were no longer His, & as if He were no longer my MASTER.
Blinded

Blinded by self-love & pride, I have made myself the end of all my actions; & my works have not been works of Life, nor those of a Christian, receiving Life in the most Holy Eucharist.

Instead of living by my GOD, I have only lived a carnal, earthly, animal life; careless to preserve the supernatural Life bestowed on me by the Blessed Sacrament, I have lost It by mingling too freely with creatures, & so neglecting the Presence of the Living GOD.

Instead of living in my GOD, & abiding in Him after receiving Him, I have hurried away from that ineffable Centre which attracted me with infinite Charity, to seek elsewhere for rest, which yet I never found. Instead of living for GOD, I have lived for created beings, & have bestowed on them the care & thought I owed to Him Alone; & with the strangest blindness, I have lived for vanity, & for the world.

O Living & Life-giving GOD, Thou True BREAD of the Spirit, & of Life, Who sustainest Soul, & heart, & mind for time & for all Eternity, I humbly beseech Thee to nourish, quicken, & strengthen me for ever. Verily, O my LORD, I see & acknowledge that life out of Thee is no life, but is very death.

Thanksgiving.

What joy & comfort, Dearest LORD, is this to me. LIFE, & its AUTHOR are mine own. Yea,

Twelfth Meditation.

Yea, truly spake Thy Beloved Apostle that in Thee *was Life; & the Life was the Light of men.* So, when Thou art mine in the most Holy Communion, mine are Life, & Light, & the SOURCE of both: the SOURCE of Life to preserve me from death, & the SOURCE of Light to drive away my darkness, to enlighten my ignorance, & to lead me in the Way of Salvation. Abide then with me, O Thou from Whom proceed the Life of Grace, & the Life of Glory. Delight Thyself in me, O LORD; destroy Thou the works of death; work in me Thine Own Righteousness, & be in my Soul a Well of water, springing up into Everlasting Life, bearing in its current every thought & wish, my heart, my understanding, & my Soul, unto that blessed Abode of Life, where there shall be no more fear of death.

By the perfect Virtue of this Spiritual & Living BREAD, Which I have received, grant me, I beseech Thee, LORD JESU, that Everlasting Life, that my Thanksgivings may likewise be everlasting; since time is too short to praise Thee for Thine infinite Mercy.

But, O my SAVIOUR, that I may be not unworthy of this Grace, vouchsafe to show forth Thy Life in me; let me now rule my life by the Pattern of Thine; let the thoughts of my mind, the desires of my will, the feelings of my heart, the sight of my eyes, the words of my lips, & the works of my hands, be perfectly likened unto Thine.

Thine. Quicken Thou them by that SPIRIT of Life, Which Thou haft given me. Let me fo fet Thee as a feal upon mine heart, that the Impreffion of Thine Image may perfectly be formed thereon.

Thirteenth Meditation.

Of the DIVINITY of JESUS CHRIST, in the moſt Holy Communion.

I.

Now let your heart & mind riſe up beyond all created things on earth, beyond all things viſible & inviſible in Heaven; yea, beyond the FLESH & BLOOD, the Entire HUMANITY & SOUL of our LORD JESUS CHRIST. That FLESH indeed is infinitely Pure & Glorious, becauſe Hypoſtatically united to GOD, Who is Very Purity Itſelf. That Adorable BLOOD is infinitely Precious; becauſe it is the BLOOD of JESUS, & the Price of our Redemption. That SOUL is infinitely Glorious; for during three & thirty years It was, yea, & now It is, the Life of CHRIST as MAN, & the moſt Glorious of all the Works of the SPIRIT. Yet, in the venerable Sacrament of the Holy Euchariſt is ſomewhat unſpeakably more Auguſt, more Sublime, & more Adorable; even the DI-

VINITY

vinity of our Lord Jesus Christ, doubly hidden beneath the Sacramental Species, & the Veil of His Sacred Humanity.

Think thus when you approach the Divine Sacrament—that, together with a perfect Humanity, infinitely exalted by the most august Union ever effected, which is the Hypostatic Union, you moreover receive Entire Divinity, veiled under the most humble Forms; a Divinity Which will enter in & dwell with you, will take complete possession of all your powers of Soul & body, & will so serve as your Food, that, if only you offer It no hindrance, you shall be transformed into Itself.

Purify your mind, animate your faith, & raise both to your God. Put far away from you all that imagination can fancy, eye can see, & reason can understand. Nothing but Faith, at once submissive & fervent, has a right to rise to God, passing all created & sensible things, & penetrating to the Bosom of Almighty God, there to contemplate His Divinity.

Think that you receive, in the All-holy Communion, That God Who created the universe with a Word, & Who preserves it by His Power; Whom Heaven & earth adore; Whose Name strikes terror into Hell; Who spake by the Prophets, & is Greater than all the Kings of the earth. To you He comes down; in you He dwells; He acts for you; He rests with you; He takes delight in you; He becomes your Food,

nourish-

nourishing you, not only with His Precious BODY & BLOOD, but also with His Very DIVINITY, & that, because He loves you, & would be loved by you.

Yea, This Almighty GOD, not content with having taken Flesh in Blessed Mary's Womb, for your Salvation, carries His exceeding Love so far as to make Himself your Food, in order to draw closer unto your heart, to unite Himself more nearly with your Soul; & that, with an Union so perfect, as to amount in one sense to Unity itself. He would that man should become the child of GOD; therefore He has become both the CHILD of Mary, & the FOOD of man. O ineffable Humiliation of GOD. O marvellous Exaltation of man.

He descends from the Throne of His Glory; & He descends to our nothingness, even as He exists from all Eternity in the Bosom of the FATHER; & He descends at the word of the Priest, His creature, obeying his voice, as if he were His Lord & God. He, the Supreme Greatness, casts a miraculous Veil over the glorious Majesty of His DIVINITY, when He communicates thus intimately with us in the Divine Sacrament; because He seeks our hearts, which He created for Himself, & wills to feed, to fill, to exalt, to transform into Himself, & to possess entirely, without reserve.

The GOD, Whom Heaven & the Heaven of Heavens cannot contain, comes in PERSON to set up His Throne within the narrow bounds of our heart.

heart. The LORD GOD of Hosts, the KING of Kings, & LORD of Lords, lays by the weapons of Almighty Power. Love disarms His Terrors. He comes to dwell among us; not, as under the Old Law, a GOD of Terror, but a GOD of perfect Love.

This is That GOD, Who, in His Holy HUMANITY, worked so many evident Miracles, which were as many certain Proofs of His DIVINITY; Who healed the sick, gave sight to the blind, & raised the dead; Who fed thousands in the wilderness, & not only cast out devils Himself, but gave that power unto others; & Who sought out, taught, touched, & converted the most hardened & wicked of sinners. This is He, Who gives Himself to you in the Blessed Sacrament of the Altar. Receive Him therefore, detain Him, & honour Him, as is most justly due, with the reverence due to the ALMIGHTY; with the love & tenderness due unto the SAVIOUR. And hasten thou unto Him with fervent eagerness; for lo, This is the SPOUSE of faithful Souls. See thou open unto Him, not only thy lips, but also thy heart & thy Soul.

II.

Consider the infinite distance between GOD & human nature; between essential Holiness, & man conceived & born in sin, & full of misery & wickedness; between that Greatness, & this nothingness; between infinite Purity, before which the

very

very Angels are not clean, & human defilement; between the glorious Light, which is the Source of all light, & the thick darkness, which is the gloomy heritage of fallen man.

Let a part of your preparation for Holy Communion consist in reflecting on these two extremes, which cannot be drawn together, but by a wondrous Miracle of Divine Love. Let such thoughts rouse in your heart & mind a lively sense of GOD's exceeding Mercy towards you; strive to respond to it by true & tender gratitude, by ardent love, & by eager desire for frequent Communion.

Yea, how marvellous is this prodigy. The exceeding Love of GOD wills to make those nigh who were afar off; to do all things in order to bring them near to Him; & to be Present on His Altar, when the Priest says the Words of Consecration. From His Altar, He wills to enter into our bodies, hearts, & Souls, that He may cleanse all our defilements by His infinite Purity; mingle His Light with our darkness, that we may see; His Strength with our weakness, that we may not fall; His Greatness with our meanness, to exalt us to Himself; His Sacred HEART with our heart, that it may be set on fire with His Own Love; & His DIVINITY with our Soul & our whole nature, that we may be wholly transformed into Himself.

After receiving the Blessed Sacrament, remember that GOD is within you, & that therefore you are a Temple, a Sanctuary, a living Altar which contains the DIVINITY, surrounded by infinite Celestial Intelligences, absorbed in adoration.

Join with these blessed Spirits in Bliss; love & adore like them; let the purity & fervour of their homage supply the faintness of your feelings; unite with them in heart, & mind, & voice, that you may think of Him, adore Him, love Him, & praise Him, if not according as is due, yet as perfectly as may be possible to you.

Consider also that it is GOD, Who comes unto you, with all the glorious Attributes of His DIVINITY, & that you receive with Him, His Might, His Wisdom & Greatness, His Mercy & Goodness, His Fulness & boundless Charity.

By a miracle of Mercy & of Love, His Immensity contracts, that it may conform to these narrow bounds. His Eternity seems to subject Itself to time, that It may gain eternal Beatitude & Glory for us. His adorable Fulness sheds itself profusely on us, that it may enrich us with most precious Treasures of Grace & Glory. His Bounty unites itself closely with us, condescends to our weakness, bows its great Heart to ours, & raises us to itself. His Divine Mercy becomes incarnate, so to speak, within us, tenderly pitying our frailty, & pardoning all our sins; & that, with a pardon so certain, that it is sealed with His BLOOD, Wherewith we are at once watered, nourished, & purified in the most Holy Communion.

Herein

Herein He imparts to us far more of His Light than in any other Sacrament. If the Soul be rightly prepared, He enlightens its darkness, & dispels its ignorance. When you have tasted of this Honeycomb, your eyes open to Divine Truth; you learn to know GOD, & to know yourself. The Almighty GOD of Glory here bestows His Strength upon you, that you may more boldly resist temptation, more patiently endure adversity, & more steadfastly labour, fearing nothing but sin.

The priceless Purity of CHRIST, here received into your heart, cleanses its most hidden stains; yea, effaces even the baneful impressions which vain pleasures may have made upon your senses. His Holiness detaches you from creatures, & from yourself; dedicating you wholly to Himself, a Sanctuary to serve henceforth no other end, but to contain Him, & to offer Sacrifice unto Him. His Divine Wisdom enlightens & instructs you; & guards you against error & delusion. His infinite Greatness impresses on you the sense of your own nothingness; cures you of your pride; & renders your adoration & worship more reverent & submissive. His Divine Love warms your heart, & enkindles in your Soul fresh ardour. His whole DIVINITY is your Sustenance; & your flesh, says an ancient Father, eateth the FLESH, & drinketh the BLOOD of CHRIST, only that your Soul may spiritually be fed by the very Substance of GOD.

Affections.

Dwell with GOD alone, O my Soul, in Grace & Heavenly Joy. For He is within thee after a Divine manner, & in His Own Divine Substance. Yet pray Him, that He would enter deeper into the most secret places of thy heart, & set it on fire with Love, & abide therein for ever. Lo, He is within thee. Strive then to feel His Presence, to hear His Voice, to yield to His Guiding, to obey His Will, & to lay down thy heart at His sacred Feet.

Blessed, beyond the Bride in the Canticles, He hath brought thee not only into His banquet-chamber, but even into His Own Heart, to give thee to drink abundantly of the Wine of His boundless Love. And thou hast brought Him not into thy mother's house only, but into thine own Soul, where now He abides. He fills thee, & His Delights are with thee. Respond fitly to His Divine Mercies; breathe, love, act, live, only for Him Alone, Who breatheth, loveth, acteth, & liveth in thee & for thee.

Thanksgiving.

How can I, frail creature, duly praise Thy Divine Majesty, O most Blessed JESU, Who hast given me Thy Very DIVINITY for Food? For when I reflect that I possess within me the CREA-

Creator of Heaven & earth, the God Whom men & Angels worship, & Hell fears, mind & imagination of man cannot grasp the thought; & my most burning feelings seem so faint, that I durst not offer them to Thee, were it not that I trust in Thy merciful Lovingkindness.

Yea, Dear Lord, I sink under Thine awful Presence. Words have I none, save the cry of Thy Servant—*What reward shall I give unto the Lord, for all the Benefits that He hath done unto me?* And with him will I make answer—*I will receive the Cup of Salvation, & call upon the Name of the Lord.*

Fourteenth Meditation.

Of the General Preparation before the Blessed Sacrament.

I.

Consider that there is a great danger, into which frequent communicants are prone to fall, & that is, of coming to the most Holy Communion from custom's sake & unprepared; & the consequences of this danger are ofttimes very sad. These lax & lukewarm persons are content, if only no great sin weighs on their conscience. They imagine habitual & allowed lukewarmness to be no hindrance to the Grace of the Divine Sacrament, nor to render them unworthy of frequent Communion. Hence, they live with careless minds, unrecollected, unmeditating, insensible of GOD's awful Presence, & ever dissipated. They lay themselves under no restraint; their passions are as violent as if they never communicated; they almost always act in a wholly human manner, & they derive no profit from the Life-giving Sacrament.

Instead of preparing themselves by Devotion & Meditation, these wayward Souls regard such an exercise as burdens too heavy for them to bear, unless they be accompanied by sensible sweetness; or else, they go through them coldly, not struggling against distractions, which, in them, are wilful, at least in principle, because occasioned by their dissipated life. But they rush into every pleasure which they can suppose innocent. They give themselves to all sorts of vain & earthly joys. They rarely speak of GOD; all their conversation being useless & worldly. Their conscience is not tender regarding such sins as they consider to be merely venial. Self-love & vanity appear in all their words & works; & their whole being is pervaded by an affected delicacy. No self-denial do they practise; nor mortification; nor recollectedness; nor sense of the Divine Presence.

Yet they must communicate often. What would be said if they did not? Long since they
made

made it a rule to do so; & then they were fervent & zealous, & always prepared themselves with much diligence; & then they deserved to communicate often. Gradually they fell into laxity, which they were not careful instantly to shake off. Hence, of two things they ought to choose one, either to keep away from GOD's Holy Altar, or to approach it with renewed zeal. But no; they prefer remaining as they are, doing themselves no violence. This frequent Communion does them honour, & gives them reputation among the devout. They are willing, therefore, to change neither their will, nor their way. They prefer to go to Holy Communion unprepared, careless of the awful risk they run; & this, because doing better would be too great a tax upon their softness, & less frequent communicating would hurt their vanity too sorely.

On the eve of Holy Communion, they scarcely give the Blessed Sacrament one single thought. Before receiving, they spend a few moments in Devotion. But even that preparation is formal, rather than hearty. They have grown so familiar with GOD, that they are devoid of that chastened & reverent awe felt by holy Souls, when such draw near unto the Blessed Sacrament of Love. Gone is all their desire, their eagerness, their fervour. They care not to draw profit from this Means of Grace, & rashly expose themselves to the danger of making doubtful, or at least useless, Communions. Familiarity is good, indeed; &

it

it is hard to carry it too far, when Divine Love is its mainspring, & great fervency its companion. But familiarity is certainly baneful, whenever it arises from indolence, whenever it is the consequence of laxity.

Examine yourself carefully, & see whether or not you are not of the number of these Souls. Where are the feelings of awe, reverence, eagerness, & love, which filled your heart, when it belonged more to GOD than it does now? Labour to revive & renew them; & strive earnestly, by all means, to preserve them henceforth more faithfully.

Ask yourself why your Communions are colder now, than then? Find out where & when you fell from that first Love, which burned within you when oftentimes you drew near the Holy Altar of your GOD? Were not your former practices neglected, because they required more application to self-examination, reading, meditation, & the sense of the Divine Presence? Did you not mingle too much with the world, whose manners, words, & false proprieties are incompatible with true Holiness?

If you own yourself guilty of this dangerous relaxation, you have found the clue to your insensibility at Holy Communion. You make no advance in a holy life, both because your want of preparation renders your Communions useless, & because you live in indifference & lukewarmness. Tremble then, lest your Communions be not worse

worse than useless. Remember that the Glorious GOD Whom you so indevoutly receive, is the Same Whom once you welcomed with such fervour. If your preparation be not more careful, you will at any rate lose those abundant Gifts & Graces which are inherent in the Precious BODY & BLOOD of CHRIST; & it may be that you will fall into profanity, which is the deepest of misery.

II.

In order rightly to prepare your Soul for Holy Communion, take the most excellent & Divine of Models. CHRIST Himself is set before you by the Church. Study, therefore, to enter into the Mind & Feelings of our Adorable SAVIOUR, at the time when He instituted the Sacrament of the Holy Eucharist, & gave Himself with His Own Hands to His Apostles. Thus He Himself enjoins, when He saith—*Do this in remembrance of Me.* Therefore, let this Divine MASTER be ever in your memory, in your mind, & in your heart, before you come unto the Holy Altar of GOD.

Notice, first, that CHRIST had withdrawn from the society of the world, though He was incapable of being distracted by it, & only appeared in it to teach, or to work Miracles. And if He went apart with His Disciples into the Upper Chamber, to institute that Blessed Sacrament before He suffered, do you also withdraw yourself

yourself from the world, & from much intercourse with men, where no place is given to Almighty GOD. Speak little, & only with the holy; for silence & recollectedness are very needful to a fitting preparation for the Celebration of Divine Mysteries.

The distracting spirit of the world, is simply ruinous to your immortal Soul, & incompatible with the Presence of the HOLY SPIRIT of GOD, with Whom you should be fulfilled, before His Sacred BODY enters within you. That fulness is a necessary preparation for this; else, you will receive, so to speak, the FLESH only of CHRIST, & not His SPIRIT; & your Communions will profit you nothing.

Therefore choose out a time & place, where no created thing may intrude to steal your heart from precious moments; & then, give vent to your affections, to love & desire; examine yourself; confess your sins; & make amends for your faults by the sacrifice of a contrite & humbled heart; & withal, have none other witness of your Devotions, if it may be so, but GOD Alone.

In the next place, our Blessed LORD prepared Himself for the Institution, & His Disciples for the Reception of the All-holy Sacrament, by deep reflections on the infinite Gifts bestowed on Him by His Heavenly FATHER; in order to bind them all together in the Divine Sacrament of His Very BODY & BLOOD, & also to communicate them abundantly to those who should re-

ceive

ceive them, with hearts duly prepared, both then, & to the end of time.

Therefore, by meditation must you prepare for the Holy Eucharistic Sacrifice, reflecting on the infinite Treasure you are about to receive; the Purest FLESH, the most Precious BLOOD, the Holiest SOUL, the most Fervent HEART, the Dearest & most Perfect LIFE that ever existed.

Yea, in a word, Entire DEITY shall possess you, & be possessed of you; shall enrich you with Grace, in proportion to the preparation of your heart & mind; shall dwell within you, feed you, strengthen you, enlighten your mind, enkindle your heart, calm & rule your passions, purify your desires, & give you fresh ones, purer & more ardent. It shall sanctify, moreover, your Soul, consecrate your whole nature, unite His HEART with your heart, His SUBSTANCE with your substance, by ties most sweet, most glorious, & most lasting, if only you desire it; dwelling in you as in a Paradise of delight, & giving you certain Pledges of blessed & Eternal Life, which cannot fail you, & which none can take away. Only prepare yourself duly to receive Him; & after reception, be faithful unto Him. Such are the weightiest matters for your meditation before Holy Communion.

In the third place, CHRIST was about to quit the world. He knew that He was now to be betrayed to His cruel enemies. To His mind were present the insults, & the agonies which He

should

should undergo, the BLOOD which He should shed, & the Death which He should suffer for the love of men. At the Institution He was a VICTIM, about to yield up His Sacred LIFE to save us from death.

Before communicating, do you seek that self-sacrificing mind, most excellent of all, & most conformable to the SPIRIT of CHRIST. Shew forth, as the Apostle saith, the LORD's Death. Shew it forth, by dying to the world & its pleasures; to yourself & your passions; to all sensual enjoyments, & inordinate attachments. Put on the spirit of a victim; be willing to accept all possible sufferings; prepare yourself for them, & if they beset you, bear them with courage, patience, perseverance, yea, even with joy. The true victim yields to GOD all it has received from GOD; & is ready to offer Him its possessions, its blood, & its life, never in any wise resisting His adorable Will.

Affections.

Dare I think, O my GOD, of so many past Communions, without a trembling fear of Thy most just Judgment? If Thou comest as a KING of Glory, Thou shouldest dwell in a Palace garnished & prepared, & the least stain must displease Thine Eyes, for Thou art Purity itself. But I have often neglected to cleanse my Soul, & to adorn it with all Virtues. If then

Thou comest as a GOD of Majesty, Thou shouldest have an Altar where the fire of Divine Love may ever burn; but in my Soul, alas, it has ofttimes been extinguished by my fault, & Thou hast found none, but that of a poor & lukewarm heart.

But consider, O my Soul, that thou art about once more to approach that GOD, Whom thou hast received with so much indifference. Remember that He is thy REDEEMER, & thy SPOUSE; & let that blessed thought kindle love & trustfulness. But yet, forget not thou that He is thy Almighty JUDGE. Love His Mercies; gratefully accept His Divine Favours; but fear to incur His Displeasure; & examine, with all possible care, whether or not thou hast worthily prepared to receive Him. Are thy passions calm & thy desires fervent? Dost thou hunger after that Pure FLESH, & dost thou thirst for that Precious BLOOD? Hast thou humbled thy pride, quelled thy appetites, subjected the flesh to the Spirit, rooted out antipathies, cast away indolence, & repented of all thy sins? Hast thou prayed & longed for this Sweet & Heavenly FOOD?

Ah, my LORD, what can I do? How can I, of myself, worthily prepare for this Thy Visit? Without Thy Grace, my efforts are too faint. Prepare me therefore, Dear LORD, by Thine Own great Mercy, for I cannot prepare myself. Take away from the heart Thou madest, all that

that is displeasing in Thine Eyes. Purify it by the Almighty Breath of Thy Good SPIRIT. And do Thou, LORD JESU, Thyself adorn Thy Palace, consecrate Thy Temple, & light upon the Altar about to receive Thee, a Sacred Fire, which never may be extinguished.

Thanksgiving.

If every breath were a Thanksgiving, I could not duly praise Thee, Dearest LORD, for the infinite Mercy which has prepared this most sweet Feast for me. To none other wouldest Thou delegate the care, neither to Apostle, Prophet, nor Angel; but Thyself didst vouchsafe to make It ready, according to those Words of Thine—*Behold, I have prepared My Dinner.* Long ages since Thou didst reveal this Truth by the Holy Psalmist, when he spake, saying—*Thou shalt prepare a Table before me, against them that trouble me.*

And not content even with this tender Care, Thou dost yet invite me to Thy Holy Altar with marvellous Loving-kindness, & tender Words of irresistible Love, saying—*Come to the Wedding; take, eat, THIS IS MY BODY: drink ye all of This, for THIS IS MY BLOOD. Come unto Me, all ye that labour & are heavy laden, & I will refresh you.* How, LORD JESU, can I worthily acknowledge this overpowering Bounty? How, but by making Thy Preparation the model of mine

mine own; preparing, namely, to receive Thee as Thou hast prepared to give Thyself to me, by desire, by eagerness, by fervent love, & by making the Psalmist's words truly mine own— *My heart is ready, O GOD, my heart is ready.* But, O Thou GOD of all Goodness, in mercy do Thou perfect what is wanting in me; & now that Thou art mine, fill me, I pray Thee, with such holy fervour, that the Communion which I have made, may serve as preparation to all those which may henceforth be vouchsafed unto me.

Fifteenth Meditation.

Of the Preparation of Faith before the Blessed Sacrament.

I.

HE *that cometh to* GOD, says the Apostle, *must first believe that He is*; & this Faith is, according to a holy Bishop, the gate of admission to the understanding of all Mysteries, & of the Knowledge & Love of GOD. But of all Sacraments & all Mysteries, none demands Faith more implicit & submissive, than that of the most Holy Eucharist.

This is, properly speaking, the Sacrament & Mystery of Faith, because It is perfectly unaccountable to reason. In the adorable Mystery of the Incarnation, I need Faith indeed, because my mind

mind cannot grasp the union of Divine Greatness with human littleness; Omnipotence with weakness; Incomprehensibility with the Form of an Infant. But yet, my eyes perceive That CHILD, my ears hear His Infant Cries, & my reason concludes that He is a Human Being about to run His Course, like others. And when I see Kings led to His Cradle, by a marvellous Star, & Angels singing His Praises, & calling on the shepherds to come & worship Him, my reason enters deeper into the Mystery, & concludes that This CHILD is more than MAN.

But in the incomprehensible Mystery of the Holy Eucharist, all is darkness; all is impenetrable; all is infinitely above my reason. My eyes behold common Bread; my ears hear nothing unusual; my hands handle nothing extraordinary; all my bodily senses are deceived; so that I can only draw near by Faith, which bids me believe that GOD & MAN are together here, hidden beneath the humble Veils of BREAD & WINE, which I see, & touch, & consume. And hence, my first act before approaching, must be an Act of Faith, to believe, & say with the Prophet—*Verily, Thou art a* GOD *That hidest Thyself, O* GOD *of Israel, the* SAVIOUR.

The DIVINITY of the Eternal WORD is much more hidden in the Eucharist, than in the Bosom of the Everlasting FATHER, because He there manifests Himself by the glories of Creation. His Sacred HUMANITY is hidden here, more than

than in the Womb of the Blessed Virgin, who was necessarily sensible of That mysterious Presence.

Thus, saith a holy Doctor, has Divine Providence drawn a curtain between us, & this incomprehensible Mystery. Human reason is a captive, & cannot attain unto it; senses are deceived; experience discovers nothing; Faith alone has the right to raise this Veil, beneath which she beholds an Almighty GOD, & an abundance of Truth, based on Revelation infallible, because Divine. This is the sight that justifies, & gives virtue to her Adoration, & her Acts of Love.

By Faith likewise, CHRIST prepared His Apostles for the Institution of, & participation in, this Divine Sacrament. It was *the same night in which He was betrayed;* & it was so to teach us, that this great Mystery should be shrouded in darkness, to those especially who would examine it with over-bold curiosity, & with reason unchastened by childlike Faith.

Yet, that humble Faith will surely lead, albeit through the thickest darkness, to the knowledge of the great Mystery here, & to the evidence of It hereafter. Bid reason cease to speak; let Acts of lively Faith prepare your Soul; & you shall know sufficiently, & you shall feel & receive the holy Outpourings & abundant Graces of this Ever-blessed Sacrament. For Faith, quickened by Love, is the most needful of all Virtues, for a

worthy

worthy participation in the BODY & BLOOD of CHRIST.

Let your thoughts carry you back to that firſt Celebration in the Upper Chamber. Look with lively Faith upon the LORD JESUS, Who, before He ſuffers, gives this bleſſed Pledge of Love unto His Own; &, by the Almighty Power of His Word, changes Bread & Wine into His Own Very BODY & BLOOD. Liſten, in deep reverence, to His Divine Words, while they work this marvellous change. See how He gives Himſelf to each Apoſtle, yea, even to the traitor, who had already received the price of His Sacred BLOOD. And now, reſtrain the action of natural ſenſe & reaſon; truſt not ſuch guidance, for it will only deceive; come to GOD's Own Altar with nothing but loving & truſtful Faith; & believe as firmly, as if with bodily eyes you ſaw, CHRIST work this great Miracle, taking the Prieſt's place, & Himſelf adminiſtering to you His moſt Precious BODY, & His All-ſaving BLOOD.

II.

Take a ſtrict account of your Faith, before you draw near the adorable Myſtery & Sacrament of Faith; & remember, that if it be not ſubmiſſive, lively, & ſtrengthened by Good Works, you are not worthy to participate in this Heavenly FOOD of the BODY & BLOOD of CHRIST.

Let ſuch examination as the following, enter into your preparation. Has your mind always, & im-

& implicitly submitted to the Truth of our Blessed LORD's Own Words of Institution? Has it never reasoned, like the Jews, saying—*How can This MAN give us His FLESH to eat?* Has it not aspired to examine what is beyond its reach? Has it not trusted too much to the experience of the senses, which can only lead it to error & unbelief? Has it always guarded against its own thoughts; been careful to repulse them; & been prompt in repelling, by an Act of Faith, every suggestion instilled by Satan, to cast doubt on the Real Presence in the Ever-blessed Sacrament? Has no such doubt been suffered to dwell in the mind, for lack of care & faithfulness?

Has your Faith become weakened & languid through forgetfulness of what you owe to this Awful Sacrament; or through laxity in multiplying Acts of Faith, Love, & Adoration; or through neglect of opportunity of communicating; or through lukewarmness at Holy Communion Itself; or through want of reverence in the Divine Presence? On these important points, fail not to examine yourself. These are some of the secret unfaithfulnesses which must be confessed & renounced, & concerning which you need to be warned before you venture to draw nigh unto the Altar of your GOD.

Then consider, moreover, for the greater perfection of your preparation, that mental Faith is not enough. The Holy Eucharist claims the heart; yet it may be said, that if the heart have yielded

yielded entire & reverent submission to the Words of Divine Institution, it can hardly fail to yield Love also, & to draw near the Blessed Sacrament with true Affection. The Faith of the heart is an evident proof of that of the mind. The one gives birth to the other; & it is, as an Ancient Father well says, its mainspring & its mother. If sincere submission is the portion of the faithful mind, sweet acquiescence is certainly that of the heart. The mind presents to the heart a Divine Truth which has been revealed to it, & which it perceives through Faith. The heart fails not to love it, especially when its beauty & blessedness are apparent. In short, that Faith which passes not from mind to heart, is a dry & barren Faith, & possesses no worth. Such imperfect Faith, existing in the mind alone, is the faith of devils; for they believe, & tremble. But the Christian man believes & loves: & hence the difference between the two. Examine, then, what is the nature of your own Faith?

Nevertheless, implicit & burning Faith alone does not form a sufficient preparation for worthily approaching this great Sacrament, & receiving all Its manifold Gifts & Graces. Good Works, the proofs of submission & love, must accompany it to the Holy Altar. Belief that our LORD JESUS CHRIST is truly Present in the Blessed Sacrament, is the beginning of Faith; belief & love, is the increase; but belief, love, & consequent action, is the consummation of true Faith. For, it costs the mind little to submit to Truth, if it be certainly revealed by GOD. It costs the heart but little, to bid the lips pronounce a few Acts of Love; words are not always accompanied by feelings; & feeling, when it does exist, is often devoid of worth, particularly when it is barren, & produces no fruit.

You will say, that you believe in, that you have no doubt of the Real Presence of the BODY & BLOOD of CHRIST in the Holy Eucharist. You declare that you would willingly suffer death to maintain that great Truth. But your protestations, however hearty & fervent, are little worth, if your life does not conform to the belief you profess. Good Works are the proof of Faith; & if Faith be not active, it must needs fail, & fade away. Holy Actions witness for Faith, & sustain & strengthen it; & without such, Faith is but a phantom & an unreality. And as long as you live in indolence, & do not work for GOD, you will not have Faith enough worthily to approach the Blessed Sacrament of the LORD JESUS.

Affections.

Ah, LORD JESU, what reason have I to mistrust my Faith, & tremble to approach this Venerable Sacrament with Faith so weak & devoid of Love & Good Works. Thou hast said once, that *all things are possible to him that believeth*; & he to whom Thou spakest believed, & his desire was granted

granted by a Miracle. If I had believed rightly, all would have been possible also unto me. I should have drawn from that Divine Sacrament of Faith all strength to conquer my enemies. I should have triumphed over the world, the flesh, & the Devil; & this Sacred FOOD would have protected me against all their assaults. I should have rooted out all vice, calmed all passion, uprooted all ill habits, practised all Virtues, endured all afflictions, if not with pleasure, at least with patience; & I should have undertaken & accomplished all labours, however rigorous. But alas, I feel almost as weak & backward in Holiness, as if I had never received Thee; because I drew near unto Thee with too little Faith; or else, my Faith was defective, either in Love, or in Good Works.

O my LORD, why cannot I too cry out with tears—*LORD, I believe; help Thou my unbelief?* Do Thou, I beseech Thee, sustain this weak & trembling Faith, & quicken it with burning Love. Give me Grace to sustain it myself by actions holy & worthy of one fed at Thy Holy Altar with Thine Own BODY, & Thy most Precious BLOOD. Increase it whensoever I approach that Mystery of Faith, until that happy moment when Faith shall be swallowed up in Sight.

Thanksgiving.

By Faith, LORD JESU, I have prepared to approach the August & Venerable Sacrament of the Eucharist.

Eucharist. With Faith, submissive & ardent, as far as mine might be so, I have received Thee at Thy Holy Altar, opening unto Thee my lips, my Soul, my spirit, & my heart. With that same Faith, O LORD, I bow before Thy Feet, praising Thy Holy Name, Who hast been pleased to give me Thy Whole SELF in Holy Communion.

Yea, LORD JESU, I believe that Thou art now Present within me, even as Thou art in Heaven at the Right Hand of Thy FATHER, although Thy Glory & Thyself be doubly hidden, beneath the Blessed Eucharistic SPECIES, & within my person. I firmly believe that Thou, within me, dost hearken to my Acts of Faith & Thanksgiving. I believe that Thou receivest them in Thy Mercy; that Thou art their Author, as Thou art their Object, their End, & their Divine Reward; & that Thou dost accept my gratitude if it be born of Faith, & quickened by Love; Virtues which I cannot have, unless Thou art pleased to give them unto me.

But, O LORD, I pray Thee, do Thou Thyself, place these Acts within my heart, while Thou art Present in it; that so, they may be more pleasing unto Thee. Purify me, hallow me, save me by the Faith of the Wonder-working Sacrament Which I have received. Say to me likewise, as to those blessed ones of old—*Thy Faith hath saved thee.* Place me too among those righteous Souls who live by Faith, & who, after the life of
Grace

Grace which Thou haſt won for them by this Bleſſed Sacrament, ſhall inherit the Eternal Life of Glory in Heaven.

Sixteenth Meditation.

Of the Preparation of Hope before the Bleſſed Sacrament.

I.

*W*HOSO *eateth My* FLESH, *& drinketh My* BLOOD, *hath Eternal Life: & I will raiſe him up at the Laſt Day.* So ſaith our Bleſſed LORD; & again in another place—*Your fathers did eat Manna in the wilderneſs, & are dead. This is the* BREAD *Which cometh down from Heaven, that a man may eat thereof, & not die; & the Bread that I will give is My* FLESH, *Which I will give for the life of the world.*

O Promiſe moſt ſure, & bleſſed; moſt ſweet to the pilgrim longing after the Heavenly Country; moſt fit to kindle in his heart bright Hope, if it exiſted not already there; & moſt ſoothing to all his fears. Yea, by thee, weak Hope grows ſtrong, & triumphs over all terrors. Therefore look on the Communion of the BODY & BLOOD of CHRIST not only as a Divine Promiſe, conſoling us in all poſſible adverſities, but as a moſt glorious Preparation for future Glory. For It is a Pledge, a Foretaste, yea a Possession of the Eternal Glory promised us in Heaven. It is verily a most true & certain Promise, a most holy & perfect Preparation, a most sure & infallible Pledge, a most pure & precious Foretaste. It is moreover an anticipatory Possession, most conformable & most similar to the Eternal Life of the Blessed in Heaven.

Let us endeavour to aid reflection by entering somewhat more into detail.

The Blessed Eucharist, then, in the first place, is a most true & certain Promise, because the Divine Lips of the LORD JESUS pronounced It, & that, not once, but many times. What more true than the Words of GOD uttered, not by the voice of Prophets, but by His Own Sacred Lips, promising, what He can give because He is Almighty, & what He will give because He is infinitely Good & Gracious. It is a Gift, at once sweet & glorious; glorious, because It manifests His Majesty & Greatness; sweet, because He enriches whom He loves, & impoverishes not Himself, because He gives for His Own Sake. Remark we also, for our comfort, that He vouchsafed to make this Promise, in the hearing of a multitude of people, & in order that we might demand it as a right, although in its original nature, it was of pure Grace. He gives a written Contract concerning it in the Holy Gospels, whereof we have the keeping; yea, to make

make that Contract more solemn & more glorious, He willed to sign It with His Very Blood. It is, moreover, a most holy & perfect Preparation, insensibly disposing the heart & spirit to their promised beatitude; the spirit, by enlightening it, that it may know God; the heart, by kindling Divine Fire within it for His Love.

Holy Communion leads us gently on, from Faith to Hope, & from Hope to Fruition. Reception here, is a preparation for possession there. Divine Sustenance received, though under a Veil, is the fittest preparation for being satiated to all Eternity with that Same Substance, Unveiled & Undisguised, in Everlasting Bliss.

The Blessed Eucharist, again, is a most sure & infallible Pledge of Eternal Glory, because It is of the same Nature as that for which It is given us, & this precious Pledge is incorporated in us, whenever we communicate worthily. If we behold within ourselves the Very God, Who shall be ours in Heaven, what Pledge more certain, & more fitted to sustain our Hope here on earth?

And it is a most pure & precious Foretaste of the Eternal Fruition of God. Holy Souls, indeed, often taste therein spiritual delights, & secret sweetnesses, more easy to feel than to express; ineffable delights, which inspire disgust for sensual pleasures, so incomparably are they purer & more precious; delights which exalt & enlighten their minds, inundating their hearts with a torrent of pleasures, like unto that wherewith Almighty God

God makes glad the Blessed; delights which purify & hallow, not defile, the flesh; & which defend it against all attacks of worldly lusts.

O most sweet Foretaste, which at last becomes, by anticipation, Possession of Eternal Bliss. For, by the most Holy Communion, He is ours Whom the Saints possess in Heaven; there, Glorious upon His Throne of Majesty; here, Veiled beneath the Sacred Eucharistic FORMS, unseen but by the eye of Faith.

Let, then, your Communions be filled with Hope, since you begin to possess that Which you long after; & can say, with the Bride of CHRIST—*My Beloved is mine, & I am His*, until the Day of Eternity break, & the shadows of this mortal life flee away.

II.

Consider that of all the Sacraments of the New Law, none is so adapted for the inspiration, increase, & perfection of Christian Hope, as is the Divine Eucharist. For It brings us closer to Eternal Joys, & not only gives the Promise, but also the precious Pledge & meritorious Cause of Heavenly Bliss, even CHRIST Himself, Who is here incorporated with the faithful in closest bonds of union.

And we must further remember, that the nearer this Blessed Sacrament brings us to Eternal Joys, the more it detaches us from the flattering hope of earthly pleasures, the usual obstacles which prevent the Soul from soaring with energy, towards

towards those blessed & everlasting Mansions. It thus relieves the Soul from some of its fears concerning the Mystery of Predestination; & only leaves sufficient doubt to induce her to work out her own Salvation with fear & trembling, by Good Works. For what usually troubles your Hope? Is it not the uncertainty of your Predestination; whether or not you are really worthy of the Love of Almighty GOD; whether or not you will eternally rejoice in GOD with the Blessed in Heaven, or weep for ever in Hell, with the lost? And does not such uncertainty oftentimes wake within you wild alarm, urging you to despair, unless you instantly strive to calm it by Resignation, & by Acts of Faith, & Hope, & Love?

Come worthily to the Holy Altar of GOD; & you will find that your faithless fear will gradually die away. You will feel quieter confidence, & firmer Hope. You will fear no more than you justly ought to fear; & such fear as you do feel, instead of being that of a slave, as at the first, will become chastened & subdued like that of a son. You will dread rather to displease a FATHER & a SAVIOUR, than an inexorable JUDGE; & this Fear, wholesome, & pleasing to GOD, will lead you gently on to perfect Love, which casteth out Fear.

Indeed, if you look on Predestination to Glory, as a gratuitous Grace, depending solely on the Good Will of GOD, you will rejoice to see your eternal

eternal lot in the Hands of that Gracious GOD, Who loves you, & desires to abide with & in you by Holy Communion, that He may so more frequently assure you of His Love. As often as possible, therefore, let this precious Pledge of Glory be yours; &, without ceasing from your own labours, leave the question of your eternal happiness to the Mercy & infinite Tenderness of a FATHER, & the Value of a SAVIOUR'S BLOOD, Which purifies, & refreshes, & marks you as His Own, whenever you have the happiness of worthily receiving Him at His Altar.

Or, if Predestination depend upon your own deserts, you will acquire the more, the oftener you participate in those of CHRIST, because by this Divine Sacrament He applies them most abundantly to our Souls. In fact, if the effectuation of Predestination contains three points, according to the teaching of learned men; namely, preparation of means, or Graces, absolutely necessary to Salvation; fulfilment of duties laid upon us; & victory over temptations; a worthy Communion certainly effects them all.

First; in the Blessed Eucharist we abundantly receive the Graces pertaining to the BODY, BLOOD, & SOUL of JESUS CHRIST. We dwell at the Source of these Graces; the Very SOURCE is within us, & its Graces are poured forth according to the degrees of Faith, Hope, & Love, wherewith we approach the Blessed Sacrament. Secondly; It bestows on us much greater facility

for

for the performance of those duties, which lead towards our blessed Home. For, Love burns brighter with every worthy Communion. The greater our love, the less our pain in labouring for those we love; & the burden of the Law grows easier to bear, whilst the hardest duties become more easy to fulfil.

Then, too, in the Holy Eucharist is Strength abundant, for conquering temptation. Satan is much weaker, because CHRIST, Who is in us, is much stronger, & leaves in our heart, after every worthy Communion, the impress of Heavenly power, wherewith more easily to resist all his attacks. As we become One Flesh with CHRIST, in virtue of our mysterious Union with Him, we suffer fewer insults from the flesh. Our human flesh participates in the glorious Qualities of His Sacred HUMANITY, Purity, Spirituality, & Immortality. It is purified, spiritualized, & acquires a right to that Immortality whereof it already possesses the precious Germ. Here is wherewith to conquer all our enemies; to assure our election; to sustain our Hope.

Affections.

Delight thyself in Hope, O my Soul; for thou hast the joy of possessing within thee, GOD, Faithful & True, the GOD of Love, Who gives His Whole SELF unto thee here, as an infallible Pledge of what He has promised thee in Heaven.

ven. Let Hope cast away fear. Hope all things, & if your Hope be sustained by the practice of Good Works, it shall never be confounded.

Rejoice with holy joy in Him, Whose Bride thou art, saith a devout Servant of GOD. Calm all thy fears. The Heavenly SPOUSE, Who gives Himself to thee, will be thy Guide in thy pilgrimage, teaching thee the right way, lest thou shouldst err; Himself thy Stay, thy Food, thy Guard, that thou mayest more safely reach thy proper Country, which is Heaven. He will watch over thy struggles; He will arm thy hands; & He will fight for thee, that thou mayest the more completely conquer all the enemies which dispute thy possession of the Eternal Kingdom, purchased for thee by His Own most Precious BLOOD.

That Adorable BLOOD thou dost possess, in certain Pledge of His Divine Promises; what canst thou fear, if thou be faithful unto Him? What enemy can rob thee of that Pledge, if thyself consentest not? This Precious BLOOD is That Which inscribes within the Book of Life the names of all predestinated. And why not thy name, if only thou dost but duly treasure It?

O my Soul, the day shall surely dawn, when clear shining shall succeed to darkness, peaceable possession to fluctuating hope, & perfect & consummate Union to that beginning of Union now contracted in the Ever-blessed Sacrament of thy LORD & SAVIOUR JESUS CHRIST.

Thanksgiving.

O most gracious LORD JESU CHRIST, I acknowledge that I owe Thee continual Thanksgiving for all Thy Mercies past, & also for those Thy Loving-kindness has promised for the future. For these are the aim of my hopes, my strength in sorrow, my comfort in exile; & I believe that Thy Promises are true, that Thou art a Faithful & True GOD, & that the performance of that Thou hast spoken, depends only on mine own faithfulness unto death.

Thou didst form me out of nothing; Thou didst seal me with Thine Own Image; Thou didst suffer bitter woes; Thy BODY was broken, & Thy BLOOD was poured out, & Thou didst even give Thy LIFE, to bring me back from death, which was my just due. Such Mercies should be alway in my mind; but, O LORD JESU, what do I not owe Thee for that Thou hast given to me That BODY, That BLOOD, & That LIFE, Which I have now received in this Venerable Sacrament of Hope & Love? What shall I give unto Thee, Who hast vouchsafed to perpetuate the Precious Gift unto the end of time, & to prepare, for me, this Sweetest FOOD, to support me for time, & to assure me of Eternal Life, by Thine Own infallible Pledge?

This, LORD, sustains & quickens my Hope. This should demand perpetual Thanksgiving.

Well truly, didst Thou say by the Wise Man, that in Thee only was the Hope of Life. That Word is confirmed, accomplished, & verified in the Sacrament of Thy BODY & BLOOD, because Thou hast bound up in It the promise of an Eternal Blessed Life—*Whom have I in Heaven but Thee? & there is none upon earth that I desire in comparison of Thee; my flesh & my heart faileth, but GOD is the Strength of my heart, & my Portion for ever.*

Seventeenth Meditation.

Of the Preparation of Love before the Blessed Sacrament.

I.

THERE is no point on which thou oughtest to examine thyself more closely before Holy Communion than on that of Divine Love. Every one, says a holy Saint, ought to examine himself, & to weigh the affections of his heart in the balance of the Sanctuary, that he may know with what love it is fulfilled; whether it is that Love which the HOLY SPIRIT inspires, or that which is excited by the Devil or by evil desire.

Nothing can be more dangerous than to communicate with an unloving heart towards GOD.

Seventeenth Meditation.

To communicate with a heart full of love for the creature is profanation; but if thou dost communicate with a heart overflowing with Love for Almighty GOD, & with earnest longings to possess Him, this will make thee worthy to receive Him. Love, then, is at the same time the most holy of all religious Influences, the most dangerous of all delusions; the most perfect of all Virtues, the most shameful of all vices. It is the most certain proof of purity of Soul, if it has Almighty GOD alone for its object; but, if it turns from Him to the love of earthly things, this is the surest proof of its corruption. True Love, says a Saint, is glorious if it ascends towards its Great CREATOR to be united to Him, as the Cause of its happiness; but it becomes degraded when, forsaking the CREATOR, it seeks after the creature whom it loves above all things, & in whom it places all its happiness. By this Love to Almighty GOD we become more worthy to draw nigh to His holy Altar, & more able to love Him; since the Love which we bring there receives new fervour each time that we communicate, & draw from the true Well of Love, which is Almighty GOD Himself, an increase of it. And from His abiding within us, we obtain the power to love Him with greater fervour & purity of Love.

In the Blessed Sacrament we are told, by a holy Man, there is a continual flow of this Sacred Fire of Love. Our hearts bring thither the Love

Love they bear towards GOD, & carry away from thence still more devoted feelings. Our hearts receive those precious Flowings of Love, & draw from them power to love GOD. But as human love is apt to wax cold, we are forced to renew it at the Fount of Love, in the most Holy Communion, where our heart obtains new strength, & receives that Divine FOOD which sustains its Love. It gives & receives; it loves & is loved; & it is always given far more abundantly than it has ever given itself. In order, then, to make this Preparation for the Blessed Sacrament with benefit, thou must first examine thine own heart well, to seek for those obstacles which prevent the practice of Divine Love, & which very often escape notice unless we pay great attention to them: Secondly, thou must banish from thy heart all that is contrary to the Love of Almighty GOD: & Thirdly, thou must endeavour to fill thine heart with this Love, by actions & deeds of Love, which will make thee worthy of possessing, of nourishing, of keeping, & of increasing it.

Begin then thy preparation with a strict examination of the affections of thine heart. Are there not some whom thou dost love with too great an affection, those who are most constantly in thy thoughts, & whom thou wouldst have the most difficulty in forsaking? Does not some one person fill the place of GOD in thine heart? Dost thou love this person in GOD alone, for the benefit

benefit of his Soul, or of thine own? Is not this love hurtful to the performance of thy duties; & is it not the cause of thy distraction in prayer? Examine thyself closely on this matter, for it is one of the most subtle & dangerous obstacles to Divine Love, & to the Benefits thou mightest obtain at the Ever-blessed Sacrament. Is it not temporal goods which fill up a place in thine heart, which thou art not aware of? Is it not luxuries which excite thy self-love, & which is not the less dangerous because it is less felt & less realised? Sometimes it only requires a trifle to fill thine heart, & to make it incapable of loving GOD; & especially is this the case with those who have to some extent renounced the world. Is it not thyself, for whom thou hast an inordinate affection? Oh, meditate on this most attentively, & let nothing remain in thine heart which will prevent thee from perfectly loving Almighty GOD.

When thou hast found out on what thine affections are placed, do what thou canst to break the idolatries which enchain thee, & which prevent thee from offering to thy Heavenly FATHER the loving worship which thou owest Him. Then wilt thou love Him more perfectly, for thy heart must love something; & when it no longer loves the creature, or itself, it will soon be fulfilled with the Love of GOD. And this it is that is needful for us to approach the most Blessed Sacrament worthily, & to obtain the Love of the Sacred

HEART of our Dear LORD, whilst He is dwelling within us. A holy Penitent practised this precept so perfectly, that he was able to say—O most Merciful GOD, it was by the Sweetness of Thy Divine Love that Thou didst banish from my heart all sinful attachments, & Thou didst fill it instead with Thine Own most ineffable Sweetness, which is a thousand times more grateful unto me than that pleasure which had so long ensnared me.

II.

The Divine Eucharist could never be approached not only by the weak & imperfect, but also by the Faithful, if it were not a Sacrament of Love to which our Blessed SAVIOUR invites us. His awful Majesty, His supreme Greatness, His incomparable Purity which, through faith, we see, would make the most perfect tremble, who know the depth of their own nothingness, & the miseries to which they are subject as long as they are clothed with this mortality. Love alone can calm their fears & make them approach the Blessed Sacrament with confidence. Oh, it is indeed Love alone which can embolden us to appear before our GOD without presumption.

Love is the Queen of all Virtues, & holds the highest place in the Sacred HEART of GOD. She has always free access to His Throne, & nothing is able to delay or prevent her approach
when

Seventeenth Meditation.

when she is striving to draw near to Him Whom she loves. Being gifted, says a Father, & enriched with the Precious BLOOD of her LORD, she flies to Him with eagerness, without any fear of falling or of a repulse, because she bears upon her brow the glorious Standard of the Cross. She puts to flight all who would prevent her from approaching her GOD, Who is the Beginning from Whom she proceeds, the End to Which she aspires, & the Centre wherein she takes her rest. Take then, O my Soul, this fervent Love as thy guide to the Blessed Sacrament; for Love, a certain Saint tells us, is the most sure, the most direct path to It, the shortest, the least troublesome, the smoothest, the most devoid of danger, the clearest & brightest without any shadows, the safest without any danger, the most pleasant & the sweetest, because this Love is ever in the Presence of GOD.

It is wonderful that he who approaches the Holy Communion without Love does not, after a manner, receive the whole Benefit of the Blessed Sacrament, & that he deprives himself by his lukewarmness, of that which is most beneficial to him, so that he makes It quite useless, & often very hurtful to his Soul. For think not that the BODY, the BLOOD, the SOUL, & the DIVINITY of our Blessed LORD, which all receive, the most imperfect of those who approach as well as the most devout, compose, so to say, the Whole of this Divine Sacrament. Verily, in this Sacred
BREAD

BREAD from Heaven there are hidden Treasures, which we only receive according to the degree of Love which we take thither, & those Treasures are Supernatural Life, Divine Strength, the HOLY SPIRIT of GOD, & an increase of Love, of Faith, & of Hope. Love, says a holy Doctor, & thou wilt receive the Whole Sacrament. Thou shalt indeed consume the Precious BODY & BLOOD of thy LORD, but thou shalt not consume the Whole Sacrament, because the Impression of It remains upon thy Soul; & as long as thou shalt preserve It faithfully, the Sustenance & the Grace of thy LORD's most Precious BODY shall be with thee. Even as love is not quenched by loving, but becomes more fervent, especially when the beloved is worthy of love, so when in the Blessed Sacrament we receive our Divine LORD in Love, He cannot be consumed, because He is eternal Love. What an inducement is this for us to prepare ourselves by Love for the most Holy Eucharist, & what a great reward it is that we are able to receive the Whole Sacrament, & to preserve It, although the Sacred Elements themselves are consumed.

Think not that this Preparation of Love consists in having made a few Acts of Love before receiving the Holy Communion, & those few perhaps without fervour. Even supposing they have been very fervent, this is not all that Love requires; for it may be that thy Love, though similar to that which is demanded of thee, is unreal,

unreal, & therefore subject to change. True
Love, which is shown forth by expressions &
Acts of Love, is something; but that thou mayest
draw near worthily to the most Divine Eucharist, thy Love must also be constant. Do not
imagine, said a holy Man, that thou lovest GOD
truly, because thou sayest that thou dost so:
deeds as well as words are here required. Thou
must think upon Him more than upon ought
else; thy lips must praise Him, & think of Him;
with delight thy heart must feel this Love, or at
least make herself worthy of feeling it; & above
all things, thy hands must be busied in good
Works. Draw near to the Blessed Sacrament with
these feelings, & in the words of a Saint of old,
leave It shining with the sacred Fire of Love, &
thus shalt thou become hateful to the Devil, &
most pleasing unto Almighty GOD.

Affections.

How blessed it is, O most Sweet LORD JESUS,
said a holy Saint, to approach Thee in Love:
though Thou dwellest in Light, which cannot
be approached, we are able to come unto Thee
with Love for our guide & our companion.
While she is my leader, there is no difficulty that
I cannot overcome, no obstacle that can stop me,
no enemy that can vanquish me, no danger that
terrifies me, no Sanctuary whose doors are closed
to me. Love opens to me Thy Sacred HEART,
that

that I may enter therein; she opens my heart to receive Thee; through her I shall abide in Thee; & Thou shalt abide in me, because Thou art Thyself this Love.

O my God, if Thou art Love, according to Thy beloved Apostle, I already possess Thee in anticipation, provided I love Thee, even before drawing near to Thy holy Altar. But if Love alone obtains for me this advantage, what infinite Blessings shall I possess when I unite this Love to Thy Divine Eucharist, which is the Sacrament of Thy Sacred HEART, & when I approach It with a heart filled with Love for Thee.

O Divine Love, what wonders dost Thou work in us; how Powerful, how Helpful art Thou, when Thou hast taken possession of our hearts! Thou raisest us unto GOD, Thou dost direct our path, enlighten our spirits, inflame our heart, & consecrate our Souls. Thou dost place in us Thy Divinity, as if we were a dwelling-place of delight; & Thou dost even purify our bodies, making them fit Sanctuaries for the Sacred Humanity of our Blessed SAVIOUR. It is by Thee, says an ancient Father, that we love GOD, that we fly to GOD, that we abide in GOD, & that He abides in us, for time & for all Eternity.

Thanksgiving.

My LORD & my REDEEMER, whilst Thou art fulfilling me with Grace, & giving me such Tokens

Tokens of Thy Love, & Thy Goodnefs, fhall my heart be fo thanklefs as to be without Love, & without gratitude? When I meditate upon Thee, either on the Crofs, upon Thy holy Altar, or in my heart where Thou art now abiding, all fhows forth Thy Goodnefs & Thy Love for a creature, who is nothing, & who deferves nothing but death. Everything accufes my ingratitude & my indifference. On the Crofs Thou didft love Thy Heavenly FATHER more than Thy murderers offended Him. Thou offeredft Thyfelf with more Love, more efficacy than they crucified Thee with malice & cruelty. Thou comeft, moft Bleffed SAVIOUR, from the Crofs to the Altar, & Thou doft there renew the fame Sacrifice of Love. For us Thou receiveft there our worfhip, our adoration, our Acts of Love & Thankfgiving, & Thou joineft them to Thine Own in offering them to Thy Heavenly FATHER. They are prefented to Him with ever renewed Virtue, & He receives them as if Thou alone didft offer them Thyfelf.

But, O Adorable LORD, by an excefs of Love, Thou art now dwelling in my heart, & it is there that Thou giveft me the Tokens of a perfect Love in Heavenly FOOD, & although Thou doft communicate to me not only all that Thou haft, but all that Thou art. Fill then my heart with this Love, from its being fo near to Thy Sacred HEART, which is always burning with the Fire of Divine Love. Pour into my heart Thy Loving

ing-tenderness; fill it with a like fervour; & make it feel all that Thy Divine HEART feels. And do Thou teach it so to love, that those Thanksgivings which I now offer Thee for having given me Thyself in this Thy Sacrament of Love, may be more worthy of the Blessing which I have received.

Eighteenth Meditation.

Of the Preparation of Purity before the Blessed Sacrament.

I.

TRUE Purity, according to the Saints of old, is nothing else than perfect integrity of the inner man, who avoids with all possible care whatever may infect him with the least stain; & that, not with the view of pleasing man, but with the hope of pleasing Almighty GOD alone, Who loves Purity above all things, because He Himself is infinitely Pure. From this it follows, that Purity is as pre-eminently needful to approach the Blessed Sacrament as is the Love of GOD. Of this Love, Purity is the fruit, the production, & the inseparable companion. Or, in other words, it is only the same thing under a different name, especially since one can be defined by the other, & we can say that Purity is nothing else but a jealous Love, which

which defiring to poffefs Almighty GOD, will not leave any other affection in the heart which may be unpleafing to Him. Therefore, on this point we muft examine ourfelves with the greateft care, as without this precaution affections, like fo many idols in the heart, will efcape us, which are hidden in the fecret corners of our heart, make it an unpleafing abode for the LORD JESUS, & prevent Him from diffufing therein all the Bleffings of His Grace.

A ftrict felf-examination is therefore required, that we may not overlook thefe affections & that we may rid ourfelves of them as foon as we know of their exiftence, by at once difavowing them; & if it be neceffary, by plucking them out by the roots; taking care by earneft repentance that they do not enter into our hearts again. *But*, fays the holy Apoftle, *let a man examine himfelf & fo let him eat of that* BREAD *& drink of that* CUP. What, fays a Saint of old, what then does the great Apoftle require of the Faithful, by fpeaking to them thus, except that they fhould banifh from their hearts every feeling of malice & every ftain of fin, fo as to approach the Ever-bleffed Sacrament with greater Purity? A Doctor of the Church afks us—Doft thou wafh thine hands before partaking of common food? Thou eateft only with men, & yet thou wouldft be afhamed if they were to fee any ftain upon them. The Pharifees even were fo fcrupulous about this obfervance, which was only a cuftom of decency, very indifferent to Religion, that they complained to our Blessed LORD that His Apostles were not particular in this respect. To what Table then art thou invited at the Holy Communion? Into what a noble Company art thou about to be admitted? What Precious FOOD art thou about to receive? The Table is that of thy LORD, the SAVIOUR of mankind, & He has Himself prepared It before inviting thee thither. The Company is also that of thy Beloved LORD. Thou art about to draw nigh to Him, & to hold sweet Communion with Him. This most Precious FOOD, so Delicious, so Pure, is designed to strengthen thy Soul & to sustain her, that she may continue her journey towards Eternity with safety. What infinite Purity then must thou have to approach so holy a Table, to rejoice in the Company of thy GOD, & to be fed with most Sweet FOOD, Which is none other than thy LORD Himself.

Consider how little profit thou hast derived from all thy former Communions; meditate on what thou oughtest to be, & on what thou art. Try to discover why thou art still so imperfect, & thou wilt find that, it is because thou hast not communicated with the Purity which so great a Sacrament demands. Thou oughtest to have followed with giant steps the most strict rules of life; & may be, thou hast performed only the essential duties of thy holy Religion with reluctance. Thou oughtest now to be all-powerful against the

assaults

assaults of the enemy, & careless to the attractions of the world; & thou oughtest to hate thy imperfect life, & so to live of the Life of GOD, as to be transformed into Him. But, alas, thou art yet as weak, as imperfect, as full of self-love, as if thou hadst never communicated, & perhaps even those imperfect Communions may have contributed to thy remissness; for there are no such things as useless Communions, since by each one of them thou dost either advance, or go backward in thy Spiritual Life.

When food, however wholesome it may be, is received into an unhealthy system, far from restoring or increasing health, it injures the constitution, weakens it, & becomes another cause of malady. The Blessed Eucharist is the most Precious, the most Delicious FOOD for our Souls, & is therefore the most able to preserve them in Purity, & to give fresh strength to that Purity, because It is the Precious BODY & BLOOD of Him Who loves Purity above all things. This Purity must be found in the BODY, in the SOUL, in the SPIRIT, & in the HEART of Him Who is about to become present in the most Holy Communion. Without It, our Communions are more hurtful than profitable, & far from advancing in the path of Holiness by frequent Communions, they weaken us, & we become more liable to fall. Oh, let us then try to purify our hearts, if we would receive worthily the Author of all Purity.

II.

II.

Before coming to the Altar of God, meditate seriously on the Blessed Sacrament which thou art about to receive, in Its Types, & Its Reality. Thou wilt find throughout a Sovereign Purity, & thou wilt acknowledge that to be worthy of receiving It, & of obtaining the Grace which is attached to It, thou canst never make thyself sufficiently pure. Under the Law, none but the Priests were allowed to eat of the Shew-bread, which was a Type, though but a feeble one, of the Holy Eucharist. It was reserved as the food of those who ministered at the Altar, & it was only in extreme necessity that the Priest Ahimelech gave it to King David, & to those who were with him, because there was nothing else for them to eat. Even then, the King was obliged to answer for the purity of those who were about to partake of it. Under the Jewish Law, he who ate of the Peace-offering with the slightest legal impurity, which in itself was no sin, was punished with death. This strict Law was published throughout all Israel, so that no one in this state could approach the Tabernacle for fear of offending the most High God, to Whom the least impurity is hateful. And yet they contracted these legal impurities every day, in spite of themselves, sometimes even without their knowledge; & these legal impurities were never able to defile their hearts. Consider, O my Soul, the

the infinite Purity of the Blessed Sacrament in Its Types & Figures.

Meditate next on Its transcendent Purity now that It has passed from a Type into a Reality. It is no longer mere Shew-bread, which was only holy because it had been offered to Almighty GOD, & had been placed on the Altar & near the Ark of the Covenant. This most Holy BREAD is the BODY of the LORD Himself. It is the Strength of faithful Souls, the BREAD of Angels, the Living BREAD Which came down from Heaven. It is the BREAD Which gives eternal Life to him who receives It with a pure heart; the BREAD which, in the words of a holy Saint, was conceived by the HOLY SPIRIT in the most pure Womb of a Virgin. It is the Only SON of GOD, says a Father of the Church, the Only-begotten through all Eternity, & Who is again begotten in the fulness of time of a pure Virgin, whose Virginity was only the more sanctified when she conceived Him by the ineffable Power of the HOLY SPIRIT of GOD. Thou art about to receive this Virgin-bread Which begetteth virgin Souls, & Which adds new virtue to their virginity each time they receive It with pure & spotless hearts. Thou art about to receive a FLESH a thousand times more Pure than the purest of those who rejoice in the Presence of GOD in Heaven.

Reflect that thou art about to become the living Sanctuary of an All-pure GOD; & that for Him,

Him, the Author of Purity, a moſt pure Sanctuary is required. When He finds this purity, He abides willingly in thine heart, He dwells there, there He takes His Reſt, He works His Grace there abundantly, & He gives thee an ever-increaſing ſupply of Purity. Be not content with a common Purity to draw near to the Bleſſed Sacrament, endeavour to make it the perfect Image of thy Divine LORD. It ſuffices not to purify thine heart from all thoſe impurities & ſinful affections of which every Chriſtian ought to be aſhamed; but thou muſt weigh well each one of thy affections, & take from them all that is unpleaſing to GOD, which many find not out, becauſe they do not examine themſelves with ſufficient care. They have not love enough, nor delicacy of conſcience enough, nor light enough to perceive theſe affections.

A holy Man once ſaid—Remember that whatever height of Purity is attained, & can be attained, in this mortal life, thou wilt always find ſomewhat to purify. The nearer thou doſt approach to GOD Who is Light & Purity Itſelf, while thou art in the fleſh, the more ſhalt thou find within thyſelf that needs cleanſing, as well as a higher degree of Purity to be attained, whilſt thou art ſurrounded by objects which captivate thy ſenſes. They will always receive ſome ſlight corruption which thou wilt hardly be able to perceive without great care, & which will ſurely penetrate into thine heart unleſs thou art ever

on the watch. If thou art defirous that thy
LORD fhould abide in thee, become a perfect reflection of His Purity. If thou doft endeavour
to do this, thy Soul, continues the Saint, will
become a Paradife for the Heavenly SPOUSE;
thy good works fhall be as a fruitful growth of
trees; thy holinefs fhall be its ornament like
fweet fmelling flowers; thy Bleffed REDEEMER
will water it with the healing Water of His
Grace, & He will Himfelf come to take His
Pleafure therein.

Affections.

Thou didft call me, moft Adorable LORD, into
Thy Sanctuary, & Thou art defirous that I fhould
approach Thee, but Thou doft require firft that
I fhould confider Who & What Thou art, &
what I am. Alas, thefe thoughts fill me with
confufion & fhame; & if Thou didft not call
me with the Loving-kindnefs of a SAVIOUR, &
a moft Beloved SPOUSE, I could only obey Thee
in fear.

When I meditate upon Thee, as Thou doft
command, I behold Thee on Thy glorious
Throne, furrounded by thofe pure Spirits who
laud Thy Holy Name, & who feem to rebuke me
becaufe I am not as pure as they are. I behold
in Thee a facred Holinefs which I adore, &
which fills me with confufion. I behold in Thee
an incomparable Purity, which I revere, but
which

which terrifies me, & which seems to reject me as unworthy of appearing before It. Concealed beneath these Sacred FORMS, I behold a SPIRIT, a SOUL, a DIVINITY, Which are All-pure, & more than this, I perceive the FLESH, BLOOD, & HEART, the Purity of Which is Infinite & Incomprehensible because they are united hypostatically to DEITY. Filled with the thought of Thine exceeding Purity, & turning mine eyes upon myself, I can no longer endure the sight of my numberless corruptions. Thine all-seeing Eye, O GOD of all Purity, beholds my impurity, & although I only see in part, & cannot endure the sight, Thou seest within me an imagination either filled, or capable of being filled, with images which are unworthy to appear before Thee; a memory which only too faithfully preserves a dangerous remembrance of things which it ought to abhor; a mind which has not always entertained pure thoughts; a will often turned from Thee to mortals; desires which have often displeased Thee; a heart which has not always loved That which it ought to love alone; & a flesh which leans only too much upon earthly gratifications.

But, O most Merciful GOD, since Thou art a consuming Fire, do Thou come & reduce all these offences to ashes. Do Thou purify all that I am, all that I have, & make me worthy to approach Thine infinite Purity.

Thanks.

Thanksgiving.

O incomparable Purity, O All-powerful God, Who, according to Thy holy Prophet, dost recompense the just after the measure of their Purity, & Who dost listen to & grant the prayers which issue from a pure heart, hearken, I beseech Thee, unto mine. Give ear unto the most humble Acts of Thanksgiving which my spirit, my heart, & my tongue offer unto Thee for having vouchsafed to bestow on me to-day, as my Food, Thy Body, Thy Blood, Thy Soul, & Thy Divinity, Which are the Sources of all Purity, & Which sanctify the Purity of those who have endeavoured to purify themselves before drawing nigh unto Thine Altar.

Whilst Thou art abiding within me, O infinite Love, O consuming Fire, O God of all Purity, do Thou inspire my Soul with the most fervent, & the purest gratitude for the infinite Grace which I have now received of Thine exceeding Bounty. Inflame & purify my heart, that its love may be that of a purified conscience. Cleanse it from every impurity & from its smallest desires & affections, which do not tend to Thee alone, & from all those aspirations which Thou hast not inspired. Destroy in my heart, wherein Thou dost now abide, its too natural leaning towards the creature. Consume with the Fire of Thine all-pure Love all that is earthly & unworthy of Thy

Thy gracious Presence. Verily, O most Adorable LORD, Thou art Powerful enough to do this, & Thy Divine Love is All-powerful to change the evil desires of the flesh into those of Thy BODY Which, veiled under these Sacred FORMS, I now possess, & Which I hope one day to behold, unveiled, in a most glorious Eternity.

Nineteenth Meditation.

Of the Preparation of Humility before the Blessed Sacrament.

I.

ALTHOUGH Almighty GOD is Greatness itself, & although creatures are nothing in His Presence, it is not by greatness, by riches, by high places, by talents that they can obtain free access to Him. Nay rather, is it because of His infinite Greatness that we can only be worthy to approach Him, & to receive His gracious Favour by being filled with the deepest Humility. *The LORD is great*, said the holy Psalmist, & yet He sees true Humility with pleasure, He exalts it, & He confounds the proud. He despises & rejects those who are filled with pride, & who rebel against His Commands, & He never honours them by holding communion with them.

He

He does not even draw nigh unto them, except to make them feel the strength of His Arm in Chastisement. But He delights in exalting those who humble themselves, & who are lowly of heart. He draws nigh unto them, & abases His Sacred HEART to their nothingness. He invites their approach with Loving-kindness. He gives Himself to them without reserve. He even abides with them, & invites Himself with the same Love as He invited Himself into the house of Zaccheus. He dwells in their hearts, pours out upon them all the Blessings & Graces which are attached to His abode there, through the Ever-blessed Sacrament.

The holy Patriarch, in pleading for the inhabitants of Sodom & Gomorrah, spoke to the ALMIGHTY with familiarity & even with boldness. It was deep Humility, strengthened by lively Faith, which obtained for him this freedom. *I have taken upon me*—said the holy Man—*to speak unto the* LORD, *which am but dust & ashes*. Following the reason of man, his acknowledgment of himself to be but dust & ashes would have prevented his conversing so nearly with GOD; but on the contrary, it was because of that confession, & of his Humility that he was able to approach his LORD with confidence. Clothe thyself then, O my Soul, with this Humility, ere thou dost draw near to the holy Altar of thy GOD; engrave deeply on thine heart the thought of the infinite Greatness of GOD, & then meditate

meditate on what thou art, on thy weakness, thy misery, & thine absolute nothingness. Make a sincere confession of this, humiliate thyself before the Majesty of GOD, & learn from this the power to approach Him with greater confidence. The more thou dost empty thyself of all thy natural inclinations, by Humility of heart & Soul, the more worthy shalt thou be to be filled with the Presence of thy GOD.

Be then assured that there is no Grace which enables us to approach our Adorable LORD more freely than that of Humility. Remember that when He dwelt upon earth, He graciously received all who came to Him with this Grace; that none, however grievously they might have sinned, none were refused the Grace which they sought. The Centurion declared himself unworthy that the LORD should come under his roof; & by his Humility he made himself meet to receive a visit from his Blessed REDEEMER. He obtained not only that which he so much desired, but as a holy Saint tells us, he also, by his Humility, obtained the power of seeing, with the eyes of faith, that Holy DIVINITY which was concealed under the FORM of a Sacred HUMANITY. The Publican, again, who smote his breast, & dared not to raise even his eyes unto Heaven, was justified, while the proud Pharisee was condemned. The sinful Magdalene prostrated herself at the Feet of her All-merciful LORD, & obtained one of the highest places in His

His Loving HEART; her tears were dried, & she became loving when she became penitent. Zaccheus, by Humility, attracted the LORD of all into his house, & into his heart; he was not despised by the Blessed JESUS notwithstanding his littleness of stature & the murmurs of the Pharisees. Our Divine LORD converses with him familiarly, treats him as a true Israelite, & brings Salvation into his house.

Follow in the steps of these holy Examples, who, though they were sinners, gained the Blessing & Favour of their Divine MASTER by Humility. Be small in thine own eyes, in order to draw down upon thee the gracious Eye of thy GOD. Meditate on thy sins, on thy wretchedness, so as to impress upon thy heart the urgent need which thou hast to be humble. Be filled with the thought of thine own littleness & the Greatness of GOD, of thy sinfulness & of His Mercy, & draw near unto Him with confidence. Forsake all false greatness with as much Humility & promptitude as Zaccheus descended from the tree into which he had mounted to see his Divine LORD pass by; & the more humble thou art, the more easily shalt thou see Him. Zaccheus was hastening to prepare his house for the reception of the MESSIAH, Who had invited Himself into it; do thou in like manner prepare the Sanctuary of thy heart, & He will even anticipate thee. Do it so that He may find therein no spot of sin, no remains of vanity, & not the

least

least particle of pride, which would be unpleasing to His Almighty Eye, & which would induce Him to leave the sooner without thy having experienced the exceeding Blessedness of His Visit, & His Abode. Confess with the Humility, the sincerity, & the fervour of the Centurion, that thou art not worthy that He should enter under thy roof; & by thy Humility thou wilt attract & keep Him there. Prostrate thyself before Him with the love, & the humility of the blessed Magdalene, & weep at His most sacred Feet, so as to gain a nearer approach to Him, & to prepare thyself for the Kiss of Peace which thou wilt receive at the Blessed Sacrament. Weep abundant tears at the knowledge of thy sins, & He Himself will graciously vouchsafe to wipe them all away.

II.

Take also here thy Divine LORD as the Example for thy Preparation. Follow with thy heart & spirit in His adorable Steps, & meditate upon all that He does. And whether it is in that which immediately precedes the Institution of the Holy Eucharist, whether it is at the time when He gave Himself to His Apostles, & to the faithful, or when He condescends to become Present under the Sacred ELEMENTS, or when we adore His Divine Presence, thou wilt see not only Humility, but the most wonderful of all Humiliations. The Ever-blessed JESUS prepares
Himself

Himself for the Institution of the Divine Sacrament by the most humble of actions—that of washing the feet of His Disciples. The Almighty GOD of all, upon His sacred Knees, at the feet of His Apostles, even at the feet of the traitor who was about to betray Him! Oh, what a wonderful Sight, what a Preparation, what an Example, what a wondrous Lesson for us, what a cause of confusion to the proud who would venture to approach GOD without Humility!

But, O my GOD, what a Posture, what a Humiliation was Thine, to touch with Thy Divine Hands, Which created Heaven & earth, the feet of Thy creatures, the feet of a traitor, & to wash them even as if that wicked One was Thy Master. And yet, it was by this Humility that Thou didst prepare for the Institution of the Blessed Eucharist, & Thou didst accomplish Thy Purpose in spite of the resistance of one of Thine Apostles, who could not suffer his gracious Master to fall at his feet. Thou didst do this, most Adorable LORD, that we might follow Thy blessed Example, & therefore didst Thou say unto us—*If I then, your LORD & Master, have washed your feet, ye ought also to wash one another's feet.*

Again, meditate on the Blessed Sacrament in Its use, where thy Divine SAVIOUR, not content with serving thee at His holy Altar, as if He was thine inferior, gives Himself to thee as thy FOOD & thy Guest. He Who is Greatness itself, comes to abide in thee, to nourish thee, & to hold sweet com-

communion with thee. He is as Great as His Heavenly FATHER; &, after a manner, He becomes lefs than thou art. Heal then thy pride with this holy Example; prepare thyfelf with Humility for the holy Sacrament; approach humbly to a Humiliated GOD, humiliated in His facred Humanity, & under the Humble FORMS of Bread & Wine. The ufe of this Divine Sacrament fo great, & yet fo humble, will affuredly produce Humility in thine heart.

Meditate, again, O my Soul, upon the Sacred FORMS of this Holy Sacrament, & thou wilt find that they contain an admirable leffon of that Humility, with which thou oughteft to prepare thyfelf for their reception. Under the FORM of that Sacred BREAD is prefent that DIVINITY Which the infinite fpace of Heaven cannot comprehend, that Perfect HUMANITY, that SOUL, that SPIRIT, that WILL, that FLESH, that HEART, & that BLOOD Which are prefent there by a Miracle of Love. Our Adorable LORD is a voluntary Prifoner beneath thefe Forms becaufe He loved us; & there He is gracioufly pleafed to wait for us, to liften to us, to fpeak to us, to infpire us in doubts, to comfort us in troubles, to animate us in temptation, to excite in us the practice of Chriftian Virtues, & to grant with bounty all thofe Graces which we fhall afk of Him.

Approach Him then with Humility, & acknowledge thy wretchednefs, thy fins, thy weaknefs, & thy corruption. In the words of a holy Saint of
GOD,

GOD, examine into the depths of thine heart, & plant firmly therein the foundations of true Humility. Know, feel, & acknowledge that thou art nothing, & confess it, so as to be esteemed as nothing, & not to be vain even of thy Humility. By this means thou shalt acquire Divine Love, & if thou wouldest make thyself worthy to keep within thee the Greatness of GOD, remember first the exceeding Humility of the LORD JESUS, & then follow in His most holy Steps, without ever wandering away from them.

Affections.

And wilt thou, O my Soul, draw near to a GOD Humble & Humiliated under the Sacred Forms, with a proud heart? Wilt thou dare to kneel before the holy Table of the LORD with feelings so little conformable to the Humility of Him Who became MAN for love of thee? Wilt thou receive the most Humble HEART of thy Dear LORD into thy proud & self-sufficient heart? O my Soul, what sorrow wouldst thou cause to the Sacred HEART of thy GOD by placing It near to that heart which is His enemy, & what a fearful punishment wouldst thou draw down upon thyself.

Filled with shame at my wretchedness, at my constant rebellion against Thee, & at my want of Humility, I approach Thee, O most Merciful GOD, as but a worm of earth, as but living dust, animated only through Thy Love. I humbly implore Thee to pardon my pride, & to grant me that perfect Humility which shall be the imitation of Thine, so as to make me worthy to receive Thee in the Ever-blessed Sacrament. Alas! I acknowledge that I am nothing; I am assured of it, & I detest my pride. Do Thou then, O Adorable LORD, sustain my weakness. Grant me both Humility of spirit & Humility of heart, & the power to keep them humble even unto my death. Give me that Humility of spirit which Love produces, that I may be assured that I am nothing, & that I deserve nothing. Oh, let my heart realise this truth, so that acting in conformity therewith, I may despise & distrust myself; that I may hate myself so as to love Thee more, & to make myself more worthy of receiving Thee at Thy holy Altar, & of possessing Thee for ever in Eternity.

Thanksgiving.

O ineffable, incomprehensible Greatness, O All-powerful GOD, before Whose Majesty the kings of the earth are mere dust & ashes, how is it possible that Thou shouldst have abased Thyself unto me, & that Thou shouldst now be abiding within me, who am but a worm of earth, & who have so often rebelled against Thee? Yet, notwithstanding my sins, & my unfaithfulness, Thou hast done for me in a marvellous & spiritual manner,

manner, that which the Prophet did in times of old, for the Widow's son whom he restored to life. Not content with having left Thy Throne of Glory in Heaven to unite Thyself closely with me, Thou hast most wonderfully abased Thyself to me, & hast straitened Thyself that Thou mightest be conformed to mine exceeding littleness. But, by the eyes of Faith, I see & adore in Thee, Who art now abiding in me, a dazzling Glory, although It is for the time obscured, a wondrous Height abased, an Immensity straitened, an infinite Greatness infinitely Humbled by a Miracle of Love & Mercy.

O GOD of all Goodness, whilst Thou art in me, teach me how to become humble, how to love humiliation, so that my eyes which have had the exceeding joy of seeing Thee in these Sacred FORMS, may become, after their degree, like Thine, which are perfectly Humble. Oh, grant that my lips, which have just received Thee, may never utter a word of pride; that my mind may reject all sorts of vain glory; & that my heart, near which Thou dost now abide, may resist all feelings of false greatness, so as to receive Thee worthily in this life, & to possess in that which is to come the eternal Glory, which Thou hast promised to all those who are humble in heart.

Twentieth Meditation.

Of the Preparation of Desire before the Blessed Sacrament.

I.

It is our Blessed Lord Himself Who has taught us to desire most earnestly to approach the Holy Eucharist, for was it not with Desire that He instituted It, to nourish us with His most Precious Body & Blood, to be with us to the end of time, to be to us our Daily Food, & to sustain us in Holiness? Did He not say at that Paschal Supper, the last He celebrated in His Life on earth, these most comfortable Words—*With Desire have I desired to eat this Passover with you before I suffer?* By the great Desire which our Blessed Lord felt & manifested to us in these wondrous Words, He showed forth two things; first, the excess of His Love, & secondly, the Preparation of Desire that we ought to bring to the holy Altar, that we may communicate with profit, in clothing ourselves with the same earnest Desire that He had.

What advantage could our Blessed Lord gain from this Institution, that He longed for It so fervently, since He gave all & received nothing? It was then His Love alone which made Him desire to unite Himself with us, to give Himself
to

to us, & to remain with us to the end of time, to attach us more inseparably to Him, & to pour out upon us more abundantly the Blessings which are enshrined in His BODY, His BLOOD, His SOUL, & His DIVINITY. Oh, what an inducement to make us long for this most sweet Union with our GOD. We give nothing that we have, we receive all that we can desire, since we receive the Almighty GOD from Whom all good things do come, & Who desires to communicate them to us. What blindness not to desire to unite ourselves intimately to Him, Who so earnestly desires to unite Himself to us, & Who, not content with only desiring it, wills to express His Desire by the most comfortable Words & Expressions.

Examine thine heart on thy Desires for the Ever-blessed Sacrament. Each time that thou comest to the holy Altar, dost thou feel this Desire; & if thou hast it not, dost thou endeavour to excite it? Dost thou suffer whenever thou art deprived of the Divine Eucharist, or when thou hast committed some sin which will prevent thee from drawing nigh to It, or when thou art deprived of It by some bodily infirmity, or when thy spiritual Guide sees fit to forbid It thee either to make thee feel the privation, or to excite in thee more earnest desires for the Holy Communion? Be assured that to feel no sorrow at this privation is a sign that thou desirest not the Blessed Sacrament; & not to desire It, & not to love It is the same thing; & if thou lovest not thy Holy REDEEMER, thou art not worthy to approach Him.

Thou must then feel a Desire to communicate, & sorrow when thou art not able to do so; but thou must also examine this Desire & this sorrow, for sometimes instead of proceeding from the ALMIGHTY, earthly feelings glide into them, to which we do not pay enough attention. To discover the reason of this delusion, search into thine heart, & see whether it is not a perverse attachment to some practice of which thou hast made a custom, & which thou wilt not discontinue; whether it is not self-love; whether it is not vanity; for, remember, that such desires are very imperfect. Control then these desires, purify this sorrow, & give them more perfect, more exalted motives. Desire Almighty GOD, for His Sake alone, & for thine own spiritual advantage. Banish all that comes from self-love & human respect; & by this means thou shalt become more worthy to unite thyself to GOD in the Holy Eucharist. Thou wilt delight in Him more, He will communicate Himself to thee more completely, & thou wilt receive the whole Grace contained in the Holy Communion. The ALMIGHTY communicated Himself to the Prophet of old, & filled him with His HOLY SPIRIT, because he was a Man of Desire; he desired only the GOD Whom he loved with his whole heart. Yet, in this life, he could only possess Him spiritually,

tually, & by love; for then there was no holy Table at which GOD communicated Himself, as He now does to the Faithful.

Be thou then also a man of Desire. Desire unceasingly to behold Him Whom the Angels desire to look into. Turn all thy Desires towards Him Who, in the language of the Spouse, is altogether Lovely. Thy Desires shall be very differently rewarded in this life, than were those of the Prophet. Thou shalt possess the LORD thy Redeemer, not only by love but in reality, such as He is in Heaven; & He will be thine & will abide in thee. In the Blessed Sacrament thou wilt receive more than His Sacred BODY & BLOOD, more than His Adorable SOUL, & if such a thing can be said with all reverence, more than His DIVINITY, for there thou dost also receive His SPIRIT, His Grace, His Strength, His Life, & the participation in His Divine Nature.

II.

Nothing prepares a Soul so completely for the Reception of the Ever-blessed Eucharist as an ardent & constant Desire to receive It. The more eager, the more famished thou art after this Sacred FOOD, the more capable is thy Soul of receiving It, the more she experiences Its Delight, the more she receives of Grace, & the more her Desires increase. Hunger & thirst are the needful requirements to receive bodily food; for food, however well prepared, does not benefit a body a body which hungers not after it; on the contrary, it is hunger & appetite which prepares the human body for its nourishment.

The Blessed Sacrament cannot be said to be of great Benefit to those who do not earnestly desire It. They must desire It, if they would receive all the Graces, all the Virtues, contained in It. A Soul occupied only with earthly & temporal desires, far from deriving any benefit, far from being spiritually filled with this most Sweet, most Delicious, & most Super-substantial FOOD, will receive It without feeling Its Sweetness; & instead of being strengthened by It, it is much to be feared that she will become weaker, & that then she will make an unworthy Communion.

Here there is a difference to which thou must pay attention. An abundance of bodily food, however gratifying it may be, soon satiates the appetite, & finally disgusts it; but the Blessed Sacrament of the BODY & BLOOD of our Divine LORD, the Sweet FOOD of Souls never satiates, but the more It is received with a meet disposition, the more is It desired & longed for. Sensual pleasures always excite desire; but these desires are corrupt, & proceeding from evil principles they tend to an evil end. The seeking for them is never without anxiety, & persons suffer even while they desire them. It often happens that the longed for pleasure, far from satisfying the desire, destroys it, & fills the heart with disgust, with sorrow, with bitterness, & with a gnawing remorse

morse—a remorse which pays dearly for those pleasures that have been purchased at the expense of their innocence.

Far otherwise is it with those longing Desires for the ALMIGHTY which Saints experience in the most Holy Sacrament. However ardent these Desires may be, there is no disquietude in them, because they proceed from GOD & end in GOD. They are all accompanied with tranquillity & resignation, which render them sweet, because they are conformed to the perfect Will of GOD. A holy Saint tells us, that when the Faithful possess in their hearts the GOD Whom they have so much desired, He enters into their Soul & fulfils It with His Divine Presence, by the pouring forth of those Graces which in the Holy Communion He gives to all who earnestly desire them. He fills them with chaste Delights, which tongue cannot express; the more they taste of them, the more our Blessed LORD enables them to taste of still more precious Joys, & the more do they desire them.

They are satiated indeed, but it is after the manner of the Saints who enjoy their GOD for ever in Heaven, without satiety & with an ever renewed pleasure; & this Fulness of Sweetness & spiritual Delights far from diminishing, increases. It is as if they possessed their Blessed LORD only to desire Him more ardently, & they desire Him only to possess Him more worthily, & more fully; & thus, instead of being troubled

troubled & disquieted by this Desire, they find in It the very completion of their repose. Turn not away, says a Saint of old, without good reason, from the sacred & Life-giving Sacrament of the Precious BODY & BLOOD of thy LORD; on the contrary, desire It as fervently as thou canst. Seek after It eagerly, & hunger always after so precious a Food as is the FLESH of thy LORD & thy GOD. Ever thirst after so grateful a Beverage as is the Precious BLOOD of thy Redeeming LORD. Desire is the hunger & thirst of the Soul, therefore receive the Ever-blessed JESUS at the Holy Altar with this longing Desire, mingled with the deepest reverence. Preserve this Divine FOOD most carefully, & lose none of the Graces that It contains.

Why are such fervent Desires required? Because much Love is demanded, & Desires come from Love, even as heat proceeds from fire. They sustain this Love, they nourish it, & give it new fervour. Desire is to Love, what flame is to fire; it proceeds from Love it is true, but it is always more brilliant, more vivid, more subtil, & always is drawn more quickly towards her Centre.

Affections.

Like as the hart desireth the water brooks, so longeth my Soul after Thee, O GOD. Thus spake the holy Prophet of old, & in very truth, most

Blessed Lord, Thou art in the most Holy Communion as a Fount of living Water, which quenches the thirst my Soul ought to have after Divine Wisdom, & the All-powerful God Who sustains her against the assaults of her enemies. Oh, when shall I come to appear before the Presence of God? Oh, when will that blisful time come when I may draw near to His holy Table, to receive that most Precious Food of His Body & Blood? I feel more than ever, O Merciful God, that I can no longer live without Thee, I need all things when I cannot receive Thee. I am nothing but weakness, I am nothing but misery, in this most sad separation from Thee. *My tears have been my meat day & night, while they daily say unto me—Where is now thy God?* I meditate on Him unceasingly, & when the long desired day dawns on which I am to communicate, my Soul expands within me in the most ineffable manner, & I say—I am about to enter into the Courts of the Lord. I shall soon hear that joyful sound which calls me to the most high Feast of the Lamb; why then art thou so vexed, O my Soul, & why art thou so disquieted within me? Hope, desire, praise thy Blessed Saviour; for the time is drawing near for thee to receive Him.

Come then, O most Adorable Lord; my whole Soul desires Thee; without Thee nothing is sweet, all is but bitterness. O Thou That givest all things, said a Saint of old, give Thyself to to me. Thou mayeſt deprive me of all that Thou canſt give me, provided only that Thou giveſt me Thyſelf. I will have nothing, unleſs He Who giveth all things doth give me Himſelf.

Thanksgiving.

Now that I poſſeſs Thee in my heart, moſt Sweet LORD JESUS, ought I not to ſay with the ſame truth, the ſame Love as the Spouſe in the Canticles —*I ſat down under His Shadow with great Delight, & His Fruit was ſweet to my taſte. He brought me to the Banqueting Houſe, & His Banner over me was Love.* More favoured than this faithful Spouſe, I have Thee not only near me, but in my heart. Thou abideſt within me to liſten unto my Thankſgivings, to ſuggeſt them unto me, to increaſe my gratitude, to give freſh ardour to my Deſires & my love, & to communicate Thy Love to me. But alas, leſs faithful than that loving Spouſe, I have not longed after Thee with the ſame fervour, I have not ſought Thee with the ſame care, even though Thou art a Beloved to be altogether deſired, Who alone art capable of filling all hearts.

O LORD, whilſt Thou doſt abide in me, teach me to deſire Thee with all my Soul, & to love only Thee, ſo that I may find Thee, & poſſeſs Thee as the Reward for all my Deſires, that I may only poſſeſs Thee in this life, to learn to deſire Thee with greater fervour. Excite in me, moſt

moſt Adorable SAVIOUR, continued Deſires to approach Thee, & to unite myſelf inſeparably to Thee in this All-holy Sacrament. Theſe Deſires will then ſerve as a continual Preparation to receive Thee more worthily, though Hidden beneath the ſacred Elements, & they will enable me to ſee Thee unveiled, & to poſſeſs Thee eternally in Heaven.

Twenty-firſt Meditation.

Of the Effects of the Reception of the Holy Euchariſt.

I.

It is moſt important, before approaching the Holy Altar of GOD, to examine into each one of the Effects which a worthy Communion produces, ſo as to become more worthy of feeling them inwardly after having communicated. This Meditation will inſenſibly lead us into an examination of our former Communions, which perhaps will cover us with a wholeſome confuſion, when we meditate on the profit which we have obtained from them, & on that which we ought to have derived. This will make us take more certain precautions for the future, to prepare ourſelves with greater care & to profit more largely by our Communions.

The Divine Eucharist being one of the Sacraments of the New Dispensation, the Sacrament of Sacraments, the most Sublime, the most Noble, the most Efficacious of all Sacraments, it is impossible for It not to produce Grace in the Soul each time that we receive It, provided there exists no obstacle of deadly sin. And the Grace which It works in us, is either weaker or stronger according to the different degrees of Faith, of Love, & of Purity, which we bring to the holy Altar. Far above all other Sacraments the Divine Eucharist gives us at once the Cause & the Effect, the Source & the Stream Itself. It applies & unites to us intimately both the Effect & the Cause, by which Grace is obtained, in giving us JESUS CHRIST Himself, Who is the Author of all Grace, & Who obtained It for us by His Sufferings, by the Shedding of His most Precious BLOOD, & by the cruel Death which He endured. This is sanctifying Grace, the principal Effect of the Holy Communion, when the conscience is not burdened with any great unfaithfulness. But remember, that this Grace will increase according to the feelings which thou dost bring with thee.

Content not thyself with this common Grace at the Altar; there are many other Treasures which it depends only on thee to participate in. A Soul who comes to the Holy Eucharist after having been in retreat, after having exercised herself with all possible care in Acts of Faith, of Hope, & of Charity, after having banished all self-

self-love, all affection for the creature, & for venial sin from her heart, filled with the thought of her own baseness & the infinite Greatness of the ALMIGHTY, with fervent desires to unite herself to Him, & to feel within her His Real Presence, & with a heart burning with fervent Love—this Soul receives far more abundant Grace than those weaker Souls, who content themselves with only a slight Preparation, & who are in danger of making an unworthy Communion. Those who communicate often are the most apt to make shipwreck on this dangerous rock, which often occasions great misfortunes. Examine then thyself on this point, & do all thou canst not to incur these troubles, because they are for the most part the reason of unprofitable Communions. The first of these troubles is, that such persons expose themselves to lose all the benefits which are inseparable from a worthy Communion, & especially that Grace of Unction, that Grace of Strength, that Grace of Union, that Grace of Perfection, which only are given by measure, & which are never received in full unless a careful Preparation has been made.

How indeed couldst thou expect to receive the whole Grace, to feel the whole Effect of a Sacrament so efficacious in Itself, if thou prayest without fervour? Our Blessed LORD doubtless will give Grace; He has more pleasure in giving than we have in receiving; but it is His Will that

that we should give Him all that we can give, our will, our desires, our good works, our love, & that we bring to the Holy Sacrament no obstacle to those Divine Graces & Feelings with which He favours all who receive Him fervently. If we would gather those precious Fruits which are offered to us, we must first of all sow the Seed of them.

The second of these troubles, & a consequence of the first, is the being responsible for the Treasure received, & even for the Graces that would have been received, had not the recipient made himself unworthy.

Oh, what a fearful thing it is to be guilty of the Sacred BODY & BLOOD of our Everblessed REDEEMER, to be guilty of It after every unprofitable Reception, & to be treated as was that idle & unworthy Servant who did not increase the Talent committed to his charge. That Talent was but a small worldly charge, but this One is a Treasure of infinite Value. That Talent was given into his care once; yet it was taken from him & he remained in poverty for ever; but this Divine Talent has been given thee whenever thou hast communicated. Meditate upon this, & endeavour for the future to profit better by the Blessed Eucharist left It be taken from thee for time, & for all Eternity.

II.

To lose none of the infinite Graces that are contained

contained in the BODY & BLOOD of CHRIST, in the Holy Communion, we will here enter into the detail of all the other Effects which It produces in the Soul of the worthy recipient. This Meditation will enable us to love the Blessed Sacrament more & more, & will create in our hearts new desires & new longings to feel all Its Effects. Verily, the Favours we receive do not end with only sanctifying Grace. We receive, besides, the forgiveness of our sins & the remission of that punishment which we owe to the Justice of GOD for the sins of our lives. For this adorable Victim does Himself bear all our iniquities, & while He abides in us, He offers up for us to His Heavenly FATHER, in satisfaction for our sins, His Merits, His Passion, His Death, & His most Precious BLOOD.

True penitents acquire at the Altar the practice of penitence, & greater ease to sustain its salutary discipline. They taste Heavenly Sweetness in its true Source, & a pure Delight which detaches them from sensual pleasures, & makes them confess how false, how transient they are. Before Holy Communion, they were only initiated into repentance, they could only offer up Acts of Contrition :—but after having worthily communicated, they obtain the habit of penitence; their contrition becomes more perfect; their resolutions are more firm; their passions grow weaker; Grace increases; the flame of evil desire grows less, & by degrees is extinguished; they

they can resist temptation more strongly. The Devil has less power over them, for he can no longer be master of a Soul which has just been refreshed with the Precious BODY & BLOOD of CHRIST Himself; & he respects, in spite of himself, the Sanctuary where his Sovereign LORD abides. Weak & sinful flesh purifies itself by its close Union with the most Pure FLESH of a Redeeming LORD; it no longer feels weak, nor has it any inclination to sin.

Consider that the Divine Sacrament enlightens a worthy Communicant, bearing into his Soul the Torch of eternal Light. This sweet & Heavenly Honey more truly opens the eyes of the Soul, than the wild honey opened the eyes of Jonathan. He finds within himself a greater knowledge of the ALMIGHTY, which induces him to fear, to reverence, to honour, & to love GOD; he finds that knowledge of himself, which teaches him to despise himself, & to lean not at all on his own strength. This Light, which he obtains from the Source of all Light, shows him the extent of his weakness, his instability, the depth of his corruption, & that of the world, all the dangerous circumstances that may occur, & makes him take precautions how to avoid them. Draw near then to this GOD of Light, & thou shalt be enlightened.

How wondrous are the Effects of the Holy Communion, when It is worthily received. It recalls our most secret sins, which either we have
forgotten

forgotten by the unfaithfulness of memory, or which are hidden by that self-love, which often conceals our most besetting weakness from our eyes. The holy Prophet felt assuredly the weight of this kind of sin, when he said to the LORD— *O cleanse Thou me from my secret faults.* And yet this noble Penitent enjoyed not the efficacious Remedy, which we possess in the Blessed Eucharist; for either It enlightens us to make us know them, or else It purifies us from those defilements which we do not perceive, & which it pleases Almighty GOD sometimes to hide from us.

Draw near then to this most Blessed Sacrament with the same faith, the same eagerness as the poor Woman in the Gospel, who suffered from an issue of blood for twelve years. She began by saying secretly those wonderful words which touched the Sacred HEART of JESUS, & which He heard, although she spoke them not aloud— *If I touch but the hem of His Garment, I shall be whole.* She finds Him in the midst of a crowd; she presses through it; she approaches Him with lively faith & real confidence; she touches Him with the greatest reverence. The Divine SAVIOUR perceived that Virtue had gone out of Him, which had worked a Miracle. He said that He had been touched, & His Apostles answered Him—*Thou seest the multitude thronging Thee, & sayest Thou—Who touched Me?*

By these words the Heavenly Physician would give us to understand that His Apostles knew
not

not that it was one thing to press upon Him, like a crowd, whose eagerness was not that of faith, & another thing to touch Him, as did that faithful Woman. Thus may it be said, that in the Blessed Sacrament many press upon Him as mere Christians, without being enlightened or cured of their secret faults. Touch Him then as did this sick Woman, & thou shalt be healed, because thou wilt touch not His Garment only, but His most Sacred FLESH. Thou wilt place It near thine heart; It will touch thee; It will abide in thee; It will act as thy Food; & thou wilt be incorporated into It. Make then good use of these precious moments; confess thyself guilty of a multitude of secret sins; weep for them, & thou shalt be purified from them.

Affections.

Whence cometh it, O my Soul, that after so many Communions thou art still the same? why feelest thou not the beneficial Effects of the BODY & BLOOD of thy LORD? Thy Faith is as weak, thy Hope as imperfect, thy Love as languid, as if thou hadst not received this Precious FOOD. Where are the faults thou hast corrected, the Virtues thou hast acquired? Where are the temptations thou hast overcome, the passions thou hast extinguished? Thy Grace, is it stronger? Thy feelings, are they more detached from things of earth? Thy thoughts, are they more pure? Thy will, is it more obedient?
Dost

Dost thou love thyself less? Oh, what cause hast thou for self-examination, what cause for confusion. This is a Sacrament of Love, of consummated Love; has then thy love become more fervent towards GOD & thy neighbour? This is a Sacrament of Grace; of what profit then has It been to thee, or has thy Grace increased since thou hast received It more frequently? This is a Sacrament of Strength, & thou art as weak in resisting temptation. This is a Sacrament of Purity, & thou art as sensual, as indulgent to thy flesh, as if thou hadst not been fed with the most sacred BODY of thy LORD. Exclaim then, with a Saint of old—O infinite Love, O Almighty GOD, Thou Who art sweeter than Honey, Milk more white than snow, Food of the strong, & Support of the weak, grant that I may grow in Thee, & by Thee; & do Thou, O my GOD, take from my heart all that is opposed to the Effects that Thou couldst produce in me by giving me Thyself. Grant that through this Heavenly BREAD my Soul may be enlightened, as was that of Thy two Apostles, to know Thee after having received Thee, & that I may say that which they said when Thou didst vanish out of their sight—*Did not our hearts burn within us while He talked with us?* does not my heart burn within me since my GOD & my SAVIOUR has given Himself to me, & since by the Blessed Eucharist He has made me feel the Effects of His Divine Presence.

Thanksgiving.

Do Thou work in me, O most Blessed SAVIOUR, the beneficial Effects which Thou dost work in the Faithful, who approach Thee with Faith & Hope & Love. Produce in my senses, in my memory, in my spirit, in my heart, in all my Soul, the most precious Fruits of Grace, which Thou dost produce in all those who receive Thee worthily. O GOD of all Goodness, grant that I may feel now that Thou art abiding in me, with all the Fruits of so Divine a Food. Thy most Holy FLESH is now within mine. It is Purity itself; destroy then in me all that is displeasing to Thine infinite Purity. Grant that It may efface for ever even those impressions which are the sad remains of my sin. Grant that It may banish from my memory the flattering remembrance of all that could incline it to sin, & that instead there may be engraven on my heart the remembrance of all Thy Goodness, of Thy Passion, of Thy Death, of all that Thou hast done for love of me. Excite within me that True Light, so that mine eyes like those of Jonathan may be enlightened, after having tasted of this Divine Honey. Excite in my heart that Love with which Thy Sacred HEART is burning, & in my Soul that Grace of Unction, of Nourishment, of Christian Strength, which are the Effects of this Holy Sacrament. But, O most Blessed

Blessed Lord, do Thou excite in me worthy Acts of Thanksgiving for the Benefit which Thou hast given me, & only regard my incapacity to thank Thee by adding to them of Thy Goodness. Nay, rather, do Thou render to Thyself, while Thou art abiding in me those Acts of Thanksgiving which Thou dost deserve, receive mine, unite them to Thine, & thus make me worthy to render Thee eternal Thanksgivings in Heaven.

Twenty-second Meditation.

Of Union with JESUS CHRIST in the Holy Eucharist.

I.

MEDITATE attentively on the Words of the holy Apostle, & thou shalt know both the glorious Union which thou dost contract with our Adorable LORD in the Divine Sacrament, & the incontestable proof of that Union—*The CUP of Blessing which we bless, is it not the Communion of the BLOOD of CHRIST; the BREAD which we break, is it not the Communion of the BODY of CHRIST? For we, being many, are One Bread & One Body, for we are all partakers of that One BREAD*: & he concludes with these most comforting Words—*Now ye are the Body of CHRIST, & Members in particular.* I speak not here

here of that simple Union of heart & spirit which each faithful Soul may contract every moment of the day by Faith & Love with her Blessed LORD; this is but a spiritual Union, & a Union only just commenced. That which is entered into by the most Holy Communion is after a manner, a consummated Union, an intimate Union, a perfect Union, which supposes, which surpasses the first, & which indeed seals it. Prepare thine heart in Faith & Love, for it is about to become the Centre where this Divine Union will be perfected. Wish for It, hasten to It with all thy Soul, bind closely together all Its most sacred bonds, & when thou hast contracted this Union, do all thou canst to preserve It & to make It eternal. This Eucharistic Union is the most holy, the most glorious, the most intimate that a Christian can contract in this mortal life. It is the most holy, because in this Sacrament man is closely united to the Author of all Holiness; & because the FLESH, the BLOOD, the SOUL, & the DIVINITY of our Blessed SAVIOUR, which are only Holy, communicate to him the precious Tokens of their Holiness, as often as he draws near to the Blessed Sacrament worthily.

It is the most glorious of all Unions, because It binds & incorporates us with our Creator & our GOD, & draws us from our own nothingness to raise us to the participation of His Divine Nature, when we put no obstacle in the way, & when we are worthily prepared. What honour, what

what glory it is to possess the Almighty GOD, & to be one with Him. It is the most intimate of all Unions. It is both Divine & human, Spiritual & corporal, natural & Supernatural. This Union is so intimate, so close, that holy Doctors have compared it to the vine & her branches, which make but one tree; & also to two pieces of different sorts of wax, which, when melted, blend together & become one & the self-same wax. Again, it is compared to water put into the wine cup, which loses its own qualities in the strength and superior virtues of the wine with which it is mixed.

It is the most incomprehensible of all Unions, for what can be more distant than the two extremes which here unite themselves, what more wonderful than the Centre where they come together? These two extremes are an All-powerful Creator, & a weak creature, who has come from His Hand & is covered with sin; an Immortal & Sinless GOD with a mortal man, subject to sin, to death, & to corruption; a Sovereign & a slave; a GOD of Majesty with a worm of earth; a Supreme Being with nothing.

What is the Centre where they unite themselves? the heart, the flesh of man. Almighty GOD, Who is the most sweet Centre where all seek for rest, came down from Heaven to seek His Rest in the heart of man, wherein He tells us that He finds His Delight. Thus the heart of a man who draws near to the Blessed Sacrament in love is made one with that of our Blessed REDEEMER, Who takes his place, Who reforms & destroys his carnal affections, to put His Own Love in their stead. A Saint of old felt thus when he said—What bliss would it be, O my GOD, if after the most Blessed Sacrament I found my heart taken from me & the Sacred HEART of my Beloved LORD placed in its stead. Nor is this transposition impossible, for the heart is far more where it loves than where it lives.

II.

To impress more strongly upon thy heart & mind the knowledge of that Union which thou dost contract with our Blessed REDEEMER in the most Holy Communion, & that thou mayest derive great profit from it, meditate upon the Divine Sacrament as a Heavenly Food, a Spiritual Union. Our Souls, being nourished with the Sacred BODY of the LORD, & becoming His Spouses, the Union which we contract with Him must be very intimate & very blessed. If we think it an honour in the world to be admitted to the table of a King, what an honour in Religion is it, to be fed at the Table of the most High GOD. What an honour to be waited on, not by servants, but by Himself. But how much greater an honour is it to be nourished with the BODY & BLOOD of an Almighty GOD. Not satisfied with inviting us, He wills to serve us, us, & He extends His Love so far as even to serve us Himself. Could our Sovereign LORD abase Himself more? Could He give us more tender tokens of His Love, & of His Desire to unite Himself to us, than by giving us Himself as our Food?

What can be closer, what can be more indissoluble, than the Union made between us & the food we eat, since it is converted into our own selves? This Union is so complete that none can separate from thee a piece of bread which thou hadst eaten, for it has now become one with thy flesh, thy blood, thy substance, in one word, thyself. Thus it is that we are united to our Blessed LORD in a most intimate Union; without there being any thing between Him & us we touch Him, He touches us; He incorporates Himself, He incorporates us. We become, a holy Saint tells us, by this Heavenly Food, the Body of our LORD & SAVIOUR not only by Faith but in reality, or as S. Paul says, *members of His BODY, of His FLESH, & of His Bones.* By the Strength of this Divine Food an intermingling is made of the sacred FLESH of JESUS CHRIST with our flesh, to purify it from sin, & to lessen its inclination to pleasure & self-indulgence. His Sacred FLESH becomes our flesh; His Precious BLOOD takes the place of our blood; & after a manner but really, we become One with the LORD JESUS. After the Holy Communion, says a holy Saint, our eyes are

are no longer our own, our lips are no longer our own, our ears are no longer our own, but those of our Blessed SAVIOUR. Make use then of these members, then, as He did; see, speak, & listen as the LORD JESUS did.

Reflect that there is this distinction between bodily & spiritual Nourishment; in the one, it is not the food which changes the person into itself, but the person who changes the food into himself: but in the Divine Food of the Blessed Eucharist that Love, which is a vivifying & supernatural Fire, changes the person who is fed into Union with the Person of our Divine LORD.

Reflect again, that our Souls become the Spouses of CHRIST, by this Sacrament of Union, where this Heavenly Espousal is completed in the Presence of GOD Almighty, of the holy Angels, & of men. It is effected by the ministry of the Priest, who communicates the Sacred Elements to us, while CHRIST Himself, Who is our great High Priest, blesses this Divine Union, & unites Himself to us, & us to Him, & performs invisibly & in a spiritual manner both the office of Priest & Spouse. So that of this intimate Union & most holy Alliance it may be said, that which Holy Scripture says of the Sacrament of Marriage—*They twain shall be one flesh.*

Oh, then, let thy Soul, as a true Spouse of JESUS CHRIST, consecrated by His All-pure BODY, & His most Precious BLOOD, by His
SPIRIT,

Spirit, by His Soul, by His Heart, & by His Divinity, enter into a participation of all the Blessings of this Heavenly Spouse. He gives thee His Faith, His Love, His Grace, His Treasures, His Kingdom, His entire Person. Do thou give Him thy spirit, thy desires, thy heart, thy pleasures, in one word, all that thou hast, all that thou art. Thy spirit He will enlighten, thy desires He will purify, that heart He will inspire, thy pleasure He will join in, thy body He will consecrate, for He will give thee all His Labours & all His Merits. And because He is so kind & so generous a Spouse, do thou give thyself entirely, unreservedly unto Him, otherwise thy gift would be valueless to Him, it would do thee no honour, thou wouldst derive no benefit from it.

Be on thy guard lest either the Devil, the world, vanity, or pleasure should separate that which God Himself has so closely bound together, & destroy this sacred Contract, signed with His most Precious Blood. Preserve with care the pure Bonds of so noble, so blessed, so holy, & so glorious a Union; never dissolve them, nay, rather die than become a faithless Spouse.

Affections.

I now see more clearly than ever, O my God, that Thou, according to Thy Word, art expressly the God Who lovest Unity. Thou art united

united throughout Eternity to Thy Heavenly FATHER as the Incarnate WORD, & as His Only-begotten SON. By a most wondrous Love, Thou dost will me to bear the Image of this Divine Union, & that in the Blessed Sacrament I should be One with Thee, even as Thou art ONE with Thy FATHER, Which is in Heaven. But Thou teachest me also by the words of Thy beloved Apostle, that by the virtue of this wondrous Union, as Thou livest by the FATHER, even so Thou willest that he who is nourished by Thee in the Holy Eucharist should live by Thee & for Thee. Thou hast contracted, O most Blessed LORD, a perfect Union with our nature in the fulness of time, in taking on Thyself human nature, because Thy Love willed not that man should perish. Not satisfied with this common Union with man, Thou didst institute before Thy Death this Divine Sacrament, to make a marvellous Extension of this wondrous Union. Thou dost most wonderfully incarnate Thyself into each one of us, & Thou dost renew this Union as often as they receive Thee in the Holy Communion. Thou dost unite Thyself to them, Thou enterest into them, Thou dost espouse them & dwell with them. Thou Who art Greatness Thyself, Thou dost abase Thyself, & Thou raisest up those who are nothing, so as to hasten this Union.

Prepare my Soul then, O most Merciful GOD, for so holy a Union; draw me to Thyself by by the sweet bonds of Love, & come Thou Thyself into my heart, that they may never be broken. My Soul would deem it bliss to wear Thy Bonds, even though it were as Thy Slave; & Thou willest, through the Ever-blessed Sacrament, that she should have the honour of bearing the Bonds of Thy Love as a Spouse. Oh, what an exceedingly powerful reason, why I should never be separated from Thee.

Thanksgiving.

How can I, O Divine Benefactor, better show forth my Thankfulness unto Thee for having united Thyself to me in this Holy Sacrament, than by exclaiming with one who loved Thee most fervently—O Sacrament of Love, O Sign of Unity, O Bond of Love, let him who loveth life draw near unto It, that he may be incorporated into It; that he may unite himself to the LORD JESU, that he may live to GOD & in GOD.

Oh, what glory, what honour, for me, O my SAVIOUR. I receive Thy most Holy FLESH. I unite myself to Thy SPIRIT, to Thy HEART, to Thy SOUL. I participate even in Thy DIVINITY. It enters into me. It unites Itself to me. I possess It. It elevates me to Itself. I must then sacrifice & lose all that I have, all that I am to make myself less unworthy of so holy a Union, & to consummate It within me.

O most

O most Blessed LORD, it is in virtue of this Union, which I have made with Thee, that I venture with confidence, even with boldness to perform my Acts of Thanksgiving for being united to Thee. Thou speakest in me & for me; & Thou dost render them on my behalf to Thy Heavenly FATHER, by Whom Thou art always heard. Now do I understand, that if I have constancy enough never to break this blessed Union, all that I shall say, or do, or think to show forth my gratitude will be received by Him, not as coming only from a weak & mortal man, but from my Divine SAVIOUR & myself together. Henceforth shall we be but One Spirit, One Heart, & One Voice; therefore have I faith & confidence that my Thanksgivings shall be heard.

Twenty-third Meditation.

Of the Advantages of frequent Reception of the Holy Eucharist.

I.

MEDITATE here with thyself alone, without taking any thought of other feelings which are in a manner opposed to so important a subject. Remember that the Centurion declared he was not

not worthy that the LORD should enter under his roof; & this humility, joined to fervent faith, drew down upon him a Miracle, & obtained for him the Entrance of our Blessed SAVIOUR not only into his house, but into his heart also. Zaccheus, on the other hand, received our Divine LORD with joy, without expressing his sense of his unworthiness, & the LORD JESUS entered gladly into his house, & heaped upon him Graces and Blessings. Again, remember the exclamation of the holy Apostle—*Depart from me, for I am a sinful man, O LORD;* & that after these words, which true humility caused him to utter, his Divine LORD drew near him, & gave him that confidence, which he seemed to have lost, by saying—*Be not afraid.* All these examples were pleasing to Almighty GOD, although they each appear to have been caused by different feelings. This ought to induce thee to judge no one, but to turn all thy thoughts to thine own peculiar needs. Examine into thine own devotion, seek thine own profit, take counsel of holy men, & of those who are specially drawn towards the most Holy Communion, & practise all that thou findest of most use in thy spiritual advance. Meditate on the Words of thy LORD, when He commanded all to eat of His BODY, & to drink of His most Precious BLOOD, under peril of losing their lives, that is the Life of Grace, & the Life of Glory. At the same time, however, forget not the Words of the great Apostle,

Apostle, who forbids anyone to approach the Blessed Sacrament unworthily, lest they eat & drink their own damnation, & be guilty of the BODY and BLOOD of the LORD.

These two Sayings ought to be the unvarying rule for thy future Communions. The first of them, by itself, would perhaps inspire thee with a dangerous confidence to approach the Blessed Sacrament too often, without a due preparation; the second, also alone, would inspire thee with too great a fear, which would prevent thee from participating in the greatest of all Benefits, & which would deprive thee of Life itself. Follow then with confidence both of these Precepts; the first which enforces thee to approach the Holy Communion in a right frame of mind, & the second which forbids thee from approaching It unworthily. The disunion of these two rules has been the cause of many disputes on this subject, & has caused love to wax cold; whereas their being united is without doubt the rule which must be followed, & which will never lead us astray.

Do then all that thou canst to receive the Divine Sacrament worthily. Be persuaded that thou canst not draw near to It too often; but also be assured that to communicate frequently, without correcting or trying to correct thy besetting sins, without having a true desire for perfection in thine estate of life, without preparing for this great Act of Worship with all
due

due care, & without correcting any attachment for venial sin, is a dangerous delusion which will lead a Soul on to mortal sin, & to profane this most Holy Communion. But to communicate seldom, from false humility, which is often the veil that conceals sloth, even though they are so advised by their Spiritual Guides, is a delusion not less dangerous. It deprives them of many Graces; it leaves the Soul in a state of weakness, because she is in need of Support & Strength; & it leads her gradually to lukewarmness & forgetfulness of God. In the early ages of Christianity, there were faithful ones who used to communicate daily, or at least who communicated whenever they were present at the Celebration of these Holy Mysteries. This Custom was commended by many; but some were scandalised, lest there should be an abuse of it; since holy men were able to receive daily, though sinful men were not. A holy Father, who had a right to decide, took no side but that of charity. He said he neither praised, nor blamed those who communicated every day. He, however, exhorted his people to communicate on Sundays, provided they were free from the will to sin, & in one of his letters he adds—If thou dost only fall into little sins, thou oughtest not to deprive thyself of thy daily Food, the Precious Body & Blood of thy Lord.

This most Blessed Sacrament is in truth our Daily Bread, said another Father to the Faithful of of his time, & ye do only receive It once a year; ye are each day expofed to numberlefs temptations, from whence can ye obtain ftrength to refift your enemies? Often are ye wounded, in thefe fpiritual ftrifes, is it not natural to feek healing when a wound is received? The Devil is your enemy, Sin is your wound, the Bleffed Sacrament is your Healing. It would, however, be perilous to advife the majority of Chriftians to do that which this holy Man advifed fome to do when he faid — Receive every day That which will do thee good, That which will nourifh thee daily. But the whole world may be told that he faid afterwards—Live fo that thou mayeft be able to receive the Bleffed Eucharift every day; for he who cannot do this, is unworthy to receive It even once a year.

II.

Examine two things which are effential in this important matter: the firft of which will act as an inducement for thee to communicate often, & the other as a precaution to induce thee to draw near worthily. The firft confifts of the many advantages & benefits which are attached to frequent Communion: the fecond, of the difpofitions thou muft bring there fo as to profit by It & not to abufe It. A faithful Soul, who communicates often, is far more united to Almighty GOD & far more detached from the world

world than one who receives but seldom. Her Faith is more lively; her Hope is more firm & more constant; her Love is more fervent & more enduring.

The three Theological Virtues find in this constant Communion their increase & their perfection. Above this, let us add, that more Grace is received, because it is nourished by the FLESH of Him Who is its Author & its Cause: & most certainly it would perish without a frequent partaking of the Divine Eucharist. All faithful Souls acknowledge that they are much weaker when they have not communicated for a long time. For even as the body feels its weakness when it has been long without its natural food, so is the Soul much weakened when she has not for a long time received her supernatural Food, the BODY & BLOOD of her LORD.

Frequent Communion, says a holy Doctor, is the firmest support, the most sure Guardian of Holiness. He who frequently receives is always on the watch against accidents which might cause sudden death; death, however, which at least is not unlooked for, & which has no fatal consequences in the next life, because we believe that he who communicates often does not lose the Grace attached to the most Holy Communion, & does not fall into deadly sin of which the Blessed Sacrament gives him a dread. It also prevents him from becoming lukewarm: nay, on the contrary, he advances in Perfection in in that state of life in which he is placed, & he preserves more carefully his first fervour.

These are thoughts on which thou oughtest to meditate carefully, so as not to abuse frequent Communicating. First thou must be exempt from all inclination to venial sin. This inclination is marked either by custom, by thy falling into sin, by thy slight sorrow for it, by the little pains thou takest to avoid it or to correct it. That thou mayest understand this the better, know that there are two sorts of Grace attached to the Blessed Sacrament. One which is called Sanctifying Grace, which all Christians receive when they place not the obstacle of mortal sin in the way of Grace: & the other is a much higher Grace, a Grace of Strength, of Unction, of interior Life, & of Support proportionable to the degrees of faith & love which we take thither.

Christians in general receive this ordinary Grace which is often very slight. When they communicate with a leaning towards venial sin, they are at least accountable for those Graces which they do not receive, & which they would receive if they were more fervent & more disinclined to sin. In this condition, when they have the misfortune to be attacked by strong temptation, having by their own fault weakened the Grace received, they are almost always overcome by it, because they have voluntarily deprived themselves of that Aid & Grace of which they were in need.

This

Twenty-third Meditation.

This detachment from sin, which the Holy Communion requires, is figured by the Paschal LAMB, which the Israelites ate standing with staves in their hands, like pilgrims who are ready to leave all & who feel no affection for anything left behind, because they have the Promised Land only in view, the Heavenly Country, which is the sole object of their desires.

Examine, on the one hand, thy Communions, & on the other thine attachments, thy habits, thy lukewarmness; & abandon either the one or the other, either thy Communions, or thy passions. But, oh! abandon not thy Communions, but rather endeavour to make thyself more worthy of them by overcoming thy desires. Think of the words of a holy Saint, to one who approached the Blessed Sacrament with a will disposed to offend Almighty GOD, even venially— Thou art less purified than defiled; & thou comest from thence laden with a terrible account, which thou must render at the Judgment Seat of GOD. With this detachment from sin, live constantly as in the immediate Presence of GOD; practise prayerfulness, for thou art not worthy to approach the holy Table of thy GOD, or to have His most Precious BODY & BLOOD as thy Food, when thou thinkest only rarely of Him, & neglectest to hold Communion with Him in prayer.

Love then retirement, & flee the world, if thou wouldst profit by frequent Communion.

Enter

Enter not into the dissipation of the worldly. Lose not, in their companionship, the inestimable Treasure which thou hast received at the holy Altar of GOD. Is it not the BREAD of Life & of the Spirit? This Spiritual & Divine Life is incompatible with the spirit & life of the world.

Love Almighty GOD with thy whole heart, & thy neighbour as thyself. Multiply these earnest Acts of thy first love & fervour; & never approach this holy Table, this Sacrament of Love & Union with the least resentment, the least antipathy in thine heart towards any person.

Affections.

What an excess of Love, O most Blessed LORD, was it for Thee to descend from the Throne of Thy Majesty to visit me, to abide with me, & to nourish me with Thy Precious BODY & BLOOD. Thou dost inspire me with Holiness; Thou dost command me to ask Thee for my Daily Bread; & Thou dost offer Thyself to become my Food, provided that I endeavour to become worthy of It, & that Thou Thyself dost aid me in preparing for It. Truly can I acknowledge now with Thy holy Prophet, that there is no nation under Heaven so favoured as ours, or who can boast of having a GOD to Whom they have such free access, & Who gives Himself to them with such Goodness, as Thou dost to us in the Ever-blessed Sacrament.

Thou

Twenty-third Meditation.

Thou doſt (miraculouſly, ſo to ſpeak) multiply Thy Divine Unity, to give Thyſelf Whole & Entire to all thoſe who deſire It. But not content with this Miracle of Love, Thou doſt multiply Thyſelf in favour of each one of the Faithful, to give Thyſelf to them as often as they draw near to Thee; for never doſt Thou refuſe Thyſelf to their deſires and longings. Thou inviteſt them in Thy Divine Bounty; & it ſeems as if we heard a gentle Voice falling on the ears of our heart, & ſaying—*Come unto Me, all ye that labour & are heavy laden, & I will give you reſt.* Come unto Me, all ye that hunger, & I will ſatisfy you: I will give you none other Food than Myſelf. Moſt Adorable LORD, I will obey Thy Voice; but awaken in me my languid faith, excite in me hunger & thirſt after righteouſneſs, after Thy moſt Bleſſed BODY & BLOOD; enlighten my Spirit, purify my Soul, inflame my heart, ſo that living in conſtant Preparation for this Holy Sacrament, I may be enabled to receive It often.

Thanksgiving.

What reward ſhall I give unto the LORD *for all the Benefits that He hath done unto me?* O moſt Bleſſed LORD, I am overcome by the multitude of Thy Bounties, & I am forced to confeſs that all mankind together could not ſufficiently make Thee worthy Acts of Thankſgiving for all the

the Blessings Thou hast bestowed on one single man. Not content with my being the Work of Thy Hands, not content with having formed me in Thine Image, & of having in an excess of Love taken human nature, not content with having redeemed me with Thy BLOOD, & of having restored me to Life as often as I deserved death, not content with having instituted this Sacrament of Love, Thy All-containing Love allows me to adore Thee & even to receive Thee, that I may be sanctified. Not content with allowing it, Thou dost call me to Thy sacred Table, Thou dost invite me to It in Love, & Thou dost allow me to make a portion of my Thanksgiving consist in being nourished with Thy BODY & Thy BLOOD, with Thy SOUL & Thy DIVINITY. I fall every day, said a Penitent of old, & instead of punishing me as I deserve, Thou dost present Thyself for me afresh each day upon Thy Altar, & Thou dost dwell in me through the Holy Communion as often as I desire it, to help me, to strengthen me, to heal me, to fill me with Grace, & to assure me of Glory. To enable me to satisfy Thy Justice, & to render Thee those Acts of Thanksgiving which I owe Thee, Thou comest to make them to Thyself in my stead, to release me from all my debts whilst Thou art within me.

Come then, O Beloved of my Soul, make me worthy to receive Thee daily, & to possess Thee for ever in that Life which is to come.

Twenty-fourth Meditation.

Of neglecting to approach the Holy Eucharist.

I.

There are four sets of Christian men, who neglect the Blessed Sacrament, & that from very different reasons.

There are some, in the first place, who keep away from It from mere recklessness; or because from their unworthiness it is deemed right to deprive them of It, for a time, that they may overcome their besetting sin; & according to the precept of the holy Apostle that they may examine themselves before they are worthy to approach It. Next, there are those who are weak & unstable, & who are for a time deprived of Holy Communion, because they have fallen into some great, but unpremeditated sin, that they may mourn over their fall during this trial, which always appears bitter to them when they truly love God; & that they may be taught to be more on their guard, & to desire the Blessed Sacrament with greater fervour. There are also others who, though in the habit of frequenting Holy Communion, keep away from It, out of profound respect, & full as was the Centurion of their own unworthiness & the infinite greatness of God, but who return as quickly as possible
with

with increased zeal to the practice of constant & regular Communion. But of whom we would now speak are those who absent themselves from various pretexts, which they excuse either by their lukewarmness, by their unwillingness to lead sufficiently pure & devoted lives, or because this frequent Communion requires them to be more on their guard, which is not pleasing to their carelessness or their self-love: or it may be, because they have some passion or habit which they cannot forego, or because they wish to excuse themselves from that preparation which is not to their taste, & which places them under restraint. In that case, persons are oftentimes found in such a state of mind that they must do either one of two things, either they must overcome themselves & their sins, or they may not communicate. They hesitate for a while between self-love and duty, & at last they make their choice. The first alternative appears to be the easiest, the most suited to their purpose & idleness. They dispense with the Blessed Sacrament, either because they will not forsake their evil habits, or abase their pride to make some reconciliation, because they will not make amends for what they have done wrong, or they will not put from them the bitterness they feel towards their neighbour, until their feelings of indignation have passed away, & they have comforted themselves with some little outburst of temper, or because they give themselves entirely

to

to external, & often to useless works which may be prejudicial to their state, & which they will not leave off because they are too much attached to them. This dispensation, which they grant too easily to themselves, attracts many another. They make a custom of it, & a law against their natural law; their Soul is no longer watchful, their spirit no longer retired, & religious dissipation succeeds. They become more full of themselves, & less filled with thoughts of GOD. They feel no longer any desire for Holy Communion. They enter into the world, whose spirit they put on, after having forsaken it. Lastly they fall into deplorable slackness. They become blind; their heart becomes hardened; prayer wearies them; religious observances become burdensome; & the approach to the Divine Sacrament formerly longed for, becomes a punishment. And should they be asked, how they fell into this sad state, if they can still answer in good faith, they will acknowledge that this slackness proceeds only from their having in times past neglected the most Holy Communion, or from their not having prepared themselves sufficiently for It. And yet, whilst lukewarm Souls complain that the Celebrations of Holy Communion are too frequent for them (& it is true they are so for them, as long as they continue in their slothful state); fervent Souls complain that they are too rare, because they have an insatiable longing for this Divine Food.

II.

To prevent thee from ever forsaking the Blessed Sacrament, meditate seriously on the wants of thy Soul, which cannot be left long without this Divine Food. Make not the specious excuse of those who say that they do not communicate often because they are too weak & too imperfect. Thou wilt become more weak & more imperfect if thou dost desist. It is because thou art weak, that thou oughtest to flee more often to That which is the Source of Strength. Without this frequent approach, that Grace in which the Life of the Soul consists would perish, even as rivers need their source to flow continually. Although this Grace proceeds from an uncreated Cause, it is amongst those things which are subject to change; desire & temperament bear it onwards to its end, & exercise a terrible ascendancy over it. Passions burst out, because they are not restrained in a wholesome manner; custom assumes its right; the Soul remains in a fearful confusion, for not possessing the HOLY SPIRIT of GOD, she must needs be filled with the spirit of the world. Her house is desolate & ill guarded, when it is so long without the Real Presence of the Strong MAN armed. The Devil, either by vanity, by pride, by idleness, or pleasure, enters into it more easily, because he finds less resistance, & because the depths of the Soul are without a Guardian or a Defender.

Thou art weak, thou fayeft, but if some great temptation were to come upon thee, who would fuftain thee, whence wouldft thou find ftrength to refift? Say rather, that thou art weak only becaufe thou doft abfent thyfelf from this Divine Sacrament. Think upon the condition in which thou wert, after having frequently partaken of the Bleffed Euchariſt; & confefs that thou wert then much ftronger, much more recollected, more charitable, more gentle; that thy devotions were more eafily, more profitably performed; that thou didft feel thyfelf better able to fulfil thy Religious & Chriftian duties; & that thou hadft lefs unwillingnefs for penitence & felf-denial.

If thou doft perfift in abfenting thyfelf, notwithftanding thy needs, thou wilt grow cold in the worfhip of GOD; & this coldneſs having become ftudied & voluntary, thou wilt throw off the yoke, & live only after thine own evil defires. Extreme felf-love, which needed to be reftrained by the Bleffed Sacrament, will take the place of the Love of GOD. Penitence, which thou hadft embraced, will become but an empty dream. Thou wilt fubftitute diffipation for retirement; the fpirit of the world for the SPIRIT of GOD; idlenefs for a right difpofal of thy time; coldnefs & averfion for the love of thy neighbour. Thou wilt either love him with an undue preference, or with a paffion more after the flefh than after the fpirit; or elfe thou wilt not love him enough, or as the law of Charity demands. From this proceeds

ceeds thy marked difference to those who communicate often, & who by their piety reprove thee for thy recklessness. From this proceeds that malicious attention, which is so eager to observe, to criticise, & even to exaggerate the smallest faults of those who draw near to the Holy Communion. Hence come those little parties & divisions which are so injurious to that Spirit of Union, which those people ought to have who live in the world, which are formed as it were insensibly, & by degrees increase against those who are most worthy of love & esteem.

See then, into what the forsaking of the Blessed Sacrament leads thee; & a slight experience will be enough to convince thee of it. Do not constrain thyself, as did the Centurion, on account of thine unworthiness. Endeavour to approach this Holy Sacrament with confidence, & make thyself less unworthy of it. What in him was a spirit of deep humility, in thee proceeds from idleness, for which thou seekest an excuse in false humility. To speak truly, the greatest Saints are not worthy to receive the BODY & BLOOD of the LORD; the purest spirits are unworthy, because of the great distance that subsists between His creature & Almighty GOD, Who abases Himself, & raises us when we do what we can to approach Him worthily. Make then a sincere profession of humility, for this is the true means of becoming more worthy to draw nigh unto Almighty GOD.

Affections.

Affections.

Oh, what blindness in a Soul, redeemed by Thy most Precious BLOOD, to absent herself from Thee, whilst Thy Love takes infinite trouble to draw her unto Thyself. Thou callest her, not to ask of her the goods of which Thou hast no need, but to give her Thy Blessing, to give her Thyself, Entire & Whole. She is poor & helpless without Thee. Thou, O Blessed JESUS, art the Source of all Blessings; she knows it, & yet she wills to remain in her poverty. She is weak, when she feels that Thou art not near her; & her frequent falls remind her of this continually. Thou art the Source of Strength. Thou willest to sustain her by the Grace conveyed by the Blessed Sacrament, & yet she prefers to be without It. Thy BODY & BLOOD are the price of her Redemption, & yet she has miserably returned to the captivity from which Thou didst deliver her. Thou hast the exceeding Goodness to renew her Redemption in the Blessed Sacrament, because Thou givest the same Precious BODY & BLOOD, which rent her bonds. When she receives Thee, she renews & as it were incorporates again for herself her Redemption; & yet she is so blind, that she chooses to remain in her chains. What then, shall I know that the LORD, my Redeemer, desires to unite Himself to me, & shall I only feel indifference towards Him? I hear Him say, that His Delights are to be with the sons of men, & shall I not take delight in His company? Shall I hear Him ask to abide in my heart, & shall I not give it to Him? He will say to me—*Come unto Me, all ye that labour, & are heavy laden*, & shall I not go to Him? Give me then, O Adorable LORD, such desire to be united to Thee, as will equal that which Thou hast to be united to me. Break the links of self-love, of idleness, & of sloth, which prevent me from drawing near to Thee. Take from me that slackness which is my disgrace. Increase my fervour for the most Blessed Eucharist; & grant that I may never approach It unworthily.

Thanksgiving.

Now that I possess Thee, now that Thou art dwelling within me, most Blessed LORD, I will endeavour to render Thee meet Acts of Thanksgiving for having willed to give me Thyself in spite of my numberless shortcomings. Notwithstanding my having forsaken Thee, Who didst invite me so tenderly to approach Thee, I implore Thee with all the fervour of which I am capable & of which Thy blessed Presence doth make me capable, that Thou wilt never forsake me, that I may never leave Thee. I will make use of the words of the holy Psalmist & exclaim —*Go not far from me, O GOD; my GOD, haste Thee to help me.* Oh, grant that my spirit may

realize

realize Thee, now that it is enlightened by Thee; for do I not now possess Thy Precious BODY & BLOOD, Thy SOUL & Thy DIVINITY? Make my heart, near which Thy Sacred HEART now abides, to feel of what profit it is for me to draw near to Thee, because I cannot live without Thee. How much need therefore have I to receive this Divine Food to sustain me in all the temptations & sufferings to which I am exposed. Increase the faith of my Soul, which is but languid; heal her slothfulness; animate her courage; induce her to overcome her carelessness. And grant that she may ever be in that state in which Thou wouldst have her to be, who often loves to draw near to a Divine Sacrament, which ought to be her daily Bread, & which would make her to walk with giant steps in the Path of Perfection, until she has the happiness of possessing Thee for ever in Heaven.

Twenty-fifth Meditation.

Of receiving the most Holy Communion in time of trouble.

I.

IF the Philosophy of the world looks with contempt upon the man who allows himself to be overcome by sorrow, without endeavouring to master

master it, by the means it affords him of either conquering or softening it, Christian Philosophy, which is infinitely more enlightened, more elevated, & the motives of which are more powerful & purer, justly condemns the weak-hearted Christian who allows himself to be overcome with his sorrow. But, as she possesses more resources, which she can draw from true Religion, she is also full of more pure & more efficacious consolation, because it is Divine. She takes comfort, first from resignation to the Will of GOD, Who never fails to comfort those who pray to Him, when consolation is sought from Him alone. Secondly, from its being more like to our Blessed REDEEMER, Who was in truth a MAN of Sorrows, though He was sinless. Thirdly, from the thought of that happiness which they will enjoy in the Life which is to come, after the sufferings of this life have been endured with resignation; which happiness can only be attained by present suffering.

Of all the remedies which Religion prescribes, there is none more speedy, more sweet, more holy, or more efficacious than the Blessed Sacrament. A Soul, who, in the first moment of grief, humbly adores the Fatherly Hand which has ordained this affliction for his good, without waiting till sorrow has obtained too great an ascendancy; who, without giving vent to those thoughts which only increase the trouble, or to bitter tears, which ordinarily are but a slight relief for distress;
& who

& who instead of seeking for comfort in the world, seeks for it only in the most Holy Eucharist—that Soul will find a certain Consolation for her trouble, whatever it may be. For when thou takest this Divine Food to support thee under affliction, & when by this means, the Blessed COMFORTER is near thy heart, it is then that the GOD of all Peace & Consolation, Who is in us & with us, bears the sorrow with thee, so as to make it more easy to be endured. He secretly whispers to us consoling words, which supports & resigns us to all.

Our Soul then, enjoying the Blessings of that Heavenly Food, gives herself up so entirely to that holy gratification, that the edge of her sorrow is blunted, & there is in her a change of feeling. As the enjoyment of Almighty GOD is infinitely more sweet than sorrow is bitter, her feeling of distress diminishes in proportion as the Love of GOD increases; because the weaker feeling must always give way to the stronger. And as our Blessed LORD has entered into our heart, as the Strong MAN armed to guard it, He fills it with Peace & Tranquillity. Thus does the Soul find not only comfort in present trouble, but also obtains from this Holy Sacrament a store of Strength & Resignation to bear more easily, & with more greatness of Soul, all other sufferings which may befall her.

Remember that there is a sadness which is the work of nature, as well as a sadness which is the

work

work of Grace. The first of these is imperfect, because it proceeds from an inordinate love which we bear for ourselves. The second is a Virtue, because it is inspired by GOD. The sufferings to which we are exposed cause the first sort of sadness. If it be humiliation, we suffer from the pride which is in us. If it be in illness, we suffer not only in body but in heart, because we love ourselves too much, & there is a sensitiveness in our heart which is alarmed at the first prospect of suffering. If it be loss of goods, or of friends, we suffer because we love those possessions & friends, not only for their own sake, but also on account of the relation they bear to us. In the Ever-blessed Sacrament this sadness changes its nature, & in changing its object, our sadness passes from the natural to the supernatural, & that which was before a weakness now becomes a virtue.

In fact, when one under affliction approaches the holy Table, to find there consolation for his trouble, one of two things usually happens to his Soul—Either his sadness is purified by higher thoughts, which no longer come from nature, but from Grace. The all-powerful Virtue of this Sacrament is felt so much, & works so effectually, that, if he sheds tears, it is no longer for having lost that which he loved, but because he knows that sin has drawn down upon him this trouble. The Soul being now taught by her Divine LORD, how to mourn for herself, mourns for having offended Him. She adores the Hand which

which has afflicted her, & exclaims with the holy Pfalmift—*It is good for me that I have been in trouble, that I may learn Thy Statutes.*

Otherwife the affliction ceafes entirely, & peace & tranquillity fucceed to care & forrow. For, fays a holy Saint, having partaken of that Divine Food, there is formed in the Souls of men a fort of fpiritual inebriation. They lofe the remembrance of their own fufferings; they reft their forrow on the Sacred HEART of their LORD; they are comforted, & they are ready to endure all things for Him. Such are the feelings which thou oughteft to have after the reception of the moft Holy Communion.

II.

Draw near to the Holy Eucharift with confidence & love; make as many Acts of thofe Graces as thou art able; make a mighty effort to overcome thy weaknefs; & fubftitute in the place of thy forrow & pain, the infinite Sweetnefs of that Divine Food, & the remembrance of the Sorrow which our Bleffed LORD endured during that Sacred Paffion, of which the Bleffed Sacrament is the perpetual Memorial. Then thou fhalt affuredly find that confolation which thou needeft, in the midft of thy trouble, & a diminution of thy faddened feelings.

What is more capable of foftening thy troubles, than the tafte of that Sweetnefs which is the pureft that can be conceived, & that from its own

own proper Source? & what is sweeter & more grateful than the Sacred FLESH & BLOOD of GOD made MAN for love of us, that most precious Food, Which, far more than the Manna of the Israelites, contains all proportioned to the various needs & wants of those who partake of It, & which surpasses that Manna as infinitely, as the Reality surpasses the shadow? When thou feelest the Presence of this Divine COMFORTER, & the abiding It makes in thine afflicted heart, oh, what sweet comfort it is to open thine heart to Him, to confide thy sorrow to Him, to hold converse with Him, & to hear Him say unto thee—*Come unto Me, all ye that labour & are heavy laden, & I will give you rest.*

Hold then this sweet communion with thy LORD, when thou feelest that He is within thee. Pray Him to sustain thee; & rest entirely on Him as the Source of all Delight. Spend the time of His abiding with thee in listening to His Voice. Speak to Him with the words of thine heart, which is the most sweet, the most consoling of all conversations, & thou shalt soon forget thy troubles. What can be more efficacious to soften thy sufferings, than the remembrance of those which thy LORD, thy REDEEMER suffered for thee? Compare His great Afflictions with thy troubles, & thou wilt be ashamed of thine own weakness. For thou knowest that the Blessed Eucharist is instituted as a Remembrance of the Death & Passion of our Blessed LORD, & that to

draw

draw near unto It thou muſt ſhew forth His Death, that is to ſay, thou muſt think upon It, expreſs It in thy memory, in thy ſpirit, & in thy heart; & thou muſt be even ready to drink of the Cup of His Sufferings if He requires it of thee.

Again, thou knoweſt that He inſtituted It on the ſame night wherein He was betrayed into the hands of His enemies. Picture then thy Bleſſed SAVIOUR at the time of Its Inſtitution, & try to repreſent It to thyſelf by conforming thyſelf to what He thought, to what He felt, to what He did. Doſt thou complain of the treachery of a friend? Remember how the LORD JESUS was betrayed by one who fed at His Table, to whom He had given His Precious BODY & BLOOD. Thy Spirit, again, is full of ſadneſs. Haſt thou the ſame reaſon for it as that Divine SAVIOUR, Who had then all His Paſſion before His Eyes, & Whoſe Sorrow was ſo great, that without the exceeding Greatneſs of His SOUL it would have cauſed His Death? Thou doſt ſhed tears, which perhaps only proceed from weakneſs & ſelf-love, which ſhew thee to be too ſenſitive to thy little troubles. Then meditate on thy LORD in the Garden, Who in His Agony ſheds Tears, & is covered with a Bloody Sweat. He then endured the moſt fearful trouble that can be conceived; for He knew that He was about to ſuffer the moſt cruel kind of Death, at the hand of thoſe for whom He was about to ſhed the laſt Drop of His

His Precious BLOOD. Doſt thou ſuffer from ſome ſlight humiliation, which thou thinkeſt thou haſt not deſerved? Oh, meditate then on the extreme Humiliation of the Ever-bleſſed JESUS, Who, though He is GOD, is deſpiſed by His creatures, reviled, rejected, inſulted, numbered with tranſgreſſors, & at laſt condemned to die between two thieves. Art thou ſuffering in thy body from ſome great pain? Think on the Sufferings to which thy LORD was expoſed. Gaze upon that Livid FLESH, wounded & torn by the ſcourge, & that Bleeding HEAD pierced by the thorns with which It is crowned. Look upon His Hands, His Feet moſt cruelly pierced, from Which proceeded four ſacred Streams of BLOOD, Which as it were watered the whole of Calvary. Art thou poor in temporal goods? Behold the mighty King of Heaven & earth deſpoiled-of all, & having no where to lay His Head.

Forget then thy ſufferings, & inſtead of them meditate upon thoſe of the LORD JESUS, which are infinite. Be juſt, without flattering thyſelf. Remember that being a ſinner, thou doſt deſerve to ſuffer, & that our Divine LORD being Innocent ought to have been ſpared. Be aſſured that thy ſufferings are ſlight in compariſon with thoſe thou haſt deſerved.

Heal then thy feelings in this moſt Bleſſed Sacrament, make of them a ſacrifice to the Immortal GOD, Who has made Himſelf a Victim for thee on the Croſs, & Who wills to become a Victim

Victim in this Holy Sacrament unto the end of time, & to bear both my sins & the troubles they deserve. Unite thy sufferings to His, when thou dost receive Him; & not only shalt thou be comforted, but they shall work out for thee an immortal crown of Glory.

Affections.

O God of Glory, & at the same time Man of Sorrows, once a Victim on the Cross of Calvary, now an unbloody Sacrifice, Who bearest in all these states the sins of all men, to deliver them from the eternal sufferings which they have justly deserved, I humbly confess that I deserve to suffer because I have offended Thee. But Thou art my Refuge in the troubles which encompass me, my Joy & my Consolation in my sorrow.—*My groanings are not hid from Thee; my heart panteth, my strength hath failed me, & the sight of mine eyes is gone from me. Turn Thee, O Lord, & deliver my Soul; O save me for Thy Mercy's sake.*

I groan, not by reason of my sufferings, but for my sins. I mourn my unwillingness to bear those passing sorrows, which would have drawn down Thy Favour upon me, if I had sacrificed to Thee the first feeling of my sorrow. I ask Thee not, most Merciful Lord, to deliver me from all suffering, for I cannot be saved without it, & I must bear my Cross after Thee, following the Bloody Traces Thou hast left, in order to attain

attain to Glory. I afk not even to be freed from that fenfitivenefs which makes my trouble more difficult to bear, provided it is Thou, Who giveft me to drink of Thy Cup of bitternefs & forrow, which Thou didft Thyfelf drink, to make me feel all the weight of pain I deferve. But I afk Thee to deliver me from that fenfitivenefs which proceeds from pride, & from felf-love. Strike, O LORD, but give me ftrength to bear Thy Chaftifements without murmuring, & without being difheartened. I renounce gladly all human confolations. I only afk of Thee that which a faithful Soul finds in Thy Grace, in patience to poffefs herfelf, in refignation to Thy fupreme Commands, however rigorous they may be. I afk of Thee that Comfort which is found in the Bleffed Sacrament of Thy moft Bleffed BODY & BLOOD.

Thanksgiving.

What Joy, O my GOD & my SAVIOUR, for an afflicted Soul to feek for Confolation in Thee alone, as there fhe is fure to find it. How happy the fidelity & wifdom that know how to bear in filence & in fecret, & to fpeak to Thee alone, to pour the fuffering only to Thee & to pafs by the confolations of the creature which are for the moft part but barren, & can only foothe for a time, but can never calm & conquer.

Yet, O moft Adorable LORD, if, according to Thy

Thy Divine Word, Thou art afflicted with those who are in affliction, & who have recourse to Thy Goodness & Thy Promises; if Thou dost never fail to soften their sorrow by the Resignation & Confidence which Thou dost inspire, when they have strength & faith enough to turn only to Thee in their deepest affliction, what infinite Comfort wilt Thou not bestow when the Soul seeks for the cure of her sorrows at Thy holy Table in partaking of Thy most Blessed BODY & BLOOD? And if she finds, as did the Prophet, true Consolation in the words which come forth from Thy Mouth, she will surely find in the Ever-blessed Sacrament both the Consolation & the COMFORTER together, Who comes with infinite Goodness into the afflicted heart, changing its sighs & sadness into tears of joy, & its bitterness into spiritual sweetness.

Thou art now present within me, O GOD of all Consolation, & I render unto Thee hearty Acts of Thanksgiving, that Thou hast inspired me to draw nigh unto Thee & hast given Thyself unto me. I would desire no other Consolation, no other Comforter: Thou art sufficient for me.

Twenty-sixth Meditation.

Of receiving the most Holy Communion in barrenness of spirit.

I.

It is very needful that thou shouldest examine here, whether that barrenness of spirit, of which thou art conscious, be not a state of idleness & constant languor, into which thou hast fallen by thine own fault. Many are in truth mistaken on this point, & fall thus into a subtle error, which is sure to have some dangerous end. Ingenious in flattering & deceiving themselves to justify the frequent Communions which they make, more from custom than devotion, they regard that as a trial from GOD, which is really a consequence of their lukewarmness. They think themselves right in approaching the holy Table often, because they fail not to say within themselves that barrenness of spirit ought not to keep a Soul from the Altar, since it is more especially not a sin but a trial which has had its effect when a good use has been made of it; & they approach with drooping faith, without fervour, without devotion, & consequently without profit. They think themselves exempt from the preparations which ought to precede the most Blessed Sacrament,

ment, because they pray in vain, & feel no love for Almighty GOD; the custom becomes habitual, they make useless Communions, which are most dangerous, & they run the risk of making unworthy ones. There is this difference between barrenness of spirit & lukewarmness: one takes away all feeling, & all inclination to devotion for a season, but it leaves the principle & the practice of it; while the other destroys devotion entirely, & finds plausible pretexts whereby to dispense with essential practice. One exerts itself, neglecting nothing to be delivered from its trouble, or at least to deserve deliverance from it, praying earnestly, humbling, mortifying itself, & acting with the same love, & the same faithfulness, as if it felt much & was filled full with all spiritual sweetness. Thus is it worthy often to receive the most Blessed BODY & BLOOD of JESUS CHRIST, to obtain that strength & perseverance which is necessary to support her in her sad estate. But the lukewarm Soul makes no exertion to be delivered from that languid state which satisfies her. She neglects prayer, the Presence of Almighty GOD, the Spirit of mortification, & it is this which makes her unworthy to approach the Ever-blessed Sacrament. Lukewarmness is like a dry & arid land, which produces nothing because it is neither tilled nor watered. It is not dryness, but a guilty languor, a Soul where love has grown cold, whence devotion has fled, which has no spirit of penitence nor prayer.

Judge

Judge, then, if this Soul be worthy to draw nigh to the Holy Eucharist. Probably after having well examined thyself before communicating, thou dost not find thyself guilty of this weakness. But thou must try to know whence proceeds that dryness, which thou dost feel; for it may proceed from three different causes. Sometimes from some slight apathy in the practices of devotion, & a growing cold of love, too free access is given to thoughts of the world. There is distraction & waste of time allowed in things that do not belong unto Salvation, & which hinder devotion to GOD & a due preparation for the reception of the Blessed Sacrament. Sometimes there is abandonment to the vain joys of the world, not sufficient watch over the heart, insensibly allowing it to become attached to the creature. This attachment, although apparently innocent, becomes too deep & takes away the Love of GOD. This is the first cause of dryness, this is the work of the creature, which stifles all feeling of devotion, & reduces the Soul to a state of barrenness the more sad because her own fault. These drynesses are sometimes just punishments from GOD, Who visits the least sins of His elect in this world, to save them in the world which is to come. A little delay in listening to Grace, a slight preference of the creature to the Creator, a little want of fervour in the Service of GOD, & numerous similar faults are sufficient to draw down this punishment. The Soul is disquieted, & ex-

& exclaims with the Psalmist—*Thou didst hide Thy Face & I was troubled;* or with the Spouse in the Canticles—*By night on my bed I sought Him Whom my Soul loveth; I sought Him & found Him not.*

Sometimes again these drynesses are real trials sent by GOD, without the creature having any part in them, that the Soul may be freed from selfishness, her Grace & Love increased by proving her fidelity, to draw her to love Him more purely for Himself alone, & to seek Him with more fervour. If thy drynesses come as a punishment, be very heedful not to ask those Consolations of Almighty GOD, which thou dost not deserve, but begin to reform that unfaithfulness, which has drawn down upon thee this punishment. If thou art in the habit of frequent Communion, deprive thyself with humility of one Reception; but do so with prudence & after counsel. Take more time to prepare thyself for the next; & whilst thou art feeling all the severity of this deprivation, say constantly to thy GOD, with a lowly & contrite heart—LORD, I am not worthy to receive Thee, but speak a word, & Thy Servant shall be healed.

II.

If dryness be thy trial, seek not to turn away from the Blessed Sacrament on that account, but prepare thyself for It with more care, because that Almighty GOD Who seems to turn away from &

no longer to act in thee, although He really does so imperceptibly, seems to will that all the preparation should come from thee. He will not however cease to aid thee with His Grace, without which thou canst do nothing; but He does not will that thou shouldest be aware of it. Increase then thine Acts of Faith, Hope, Love, Desire, more than in the time when thou art more sensibly helped by the ALMIGHTY, both in thy Preparation, & in thy Acts of Thanksgiving. Pray more earnestly, hold more communion with GOD though He wills not in His inscrutable wisdom to speak to thine heart those Divine Words which formerly thou didst hear with so much pleasure. If thou canst not feel the Almighty Presence, as thou wouldest, feel thine own nothingness, thine own weakness, thy wretchedness, & thy poverty. Thy faith & thy reason will make thee feel this; but be not disheartened, & draw near to the holy Altar with more humility, & more reverence; let these Virtues supply the places at present of the love thou dost not feel; & if thou feelest not, remember thou wert formerly wont to do so. If thou art in darkness, remember that once thou wert enlightened, & act thou in conformity therewith.

Take for thy rule in thy misery these words of a holy Saint—Let no one turn away from the Holy Eucharist, although he feel no devotion, he would be guilty of a sin were he to do so for so slight a reason. Divine Wisdom delights in pouring His
Grace

Grace in various ways into the Souls of those who serve Him, & we are not allowed to search into His incomprehensible Mysteries. Thus, continues the Saint, to feel no longing for God, when that deadness is not wilful, is no reason for turning away from His holy Altar, provided the life led by those who suffer from it is Christian, their conversation pure, that they acknowledge their own wretchedness, & approach the Holy Sacrament with reverence. Even when they do not feel all the effect of this Divine Sacrament, let them still feel spiritually refreshed by It, for It is a hidden Manna which contains in abundance all spiritual Delights, even though It does not continually pour them forth so as to be felt.

Seek then in this Blessed Sacrament not thine own consolation, but the Glory of God, & thine own sanctification. Bear this trial, however long it may be, with patience, resigning thyself to this dryness of spirit, which is of more benefit to thy Soul than sensible Devotion, because it comes from God. Acquiesce meekly in this privation, & thou wilt assuredly find in this Blessed Sacrament the Grace, the Life, the Strength which thou needest for thy support, both in the practice of Holiness & against all temptations which may assail thee.

Again, if thou bearest this trial with patience & resignation, not only will it not be an obstacle to thy Communion, but it will stand to thee in the stead of a most devout preparation. For this
dryness

dryness of spirit, especially that which is sent for our trial, assuredly leads a Soul to the practice of those Virtues which are the most needful to dispose her to approach worthily to GOD's Altar. It leads her certainly to Humility; it cures her of Pride, of Vanity, of Self-Love. The conviction of her own nothingness, her own weakness, her sterility in spiritual things, humbles & cures her of petty secret self-applause, which self-love knows how to extract from Piety itself, & it makes her feel her unworthiness & indigence.

When the Soul is unconscious of anything unworthy of being presented before Almighty GOD, & when she cannot even examine herself as she would desire, her dryness of spirit exercises her faith by the darkness with which it surrounds her, & purifies her love from that earthly selfishness which is oftentimes only the work of natural temperament. Still it is not forbidden thee in the most Holy Communion to ask of GOD to be delivered from it, & to feel how sweet He is: only thou must ask it of Him with great Humility, & with perfect Resignation to His Divine Will. For thine instruction, remember that when the Prophet of Israel, after the three years of drought, asked for rain, that the famine might cease, he prayed for a long time; & Holy Scripture tells us that each time he prayed, he sent his servant to see if he could not perceive a little cloud in the horizon to give him hope of that rain for which he prayed. But it was only at the seventh time

time that he perceived a little cloud, like a man's hand. This cloud grew larger & larger; & soon the rain fell in abundance. Pray then, as did this Prophet, who was a man burning with Heavenly Love. It is at the most Blessed Sacrament that the dews & rain of Divine Grace will descend most abundantly, to water, to soften, & to replenish the barren land of thy heart.

Affections.

I hear Thy Voice no longer in my heart, O my GOD: it is deprived of feeling. My spirit is in darkness & cannot turn to Thee, if Thou enlighten it not. Oh, when shall I say with the Psalmist—*My heart & my flesh rejoice in the Living GOD?* Now am I wanting in everything. Thou art no longer within me. Help me in my sorrowful estate to say with the Spouse—*Let me see Thy Countenance, let me hear Thy Voice, for sweet is Thy Voice & Thy Countenance is comely.* Water the barren earth of my ungrateful heart which can no longer feel that it loves Thee; & melt its iciness by the Fire of Thy Love. As Thou, O most Merciful GOD, in the days of old, didst open rocks in the desert, whence the waters gushed out, & ran in dry places like a river, & didst give Thy people drink as out of the great depths, causing the sweetest, the clearest, the most abundant springs to flow in the most barren places, so do Thou strike my heart which is harder than

than the desert stone, & than the rocks, & let a flood of tears gush out. Water this ungrateful heart, which has only deserved barrenness, because it brought not forth in time those fruits for which Thou didst look, Blessed LORD; for if the rod of Moses, striking the rock, drew forth a living Fountain which rejoiced all Thy people, may I not hope for an abundant Stream when Thou comest unto me in the Blessed Sacrament?

Thanksgiving.

How is it possible, O my GOD, that my heart should still be in dryness of spirit, now that Thou, Who art the Source of the most perfect Love, dost abide in me? Whilst Thou art with me, O GOD of Love, wilt Thou not strike this hard rock, as Moses did of old, that healing Waters may flow from it abundantly? Wilt Thou not water this barren & ungrateful land with a gentle rain, & the Heavenly Dew of Thy Blessings, so as to heal its dryness, & to make it fruitful in good works? How could it bring forth fruits worthy of being presented before Thee, if Thou didst not soften it with those living Waters, which flow even unto Life Eternal, & which make it find sweetness in the yoke which Thou dost impose, strength in the trials & sufferings which Thou sendest, & courage & patience in the temptations which it is obliged to endure? Ah, LORD, I have drawn down upon myself this privation by my my unfaithfulness; but I implore Thy Mercy to forgive me. I will return to Thee twofold Thanksgiving for having forgiven me the sins which drew down upon me this disgrace, & for having delivered me out of my trouble by Thine adorable Presence in the Holy Communion, which I have just received. If it be a trial, I must submit to it, adoring Thee. I know that dryness of spirit is not always hateful to Thee. Thy Ark & Thy chosen People remained long in a barren & dry land, & Thou didst never cease to protect them with this Heavenly Manna. Israel passed through a dry sea; it was necessary for them that they might arrive at the Promised Land. And I am content, provided that I love Thee, & that I love Thee as Thou wouldest be loved, & that Thou wouldest lead me on to that Heavenly Country of which the Promised Land was but the Type.

Twenty-seventh Meditation.

Of receiving the most Holy Communion in lukewarmness of spirit.

I.

COMMENCE thy Meditation by convincing thyself of this awful truth, to which thou hast probably not paid sufficient attention, & which ought to to make all lukewarm spirits tremble, that except a sacrilegious Communion, which is the greatest of all profanations, there is no state more dangerous than that of a Christian who, being lukewarm, communicates often without endeavouring to amend. There are three reasons which thou must seriously consider, so as not to incur this misfortune which is always followed by sad results.

The first reason is, because thou dost deprive thyself of the most important of those Graces which are attached to this Holy Sacrament. The second reason is, because he who communicates habitually with lukewarmness nearly approaches an inclination to make an unprofitable Communion. The third reason is, because people often blind themselves, thinking themselves only guilty of a little want of fervour when in truth they are slothful, which is a deadly sin.

In the first place, every one acknowledges that sanctifying Grace is always received at the Holy Communion, provided they do not place the obstacle of deadly sin in Its way. This it is that lukewarm spirits carefully bear in mind, so as to excuse their carelessness, to stifle their conscience, & to put an end to those wholesome fears with which true Christians ought to be filled, whenever they approach the Blessed Eucharist. But oh, how weak is this Grace, when people communicate without due preparation, & without fervour. Let us imagine the case of some

Soul who has entered zealously into a life of devotion, & full of anxiety to perform her duties. She has scarcely communicated ere she thinks of her next Communion. She neither neglects her Thanksgiving nor her Preparation. She makes her Thanksgiving consist in a constant meditation on this Holy Sacrament, as the most meet Object for her thoughts, in living in retirement, in the Presence of GOD, in the spirit of repentance, & in looking forward to her next Communion.

As to her Preparation, she makes it with all possible care, & performs with fervour all those Acts which precede it. She examines herself strictly, & confesses her sins with equal severity; so that her LORD may find nothing to disapprove of in her heart, nothing that may offend His absolute Purity. Thus does she receive all the Fulness of Grace, which may be obtained at the most Holy Communion; for her sanctifying Grace is stronger, & with this Grace she also receives a Grace of Unction & of spiritual refreshment, & a Grace of Life & Strength according to the different degrees of Faith & Love she possesses.

But such is the weakness & instability of men, that they gradually become accustomed to the most holy things, so that they do not make such an impression on them. Indifference succeeds to their first fervour; sloth & weariness, from which they do not try to rouse themselves, induce carelessness; & by degrees they lessen that time which they formerly employed in Preparation & in Acts of Thanksgiving. As the love & spirit of the world increases in them, the HOLY SPIRIT of GOD departs. They fall into indifference: they no longer feel a desire for the Blessed Sacrament: & in fact It becomes a burthen to them, & they fall into lukewarmness almost without perceiving it; whilst the habit of it increases, & rarely do they forsake it.

Not being on their guard, & having of themselves weakened the Grace received at the Holy Communion, the senses are open to dissipation. Self-love takes the place of the Love of GOD, which becomes weaker in proportion as the other increases; & they gradually give themselves up with delight to the pleasures & joys of the world, which at length ruin the little that was left of devotion to the ALMIGHTY.

However, they still communicate as before, either because such is the rule they have imposed upon themselves; or because others have imposed it upon them; or else their vanity grows used to frequent Communions, which cause them little trouble, since they have diminished their preparations; or lastly, because human respect will relax nothing left they should be esteemed careless. Hence it is, that they receive the Divine Eucharist without Its Virtue, because, says a holy Man, Grace loses its power in careless Souls, for she is neither received with reverence, nor preserved by faith,

faith, nor increased by fervour. He who receives the Holy Sacrament uselessly grieves the HOLY SPIRIT of GOD, Who is the Author of Grace, & must be prepared to give a strict account of the same to GOD.

II.

Remember also, that he who communicates without fervour is in the state of mind which leads to, & is in the great peril of, making unprofitable Communions. In truth, says a holy Man, there is nothing more dangerous than to approach the Divine Eucharist without zeal; for It is a Sacrament burning with the most pure Flame of Love. And especially is this the case when, having meditated on this coldness & finding that it is their own fault, men do not endeavour to overcome it.

For we must know, that he who communicates thus is deprived of that Strength which is attached to a profitable Communion, & which is only given to fervent Souls. He cares not to be favoured with that most sweet feeling of Divinity present within him, for he deserves it not. He feels not in the most Blessed Sacrament that pure Joy, that Sweetness, that fulness of the ALMIGHTY, that sublime Satiety which holy Souls feel after having communicated, & which makes them afterwards so full of strength & of love towards GOD.

Deprived by his own fault of these Blessings, he

he that is lukewarm feels no more desire for the Holy Communion. He only receives It from habit; & performs this most holy Action in the same sort of way as he does the indifferent duties of life, except that he repeats a few acts of Love & Faith, in which his heart takes no part. His love becomes weak, says a Saint, because it is no longer nourished by fervent acts of Love; & at last it becomes extinct. His devotion passes away, because it is no longer sustained by practices of Devotion. His Virtues are no longer virtues, because they are destitute of love. His body grows dull, & communicates its dulness to the spirit. His faith is dead; his hope degenerates into presumption; he loves no longer. Think how dangerous it must be to communicate in such a state!

It often happens that people deceive themselves, & think they are only a little lukewarm, when really they are in a most perilous state of sloth. It is difficult to distinguish these two conditions; for he who presumes on his own judgment, & who thinks himself safe, when he does not feel himself guilty of deadly sin, is hardly capable of reflecting on his own conduct as regards the ALMIGHTY & himself. For he either does not examine into the cause of his lukewarmness, or else he spares himself after having examined, & found himself guilty; because he is always prepossessed in his own favour, & self-love blinds him, so that he does not thoroughly know himself; whilst

whilst his lukewarmness, which pleases him, prevents him from taking real measures to learn the truth & to acquire fervour of spirit.

But alas, it is in this state that he draws near to the holy Altar without a scruple. Thus it is, says a Saint of old, that a lukewarm Soul is always near to death without knowing it. O lukewarm Soul, said a holy Man, change then thy life if thou wouldst receive Life in this Holy Sacrament: live by faith, live by love, live by good works; for if thou wilt not change thy life, be assured that thou wilt only receive that GOD of Life for thy judgment & thy condemnation, & that far from receiving health & life, thou wilt only find sickness & death. For what likeness can there be found between the Sacred HEART of the LORD JESUS & that of a lukewarm man; or between the Loving HEART of that Adorable SAVIOUR, & the icy heart of that creature for that GOD Whom he has just received; between that Infinite Love & this careless indifference? What a neighbourhood for Him Who takes His Delight to dwell among the sons of men, especially when they respond to His Divine Love, & how sadly must He dwell with those who are without love or fervour; who do not care to please Him; who feel nothing for Him because they are unworthy of such feelings; who say nothing to Him whilst He abides in their hearts, & is always disposed to listen to them with favour; & who ask nothing of Him Who can give all things, because
He

He is infinitely Rich, & Who will give all things because He is infinitely Good ?

This then is the subject for one of the most serious meditations of thy life; & perhaps the one subject on which thou oughtest most seriously to examine thyself before receiving the most Holy Communion.

Affections.

From henceforth, O my Soul, wilt thou approach the greatest of all Sacraments with lukewarmness? Shall the Loving HEART of thy Sacrificed LORD ever again abide with thee without thy feeling all the love & fervour with which that Sacred HEART is burning? Dost thou will that the Devil should triumph in thee & by thee, or that, even as the three Children were miraculously preserved in the fiery furnace, thy heart, by the malice of the Devil, should not burn in this Furnace of Love? Go then to this mystic Furnace, to this Throne of Fire, to this Burning Bush, to the GOD of Goodness, Who is a Consuming Fire. In opening thy lips to receive Him, open to Him thy heart, by the most ardent longings, by the most fervent acts of Love.

Instead then of giving the Devil an occasion to triumph by thy lukewarmness, become terrible to him by leaving the holy Altar as a mighty Lion, only breathing flames. Prepare thyself by thy

thy fervour, fustained by this Food of the strong, to overcome him on every occasion.

Say to Almighty GOD with thy whole heart —O most Blessed LORD, I abhor with all my Soul that lukewarmness with which I have so often approached the Blessed Sacrament. Fill my heart with constant & ever new Love, which may never be extinguished nor grow cold. Destroy in me all that is opposed to Thy Divine Love. Awaken me from that sloth & indifference which have made me unworthy to approach Thy Ever-blessed Eucharist. O Thou Who art about to dwell in me, speak to my heart, make it understand that language which Thou dost address to those who love Thee, & who are loved by Thee. O GOD of Love, when Thou art with me, grant that I may feel what Thou art, so that my Communions may prepare me to glorify Thee, & to love Thee for ever in Heaven.

Thanksgiving.

O Thou Who art now dwelling within me, how wouldst Thou receive my Acts of Thanksgiving if they proceeded from a lukewarm heart, whilst it felt Thee to be near it, Thou Who art a consuming Fire? But, O Blessed LORD, can I say without boldness that I feel Thy holy Presence within me? And am I not rather indifferent at that precious time when I ought to be full

full of Love for Thee? Animate then & fill my Acts of Thankſgiving with that Divine Fire of Love, which Thou didſt come to kindle upon earth.

And thou, O my Soul, bleſs thou the LORD, & all that is within me bleſs His Holy Name; & let me ſtrive that my memory, my ſpirit, my heart, all my members, & all that is within me may join together & offer to the LORD Acts of Thankſgiving as a ſacrifice, that my love may be the fire to conſume it, & to bear it up even to the Throne of His Grace.

Oh, that my memory may bleſs & thank the LORD, & engrave deeply on herſelf the precious remembrance of His Marvels & of His Goodneſs in giving Himſelf to me. Oh, that my ſpirit may bleſs & thank the LORD, & may think inceſſantly on its preſent happineſs, & on that which it may hope to poſſeſs if it approaches the holy Sacrament worthily. Oh, that my heart may bleſs & thank the LORD & love Him unto its lateſt breath. Oh, that my voice may bleſs & thank the LORD, & that it may only utter His Praiſes & ſpeak of His Mercies. Oh, that my hands may bleſs & thank the LORD, & may ſhow forth their gratitude by working without ceaſing to promote His Glory, & to multiply their good works ſo as to be made worthy for that eternal Happineſs of which this moſt precious Sacrament is at once the token & the pledge.

Twenty-eighth Meditation.

Of receiving the moſt Holy Communion in Reparation.

I.

As it is difficult for thoſe who are in the habit of frequent Communion always to draw near to the holy Altar with a new heart & with equal fervour, & that very often through the weakneſs of their nature many faults & many diſtractions creep into their hearts, it is well from time to time to make Acts of Reparation: & the Acts of Reparation cannot be more profitably made than by attending the Holy Communion, after having made an Act of Repentance, & after having implored the pardon of Almighty GOD. For indeed what can the creature do of himſelf to make reparation for the faults he has committed againſt his Creator, unleſs he is aided by his Creator Himſelf? What can he offer of himſelf, which will be a Reparation, ſince his faults have been committed againſt GOD Himſelf, in His very Preſence, in His Sanctuary, againſt His moſt Bleſſed BODY & BLOOD, His SOUL & His DIVINITY, at the ſolemn moment of Reception?

Enter then into thyſelf, my Soul, before communicating in reparation for all the diſtractions, all the irreverence with which thou haſt ever approached the holy Altar. Remember that thou art about to receive not only a Creating & a Saving GOD, but alſo an Atoning GOD on Whom thou canſt lay the burden of thy ſins, & Whoſe Merits thou canſt appropriate to thyſelf; that is to ſay, all His Labours, all His Sufferings, all His Satisfactions, which are of infinite value. Behold in this the precious Money with which thou canſt ſatisfy Divine Juſtice. Loſe nothing of it; profit by all it contains. It is only needful for thee to love Him, & to prove thy love by good works, to be ſure of His protection & to ſhare all that He poſſeſſes, & to be enabled to offer Him to the Eternal FATHER as a Poſſeſſion that is thine own, & of which thou canſt not be deprived, unleſs it is by thine own will, or unleſs thou makeſt thyſelf unworthy of It.

This Divine Atoner, Whom thou art about to receive, is an All-powerful GOD; it is impoſſible that He ſhould be refuſed, becauſe He is in all things equal to our Heavenly FATHER, to Whom He offers Reparation for our ſhortcomings, & by Whom He is infinitely loved. And beſides, He alſo offers in atonement all that He did & ſuffered, whilſt He was on earth, & He offers up all that He poſſeſſes whilſt He abides in thee. Therefore, when this Adorable LORD abides in us, whilſt His moſt Sacred BODY touches us, whilſt we are cleanſed by His moſt Precious BLOOD, He prays for us, & He teaches us to pray

pray succesfully, becaufe we pray in His Name. Then we are only His Inftruments, & we only offer to Him thofe prayers which He Himfelf infpires in the depths of our Soul, not to the Throne of His Juftice to afk for vengeance, but to the Throne of His Mercy to afk for that pardon which we deferve, becaufe we afk it in His Name, & He demands it for us.

But the Atonement of CHRIST is All-powerful in our favour. He requires from us at this moft Bleffed Sacrament all that we are capable of offering to Him, a living Faith, a fteadfaft Hope, fervent Love & Defire, & above all a firm refolve to make each one of our Communions henceforth as if it was to be our laft. Thy Acts of Virtue which thou doft then make, & by which thou doft endeavour to make reparation for what was wanting in thy previous Communions, are no longer efteemed by Almighty GOD as the Acts of a mere mortal, but as thofe of the LORD JESUS Himfelf; for whilft He abides in us after receiving the Ever-bleffed Eucharift, He teaches us how to make them, He purifies them, He unites them to the Acts which He produces in us Himfelf. He not only acts in our body, there dwelling that He may confecrate it, but He alfo acts in our Soul in a myfterious manner, when fhe is well prepared for it. He thinks in our fpirit, He loves in our heart, & makes it feel His ineffable Sweetnefs when we only love Him, & for Him, we become a living Sanctuary where this Divine Atoner

Atoner adores whilst He is Himself adored. And He presents us to His FATHER, when He offers up Himself, as if we were One with Him.

Let us then enter with our most Blessed REDEEMER into His Spirit as Victim; let us offer up ourselves with Himself, since we have the means of doing so & are clothed with a portion of His Priesthood. Let us be assured that if, in the Old Dispensation, Almighty GOD was pleased to receive the Sacrifice which was offered to Him in Reparation, although the Victim was but an animal, He will gladly accept this Sacrifice, the most August of any that has ever been offered, & of which His Own most Beloved SON is the Victim. GOD will be pleased to be content with the abundant Reparation He makes with thee for all the sins which thou hast committed in drawing nigh to this most Divine Sacrament.

II.

It is not enough that thou shouldest be convinced of the Merit & the Efficacy of that Reparation which thou canst make for unprofitable Communions by a Communion with careful preparation & fervent Acts of Grace; thou must also make an examination into those faults of which thou hast been guilty at this most solemn time, thou must feel a true sorrow for them, take precautions to avoid them for the future, & make a firm resolution to approach the holy Altar

Altar from henceforth with more faith, more purity, more recollectedness, & more love. Examine into all thy past Communions. Hast thou prepared thyself as thou oughtest to do for so high & holy a Sacrament? Hast thou not neglected to make thy Preparation carefully, which consists in living in the spirit of penitence, of self-denial, of retirement, & of prayer, without which no one can be worthy to communicate often? Hast thou not, & dost thou not, live too much for the pleasures of the world? Hast thou not sought after its followers with too much eagerness? Hast thou not spoken its language & followed its precepts? Hast thou not given thyself up to its false pleasures, which are so opposed to that spirit of retirement, & to the Presence of God, which are indispensable for an approach to the Blessed Eucharist frequently? Hast thou not, without necessity, employed thyself too much with business thou mightest have avoided, & which is opposed to thy state of life & thy profession, & which have prevented thee from meditating on the Holy Communion as the most important business of our lives?

Didst thou on the evening before reception think on the Blessing which thou wert about to receive on the morrow? Didst thou endeavour to excite desire for It in thine heart? Didst thou retire from the world to meditate? Didst thou rejoice in the thought of soon kneeling at the Altar-Throne of thy Sovereign Lord? Didst

Didst thou go to rest with this thought, & didst thou arise, saying to thyself—To-day I shall be the living Sanctuary of my GOD; I shall be sustained by His very Presence; I shall be nourished with the most Precious Food of His BODY & BLOOD? Hast thou seriously examined thy conscience as regards thy sins, meditated on thy habits, thy besetting fault, thy ruling passion, thy negligences, & thy loss of time? Hast thou not drawn near to the holy Table with some inordinate passion, which has divided thy heart, & has made thee unworthy of those feelings which Almighty GOD would have imparted to thee, hadst thou been more detached from earth? Hast thou not also drawn near, with some feeling in thine heart of antipathy, or resentment towards those with whom thou art forced to live; or with some secret envy which thou hast not well rooted out because it is pleasing to thy self-love, & thou wilt neither examine into it, nor correct it?

Again, art thou not often content with repeating thy wonted Acts of Christian Graces before Holy Communion without reflection? In the Blessed Sacrament Itself hast thou not often by thine own fault been distracted, because thou art too easily occupied with those thoughts which are the cause of thy distraction, & which in consequence become voluntary at least in their principle? Hast thou given proper time for thy Acts of Thanksgiving? Hast thou taken care to to hold sweet converse with thy Lord whilst He remained with thee? Hast thou preserved the Grace of the Holy Communion after having received It? Is not the impression which It ought to have had upon thee effaced by worldly pleasure? And how didst thou spend the remainder of the day after reception? Didst thou not in the company of creatures lose the precious Treasure thou hadst just received?

Examine lastly the profit thou hast derived from so many Communions. Thy pride, is it cured as it ought to be, if thou hadst benefited by this Holy Sacrament, where God, Who is Greatness Itself, humbles Himself even to become thy Food? Hast thou more devotion to, & more love for the Almighty than thou usedst to have? Art thou more charitable towards thy neighbour? Art thou more patient & more submissive to the holy Will of God in all thy troubles? Art thou less rebellious, when despised & humiliated? Hast thou less delight in the pleasures of the world? Art thou more retired? Dost thou restrain thine external senses more? In a word, art thou more united to thy Lord, & more detached from the world & from thyself?

Oh, acknowledge that this examination is capable of overwhelming thee with confusion, & of making thee know thyself to be guilty of innumerable sins to which thou dost not pay enough attention. Thou must absolutely make reparation,

tion, that thou mayeſt henceforth worthily communicate, & no longer be accountable to Almighty GOD for many uſeleſs Communions. Make therefore an Act of Reparation for them with all the ſorrow & all the love of which thou art capable.

Affections.

Proſtrate before Thee, O Bleſſed LORD, as one who feels himſelf guilty of many ſins againſt Thee, in Thy moſt Holy Sacrament, I implore Thy Divine Mercy to forgive me, a debtor, overwhelmed with debts, who has not profited by the precious Treaſure Thou haſt offered him in the Bleſſed Euchariſt. I confeſs myſelf guilty of innumerable ſins & diſtractions; & as I cannot myſelf atone for them, ſince I can do nothing, ſince I am nothing of myſelf, I beſeech Thee by that Sacred BODY which Thou art about to give me, & by that Precious BLOOD which Thou didſt ſhed for me, to be Thyſelf my Mediator & my Atonement, even as Thou art my SAVIOUR.

I confeſs that I have approached Thy holy Table as a common table, where there is only common nouriſhment to ſupport the body, without having prepared my Soul ſufficiently for this moſt Holy Food. I have approached this Myſtery of Faith without fervent faith, & with a lukewarm heart. I have been moſt juſtly deprived

prived of those feelings which holy Men experience in this Heavenly Food, because my heart, destitute of love, was unworthy to feel them after having received Thee so often unprofitably. These Communions ought to have strengthened, consecrated, & united me to Thee, to have transformed me into Thee, if I had communicated with more faith, more purity, & more love; but, in truth, & to my sorrow, I have felt myself as weak, as full of myself, as if I had never received Thee.

Pardon then, O Divine Atoner; remember that in the Holy Eucharist Thou art not an inexorable Judge on the Throne of Justice, but a Saviour-God on a Throne of Love, having Mercy on those who ask it with contrite & humble hearts. Receive my sorrow, my tears, my desires, & my resolutions. Offer Thyself for me at Thy Heavenly Father's Throne burdened with my sins, & covered with Thy Precious Blood; & this all-sufficient Atonement shall be my safeguard & my surety in the Day of Judgment.

Thanksgiving.

O Divine Mediator, O Lamb of God, Who takest away the sins of the world, what Acts of Thanksgiving ought I not to offer Thee for having voluntarily taken upon Thyself my debts, & for having paid them with usury to Thy Heavenly

venly FATHER, at the price of Thy moſt Precious BLOOD? But, O Bleſſed LORD, what gratitude do I not owe Thee, for having added to Thy former Favours that of coming to me to-day to help me to make reparation for the innumerable faults which I have committed in receiving Thee, at Thy holy Table, through my negligence, my ſlight preparation, my want of faith, my want of love; by my continual diſtractions; by the want of fervour in my thankſgivings; & above all, by the little benefit I have derived from my Communions. Plead then my cauſe, O Divine Mediator; & whilſt Thou art within me, do Thou fulfil my Soul with Thy Love. Teach it with more devotion to make Acts of Reparation for its failings. Fill it with the fervour with which Thy Sacred HEART is filled, ſo as to prepare it worthily for all future Communions, & to make them with ſuch holy deſires, ſuch purity, ſuch faith, ſuch fervour, & ſuch benefit, that no future Act of Reparation may be needed.

Receive then, O LORD JESU CHRIST, my Acts of Thankſgiving & Reparation as coming from Thyſelf, for Thou in Thy Mercy & Love, didſt inſpire them.

Appendix:
FROM VARIOUS SOURCES.

Acts of Christian Virtues
IN PREPARATION FOR THE BLESSED SACRAMENT.

Sunday.

ACT of Faith.—I. O LORD JESU CHRIST, my LORD & my GOD, I believe with a firm & lively faith, that in the most Holy Sacrament there is present Thy BODY, Thy BLOOD, Thy SOUL, & Thy DIVINITY. I believe that I shall receive Thy Sacred BODY, Which was conceived by the HOLY GHOST in the Womb of the Blessed Virgin Mary. I believe that I shall drink of Thy most Precious BLOOD, Which was shed for me on Calvary. I believe that I shall receive Thy most Holy SOUL, Which is enriched with all Heavenly Treasures. And I believe that I shall also receive Thy Adorable DIVINITY. I believe that I shall receive Thee, wholly & entire, Who art my GOD, my Creator, my Preserver, my Redeemer, & my Judge. I believe, O my GOD, but do Thou increase & strengthen my faith; & give me an ever-deepening sense of loving adoration of Thyself,

self, present in this Blessed Sacrament. Quicken & enlarge this faith, I pray Thee, LORD JESU, not only in me, but in the hearts of all Thy faithful ones; & grant that it may enlighten those that sit in darkness & in the shadow of death. Do Thou kindle within my Soul a lively remembrance of Thy Cross & Passion, & grant that being cleansed by Thy BLOOD, I may be made worthy to receive into my Soul Thyself.

Knowest thou, then, O my Soul, what thou art about to do, & what is about to be done unto thee? Thou art about to receive thy GOD into thine house & beneath thy roof. But this is not all. Holy Communion is something still more wondrous than this. Thou art going to receive Him into thy very Soul, into the lowest depth of thy being. Thy GOD is about to come unto thee, to enter within thee, to abide with thee. All that is Greatest, most Perfect, most Lovely, most Wise, is about to visit thee; the Creator of all things, the Sovereign LORD of the universe, the Most High, the Infinite, the Incomprehensible, Whose Majesty, Goodness, Power, & Perfection it is impossible to describe, is about to come unto thee, in one awful word—GOD is coming unto thee. And this GOD is thy GOD, O my Soul. This GOD is the GOD that created thee, that redeemed thee, that preserves thee. This is the GOD Who is about to make His abode with thee in the most Holy Sacrament of the Altar.

II. Humbly kneeling before Thy Divine Majesty, LORD JESUS, I firmly believe all the Truths contained in the Creeds of Thy Church, & all that Thou dost intend me to believe, in order to save my Soul alive. Especially do I believe Thee to be Present in the most Holy Eucharist; & I believe it because Thou, Who art

the

the eternal & infallible Truth, haft revealed it. I believe, O my GOD, that Thou, the Very & Eternal WORD, art really Prefent on Thy Altar, veiled beneath the facred Euchariftic Forms of BREAD & WINE; the Same LORD, both GOD & MAN, Who was Incarnate by the HOLY GHOST; Who was born of the Bleffed Virgin Mary of her fubftance; Who lived a humble Life upon earth; Who fuffered a fhameful Death upon the Crofs; Who rofe again after three days; Who afcended into Heaven; & Who fhall come again to judge both the quick & the dead. Thefe Truths I believe, but cannot underftand; I adore, but cannot penetrate. LORD, do Thou increafe my faith, & grant that Whom I receive in Faith, I may hereafter behold Face to face in Glory. For I believe, moreover, that in this Bleffed Sacrament Thou doft renew the Myfteries of Thy Holy Gofpel; the Myftery of Thy fupernatural Birth, when Prefent in Thy Sacrament; the Myftery of Thy Epiphany, in the offerings of the Faithful; the Myftery of Thy hidden Life, in the neglect & forgetfulnefs of mankind; the Myftery of Thy facred Paffion, in the Bread broken, & the Wine poured out; the Myftery of Thy Death, when Thou art offered up to the Eternal FATHER on the Altar of Thy Church; the Myftery of Thy Burial, in being confumed yet incorruptible, in being divided, but ftill perfect & complete; & laftly the Myftery of Thy glorious Refurrection, when Thou doft feed us with Thy Sacred BODY, & nourifh us with Thy moft Precious BLOOD, unto Everlafting Life.

O my LORD, I believe in all thefe Myfteries; I believe that all thefe Myfteries were fulfilled for my fake. *What reward fhall I give unto the LORD, for all the*

the Benefits that He hath done unto me? Thou haſt ſacrificed all for me. Why cannot I ſacrifice all to Thee? Why cannot I return love for Love, poverty for Poverty, humility for Humiliation, ſelf-denial for Sufferings, penitence for Sorrows, croſs for Croſs, & death for Death? Alas, Lord Jesu, this cannot be. At leaſt ſuffer me therefore to give Thee what I can, Who haſt given all thiugs to me. I conſecrate to Thy Service my body, my Soul, my faculties, my memory, my will, my life, my thoughts, my affections, my deſires, & my actions, to be employed for Thy greater Glory. Do Thou be pleaſed to accept the ſacrifice, for Thine own Sake.

Monday.

Act of Hope.—I. I believe, & therefore I hope in Thy Words, Lord Jesu, which Thou haſt ſpoken—*Come unto Me, all that travail, & are heavy laden, & I will refreſh you;* the more hardened, the more wearied, the more diſtreſſed, ſo much the more conſolation ſhall ye find. My ſinfulneſs is great, & I acknowledge it; but Thy Compaſſion, O Lord, is infinite, & therein I place all my confidence. Hope, O my Soul, hope in thy God. He is thy Saviour; He Himſelf hath ſaid ſo, He Himſelf calleth thee; hearken to His Voice; liſten in faith; believe in hope. It is true thou haſt ſinned; but it is alſo true, that to ſave ſinners Jesus came. It is true thou haſt diſobeyed His Law; but, it is alſo true, that He is ever ready to accept a repentant heart. He calls thee, in order that He may pardon thee. He comes to thee to fulfil thee with His Bleſſings. Open wide then the door of thy heart, &

give

give free admittance unto Hope. Thou canst do nothing; but thy Saviour can do all things. O my God, I hope all things, inasmuch as I hope in Thee, even in Thee, Who lovest me so much, as to be willing & ready to descend from Heaven, into this my miserable & sin-sick Soul.

In this Goodness, then, is all my Hope; & in Thee alone, O most sweet Lord Jesus, do I place my Hope, for Thou art my Health & my Strength, Thou art my Refuge & my strong Rock, Thou art the Source of all good things. For how shall I dare to offer up this dreadful Sacrifice to God the Father, & to partake of Thee therein, unless Thou shouldst give me boldness, Thou Who hast redeemed me with Thy Blood? Therefore, trusting in Thy Loving-kindness, I come to Thee, as a sheep to the Shepherd, as one sick to the Physician, as a prisoner sentenced to death to the Deliverer; that Thou mayest save me from the sentence of sin & death, as my merciful Intercessor; that Thou mayest strengthen & heal me as my skilful Physician; & that Thou mayest tend & cherish me, as the watchful & true Shepherd of my Soul. The deep of my nothingness calleth unto the deep of Thy Goodness; for although my sins are very many & very grievous, though they be grievous even unto death, & as the sand of the sea for multitude, yet are they as nothing, O Lord Jesu Christ, when compared with Thy Compassion, & with the price of Thy Precious Blood. In Thy Mercy then, O my God, is placed all my hope; for in myself is there nothing on which I may rely. Have mercy upon me & save me, O Thou Who never forsakest them that hope in Thee.

II. O Thou Source of all Goodness & Mercy, how

great foever may be the multitude of my fins, & however unworthy I may be of Thy Grace, by my ingratitude & wickednefs, I hope to obtain, in this Bleffed Sacrament, relief in my diftrefs & pardon for my fins. Thou doft declare, that *GOD fo loved the world, that He gave His Only-begotten SON, to the end that all that believe in Him fhould not perifh, but have Everlafting Life.* Wilt Thou then reject me, when I would fhare this bleffed promife; or forbid me to come nigh unto Thee, to be refrefhed, when I am heavy laden? At Thy Sacred Altar Thou doft offer Thyfelf to the Eternal FATHER on my behalf; Thou doft nourifh me with Thy Precious BODY & BLOOD; & Thou art Prefent to hearken unto my prayer. Doft Thou do all thefe things for nought? No, LORD JESU; that be far from Thee, Good LORD. Thou wouldeft thereby leffen my mifery, pour benefits upon me, & enrich me with all Thy Treafures, & I have hope therefore in Thee, O my GOD. I hope that, by virtue of Thy bitter Paffion & Death, I fhall be reconciled with my offended FATHER, & fhall obtain forgivenefs of all my fins. I hope that Thy Divine FLESH will heal all my fpiritual infirmities. I hope that Thy Precious BLOOD will wafh away all my flefhly fins. I hope that the Bleffed Sacrament will communicate to me Thy Sanctity; that It will be to me a fource of Grace, Knowledge, Love, & Strength; that It will become alfo my ftony Rock & my Refuge, my Might in Whom I may truft, my Buckler, the Horn alfo of my Salvation, & my Refuge. O my Soul, be conftant then in the hope of receiving from thy Bleffed LORD the Grace which thou doft moft chiefly need. From the Love, of which thou haft the fureft proof, in the Divine Sacrament of the Altar, expect

pect nothing short of infinite Gifts & Graces; & prepare thyself to receive thy GOD worthily, by the firmness of thy hope, the fervour of thy love, & the completeness of thy faith.

Tuesday.

Act of Divine Love.—I. O LORD JESU CHRIST, whose heart can be so hard & unfeeling, as not to rejoice at the sight of that exceeding Love which Thou showest us in the Blessed Sacrament, the perpetual Memorial of Thy Passion & Thy Death? O my GOD, Thou GOD of my Soul, my highest & chiefest Good, I love Thee with all my heart & all my Soul, & with all my might & all my strength. I love Thee more than myself. I love Thee above all things. Oh, that I had countless hearts to love Thee with, & tongues to praise & bless Thy holy Name, & lives to dedicate to Thy Service. Would that my sole desire were to love Thee Who alone art worthy of Divine love. Would that I might make some amends for the many years in which I loved Thee not.

Ah, dearest LORD, if, in past times, I have not loved Thee, from this moment I will strive to love Thee with all my heart. I know Thou desirest me to be Thine; I know Thou wouldst reign alone within my heart; I know Thou longest that I should consecrate myself entirely to Thee; I therefore renounce every other love, that I may love Thee alone. O most Loving JESUS, give me that burning Charity, that perfect Love which Thou desirest I should have. Draw me to Thyself with the sweet chains of Thy Perfections; take my heart & unite it to Thine own most loving Heart with the bonds of everlasting Love. Thou,
Thou

Thou alone, shalt henceforth live within my heart, which shall have no life but within Thy Sacred Heart, there to die to every other love but Thee, O most Loving JESU.

II. Oh, what Divine Love enflamed Thine Heart, most Loving JESUS, when about to leave this world, to go unto the FATHER, Thou didst prepare for us a Table that hath every Delight, & all Sweetness. Great indeed, & marvellous was the work of Thy Love, in that Thou didst humble Thyself for our Redemption, & didst deign to take upon Thee the infirmity of our nature; but far more exceeding & more marvellous is it, that Thou didst leave us Thy BODY for Food, & Thy BLOOD for Drink. In that, verily, Thou didst take our humanity; in this, Thou didst impart Thy DIVINITY. If Thou hast thus poured out upon us the whole treasure of Thy Grace, grant that this unbounded Love preventing us, we may strive with all our power to repay Thee the just meed of Love. Therefore, LORD JESU, I love Thee, my only Consolation in this exile, the only Hope of my fainting Soul, my only Joy, & the greatest Good I can enjoy on earth. I love Thee with all my heart, with all my mind, with all my Soul, & with all my strength; & would that I always loved Thee every moment more fervently. This is my ardent desire, which I desire with all the affections & aspirations of my heart. For Thou drawest all the powers of my Soul unto Thee, whilst Thou dost infuse Thyself into me; &, as far as it is possible, Thou makest me like unto Thyself, whilst Thou dost feed, nourish, & satisfy my hungry Soul, not with any earthly food, but with Thy Precious BODY, & Thy All-saving BLOOD. For this Thine unspeakable Gift,
I love

I love Thee, O my GOD; & that I may never cease to love Thee, enkindle the flame of my love with Thyself, Who art the Food & Sustenance of Divine Love. O Fire that ever burns, & never languishes, inflame my reins & my heart, that they may burn with the love of Thee. Thou camest to send fire upon the earth; enkindle it then, & fan it, that it may ever increase. For I will love Thee, if Thou wilt bestow on me the power of loving; & the richer the grace of loving Thou bestowest, the more will I love Thee; & yet I shall never love Thee, LORD JESU, as Thou art worthy to be loved.

Wednesday.

Act of Desire.—I. O JESU, LAMB of GOD, Redeemer of my Soul, Whom I desire to receive, though most unworthy of so inestimable a Blessing, vouchsafe to look on me with the eyes of Thy Mercy, for without Thee I can do nothing. Receive me, O my Redeemer, into the everlasting Arms of Thy Mercy, who, with all the affection of my Soul, do consecrate myself wholly unto Thee. O my GOD, the most fervent Desire of my Soul is to be united to Thee, & to be employed in doing Thy sacred Will, & advancing Thy greater Glory. Oh, let the time past of my life suffice for me to have acted according to mine own ways; & grant me Grace to spend the residue of my days entirely in Thy Service. Pardon, purify, & deliver me from the guilt of all my sins; & do Thou implant within my Soul the Graces of lively Faith, firm Hope, fervent Charity, & Angelic Chastity. For this purpose, be pleased, Good LORD JESUS, to visit my Soul in Mercy; take full possession of my heart, which

I offer

I offer unto Thee without reserve; & do Thou be pleased to make me a worthy partaker of these Divine Mysteries. O my GOD, I believe that Thou art truly, & really, & substantially Present in this most august & venerable Sacrament. I believe that It contains Thy BODY & BLOOD, Thy SOUL & DIVINITY, because Thou Thyself hast revealed it; & I am ready, Thy Grace helping me, to shed my blood in testimony of this Divine Truth. I confess that I am not meet to approach unto Thee, being so great a sinner; but Thou art the Light of my countenance & my GOD.

O LORD JESU, my desire is fixed on Thee, because Thou art my GOD; & though most unworthy, yet I firmly trust in Thy Goodness, that Thou wilt never forsake one, who thus entirely depends upon Thee, & for whose Soul Thou hast done such great things. For all Thy Blessings towards me, I desire, O my GOD, to love Thee, to bless Thee, & to offer myself to Thy holy Service for ever. I desire to love Thee with all my heart, & Soul, & strength, & mind; to love Thee above all things; to love Thee only, for Thou only art worthy of love. Come then, O my GOD; come quickly, LORD JESUS; infuse Thyself Wholly into my Soul, which longs to receive Thee; send me not empty away, whose whole dependence is upon Thee; but pour into my heart Thy Heavenly Grace, that I may be perfectly united to Thee, & never may be separated from Thee.

II. Behold, O LORD, in Thee is all whatsoever I can or ought to desire. Thou art my CREATOR, my Salvation, & my Redemption, my Beginning & my End, my Hope & my Strength, my Honour & my Glory. I long to receive Thee with devotion & reverence. I desire to bring Thee into my house, even under the
roof

roof of my sin-sick Soul, that Thou mayest speak the word only, & Thy servant may be healed. My Soul longs to receive Thy Sacred BODY, & Thy most Precious BLOOD. My heart desires to be united to Thee. Turn not Thou then away, Dearest LORD, Thy Face from me; delay not Thy Visitation; & withdraw not Thy Consolation from me. But come, LORD JESU, come to Thy Servant & make him joyful; come & satisfy him with Thy Presence, for without Thy Presence there can be no true joy. Come then, O my GOD, haste Thee unto me, & tarry not. O my GOD, my whole being desires & longs after Thee, with that love & fervour with which the most loving Souls amongst Thy Saints have ever received Thee; & with their blessed Communion, I humbly desire to join this my unworthy one. Come then, O my LORD, *for like as the hart desireth the water-brooks, so longeth my Soul after Thee, O GOD;* give me Thyself, & it sufficeth me, for beside Thee no consolation availeth anything; without Thee I cannot exist, for if Thou visitest me not, I die. Therefore I desire to receive Thee, LORD JESU, most fervently, that I may become One with Thee. Come into my Soul, I pray Thee, & sanctify & replenish all her faculties; come into my body, & purify all its senses & feelings; come into my heart, & possess all its affections; so that, to my life's end, I may be entirely consecrated to Thy boundless Love.

Thursday.

Act of Gratitude.—I. Who am I, O infinite Goodness, that Thou shouldest have willed me to approach Thy Holy Altar, & to join in offering unto Thee, of Thy gifts

gifts a holy Sacrifice, a spotless Victim? Whence have I found this favour in Thine Eyes, that Thou shouldest show forth in me the riches of Thy Mercy? Come ye & hearken, all ye Angels & Saints of GOD, & I will tell you how great things the LORD hath done for my Soul. For when I was laid low in my house, He raised me from the dust, & set me among the princes of His people, that I might eat Bread & drink Wine at His holy Table all the days of my life. What thanks, therefore, can I render to Thee, most Merciful JESUS, Thou SAVIOUR of the world? or what reward can I offer unto Thee for all the Benefits which Thou hast done unto me? Truly of Thee, the Bridegroom of the Church, that saying of the Canticles is most true—*If a man would give all the substance of his house for love, it would utterly be contemned.* Thou hast lavished all that Thou hast upon me, Thy BODY, Thy BLOOD, Thy SOUL, & Thy DIVINITY; & if I should give Thee all the substance of my house, my body, my Soul, & my spirit, with all that I now have, & all that I ever shall have, this would be esteemed as nothing, in comparison with Thy boundless & inestimable Gift. I owe Thee as much as Thou art capable of receiving, Who art Infinite; wherefore my debt surpasses all my power to pay it. Yet I dare to ask Thee, for Thou art Pitiful, & full of Mercy, & knowest my poverty, I dare to ask Thee not to despise the mite which I offer unto Thee in the simplicity of my heart, saying with the Spouse in the sacred Canticles—*My Beloved is mine, & I am His.* For as Thou hast given me Thy Whole Self, for the nourishment of my Soul, so do I consecrate my whole self to Thy Service, & give wholly to Thee whatever I have, whatever I am, whatever I shall become,

come, that Thou mayest claim me wholly for Thyself, nor suffer aught of myself to remain to me.

II. Oh, what Gratitude can I render unto Thee, my GOD, for having vouchsafed, of Thy infinite Mercy, to descend from Heaven, into this Vale of Misery, to take upon Thee our nature, of the substance of the Blessed Virgin; to suffer Death upon the Cross; & to leave us Thy Precious BODY & BLOOD to be our Divine Food & Sustenance. For of a truth, LORD JESU, I have deserved nothing of Thy boundless Mercy towards me; nor is there anything in me which could move Thee to bestow so many & great benefits upon me, both of body & Soul, upon me who am so incapable to return to Thee due & grateful thanks, for having created me, redeemed me, preserved me, & fed me with the Bread of Angels, & the Cup of Blessing. Moreover, O LORD, Thou hast given me Faith to believe in Thee; reason to know Thee; an understanding to find Thee out; a disposition to serve Thee; & Grace to please Thee. And what daily Favours hast Thou not showered down upon me? From how many perils of body & Soul hast Thou not by Thy Fatherly Providence, preserved me? With how many Spiritual Gifts & Graces hast Thou not enriched me? And how often hast Thou not given me Thy very Self, at Thine own Sacred Altar? Accept then, O my GOD, I most humbly beseech Thee, my hearty gratitude which I offer up in union with Thy All-prevailing Sacrifice; & grant, Gracious LORD, that my life may henceforth become a continual Act of Thanksgiving, to Thy Divine Majesty, for all Thy Blessings bestowed upon me.

What then shall I render unto the LORD, in Gratitude, for all the Benefits He hath done me? I will receive the Cup of Salvation, & will call upon the Name of the LORD. I will do more, however. Behold, LORD JESUS, I renounce myself to Thee; I fully resign myself, body, Soul & spirit to Thy Will; & all that is mine I dedicate to Thy good Pleasure, & to Thy greater Glory. But, O my GOD, what have I that I have not received? What is man compared with his Maker? What can a creature, a sinner, an unprofitable servant give unto his GOD, his Judge, his absolute LORD & Master? I acknowledge—nothing. Therefore, do Thou, O LORD, as my Advocate, & Mediator, rich in Merits, & boundless in Mercy, do Thou undertake for me. Do Thou, Blessed JESU, plead my cause; do Thou help my needs & supply my deficiencies; & by offering it up in union with Thy ceaseless Intercession, do Thou fulfil all that is wanting, in this my humble Act of Gratitude.

Friday.

Act of Godly Fear.—I. Called & invited to the Table of Thy Holy Feast, LORD JESU, my chiefest Good & eternal Joy, I would indeed wish to obey Thy Voice, & partake of Thee lovingly & devoutly; but I exceedingly tremble when I contemplate my own sinfulness; I am afraid at the words of Thine Apostle, who saith—*Whosoever shall eat this Bread & drink this Cup of the LORD unworthily, shall be guilty of the BODY & BLOOD of the LORD.* It is a wondrous thing & one surpassing comprehension. I feed on Heavenly Bread, with which the world can be satisfied; I drink of the most Precious Wine, wherewith the thirst of Angels might be quenched; & yet, I am consumed with

with mere worldly hunger & thirst. I bear about within me the very Joy of Heaven; & yet I cease not to be entangled in the allurements of earth, & seek vain comforts of the creature. I come to the most High GOD, the Fountain of all Good, & partake of Him under the sacred Eucharistic Forms of Bread & Wine; & not only am I not caught up with the Apostle to the third Heaven, but I wholly cleave to the world, & all my thoughts are bestowed upon earth, none upon Heaven.

These are some of the thoughts which distress me; this is the cause of my great fear & disquietude; for I dread lest that which Thou hast appointed for my health, I should receive to my hurt & eternal condemnation. Shall I then fly from Thy Face with despairing Cain; or, with disobedient Adam, shall I hide myself from Thee, because I am spiritually naked, & hear Thy Voice in the garden of my Soul? GOD forbid. For I know that Thy Mercy is greater than my wretchedness; that Thy Clemency is more boundless than mine iniquity. If I am unclean, or sick, or naked, Thou canst cleanse me, Thou canst heal me, Thou canst clothe me. To Thee therefore I fly with Godly fear, that Thou mayest clothe & heal & purify me. Draw away my heart, I pray Thee, LORD JESU, from everything but Thee; for in aught else there is nothing but vanity & vexation of spirit. May my mind realize the sweetness of Thy Presence. May it taste how Sweet Thou art, that absorbed by Thy Love, it may seek nought save Thee, O Thou GOD of my heart & my Portion for ever.

II. Who am I, LORD JESU, that I presume to receive Thee into my Soul? Who am I that venture to put

put aside Godly fear in order to receive Thee? And Who art Thou, O my God, that dost vouchsafe to come unto me, & to visit my sin-sick Soul? Thy Greatness has no limits; Thy Wisdom, no measure; Thy Bounty, no end. Thou art infinite in Holiness, wonderful in Counsel, fearful in Judgment, & perfect in all Thy Attributes: whilst I am but dust & ashes, a child of wrath, the destined food of worms, full of wickedness & sin, & fitted for destruction. In all things I acknowledge, with fear & trembling, that I am miserable, & spiritually poor & blind & naked; uncertain in judgment, vain in action, sensual in appetites, full of ambition, & overpowered with self-esteem, powerless to do good, & powerful only to work wickedness. What am I then, before Thee, O my God, in Whose Presence the very Angels veil their faces, the Seraphim tremble, & the Heavens are not pure? Shall a creature, so sinful, venture to approach a Creator, so sinless? Undeserving as I am, do I dare to draw nigh unto Thee? Ah, Lord God, go not far from me, I pray; do not make as if Thou heardest not; withdraw not Thyself from me, if I make bold to come unto Thee. My unworthiness is great; but Thy Mercies are infinite. Subject to so many ills, what can I do but hasten unto Thee for relief, with Godly reverence & fear. Nor wilt Thou reject me. For remember, Lord Jesu, that during Thy mortal Life Thou didst not only allow the sick to approach Thee, but Thou didst also heal them when they came. To whom then shall I come in my distress, but unto Thee? Hence in drawing nigh unto Thy Altar, I will put far from me all unworthy fear; I will be assured that Thou wilt shew forth Thy Mercy unto me; I will believe that

Thou

Thou wilt welcome me to Thy Heavenly Feast. Listen then unto my prayer, O my Lord; & graciously receive me, whilst I give myself entirely unto Thee. Take full possession of my Soul, most Blessed Jesu, & make it Thine. Give what Thou commandest, & command what Thou wilt.

Saturday.

Act of Adoration.—I. O my God, with the most profound humility of Soul, I venture to come before Thee, & to offer up unto Thee, by the hands of Thy servant the Priest, the most adorable Sacrifice of the Body & Blood of Jesus; thereby rendering unto Thee, O Lord God, that supreme & undivided Homage & Adoration which is due to Thee, from all Thy creatures. I offer It up, O Heavenly Father, in acknowledgment of Thy supreme Dominion over all things, & of our perpetual & entire dependence upon Thee: thereby confessing Thee to be my first Beginning & my last End, my chief Good, my only Desire, my perfect Happiness. In Union with this Adorable Victim, I offer up to Thee all the love & affections of my Soul; & consecrate & present unto Thee my self, my Soul, & my body, to be a reasonable, holy, & lively sacrifice unto Thee, for ever. I offer it up in Thy Praise & Honour, for all Thy glorious Works; for Thine own infinite Perfections; for all the sacred Mysteries of our most Holy Faith; for Thy inestimable Love, in the Redemption of the World, by our Lord Jesus Christ, both God & Man; for all Thou hast done for Thy Holy Catholic Church: & for all Thou hast done for all Thy Holy Saints in Heaven, & for Thy servants militant here in earth. I offer It, also, in hearty thanksgiving to Thee, for the numberless benefits & favours Thou hast bestowed upon me from my birth until the present hour; for creating me out of nothing, in Thy Image; for redeeming me with the BLOOD of Thy Well-beloved SON; for sanctifying me with Thy HOLY SPIRIT; for preserving me amidst all the changes & chances of this mortal life, for making me, & keeping me a member of Thy Holy Catholic Church; for vouchsafing so often to feed me with this Blessed Sacrament of CHRIST's BODY & BLOOD, that my sinful body may be made clean by His BODY, & my Soul washed through His most Precious BLOOD; & for Thine infinite Goodness towards me in many ways. For these, & all Thy Mercies, O LORD, my Soul, & all that is within me desires to laud & magnify Thy glorious Name. I humbly prostrate myself before Thee in hearty adoration. I offer to Thee this All-prevailing Sacrifice of Thy Dear SON. Accept of me, in Mercy, O my GOD, & make me entirely Thine, for the sake of the same Adorable Victim, the Holy Child JESUS.

II. O GOD, the invisible Creator of the world, its Protector, Redeemer, & Sanctifier, THREE in ONE, & ONE in THREE, how wonderfully dost Thou deal with us, how sweetly & graciously dost Thou dispose of all things, making them work together for good to them that love Thee, & to Thy faithful ones whom Thou dost feed in this All-holy Sacrament of the Altar. Rejoice, O my Soul, & give thanks to GOD for so great a Blessing, so singular a Consolation in this vale of tears. Yea, LORD JESU, with the profoundest & most humble respect of my Soul, prostrate both in heart & body before Thy Sovereign Majesty, I do adore & acknowledge Thee,

Thee, the Sovereign LORD of my life & being, Who canst again reduce me unto that nothing out of which Thou didst first create me; & Who by Thy mere boundless Goodness hast preserved me from it until this present day. I render Thee, O LORD, all Adoration & Homage, as Thy submissive & humble creature, depending entirely upon Thy blessed Will & Pleasure. And since that Honour which I am able to render to the Merit of Thy Infinite DEITY is so inconsiderable; to supply that great defect in this Immaculate Sacrifice I offer to Thee the adoration which Thy Saints & Angels render to Thee for all Eternity; & my great desire is, that all the creatures of Heaven & earth may bless, adore, & glorify Thee, with endless Praise, for ever & ever.

I also wish to adore Thy sublime Goodness, O my GOD; for of all Thy Attributes, this is the one which more especially is exhibited in this All-holy Mystery; & as the consideration of it excites my Faith & Confidence, so does it force me to adore Thy boundless Mercy. Consider then, O my Soul, all that thou hast, & all thou art. Does not all flow from GOD's infinite Goodness; & dost not thou owe Him Adoration for these His Blessings? What hast thou of thyself? Thou hast nothing, thou art nothing. O my GOD, it is from Thee that I have received all that I possess; & unto Thee I desire to give back all. I would give Thee back all that Thou hast given me; & I would I could annihilate myself in Thy sacred Presence, that I might become one with & absorbed into Thee, my GOD. I bless Thee, for all Thy Gifts & Graces; & I adore Thee. Above all I adore Thee in this Divine Sacrament, wherein Thou art Present of Thy own free Goodness; & the more Thou dost conceal

ceal Thy Majesty, the more do I desire to abase myself before Thee, & to sink into my own nothingness, acknowledging Thee only, LORD JESU, for my LORD & my GOD.

Conferences
BETWEEN THE DISCIPLE & THE DIVINE MASTER AFTER HOLY COMMUNION.

Sunday.

I. Behold with the eye of Faith our LORD JESUS CHRIST in the depth of thy Soul, opening His Sacred HEART to thee, & saying—Come unto Me, thou who desirest Me, for I will give unto him that is athirst of the Fountain of the Water of Life freely. And do thou, O my Soul, answer Him thus—I sit down under Thy Shadow with great delight, & Thy Fruit is sweet to my taste: I will look for rest & joy & satisfaction no where else in the world.

Ask our Blessed LORD, not to suffer thee to be separated from Him for one moment, & say with a holy Man of old—Draw me wholly to Thyself, Dearest LORD, that my being may be inseparably united to Thine; & whenever I am obliged to occupy myself with things of this world, for the good of my neighbour, grant to me, O LORD, to return to Thee, as soon as I have done my work as perfectly as I can, to Thy greater Glory.

The continual Presence of our LORD is so precious a Gift, that the slightest act of faithlessness, intentionally committed, may deprive thee of it; ask therefore of thy LORD for that clearsighted Love, which discovers

the

the slightest imperfections in thy Soul, in order to mourn over them, or to flee from them.

II. Behold with the eye of Faith our LORD JESUS CHRIST, Who says to thee—Look around, & behold in the ways of sin so many highly gifted Souls, whom I might have drawn to follow Me. Does it not seem as if I had set aside all thought of My own Glory, in order to save thee from perdition, preferring thee to so many great intellects and gifted minds? And do thou, O my Soul, answer Him thus, prostrate at His sacred Feet & full of gratitude—My LORD, Thou hast left these gifted Souls, these tender hearts, these noble minds to themselves, & they have been unable to rise to Thee, they have set their affections on creatures like themselves, without being able to find the only true rest, the only true love in Thee. What shall I do, how shall I thank Thee for all Thy Benefits, & especially for having given me Grace to believe in Thy Love alone? By what prayers can I move Thee to draw other Souls too unto Thyself?

Listen to our LORD, Who answers thee—A faithful Soul looks upon all those that are lost, as upon so many precious pearls fallen out of My Crown; she prays unceasingly, that no other Soul may be lost, & asks for My Love, not only to win her own heart, but to overflow all hearts, & draw them away, so as to become one in My Divine Love. If thou wouldest work together with Me in drawing these Souls & saving them from perdition, sanctify thyself more & more every day. I can refuse nothing to a Soul, which gives itself to Me without reserve.

O wondrous Law of Love! If GOD bids thee love thy brethren & pray for them, He inspires them also with

with the same ardent Love for thy Soul. How many Souls have prayed & wept & wrestled with GOD in prayer for thee, without thy knowing it. Love thy LORD more & more fervently, Who in the Holy Eucharist is the bond of the Communion of Saints, according to the Apostle's word—*For we, being many, are one Bread & one Body, for we are all partakers of that one Bread.*

Monday.

I. Behold with the eye of Faith our LORD JESUS CHRIST, Who not only lets thee approach His Table, & sit by His Side, but Who also condescends to enter into the very depth of thy heart, satisfying it, & delighting it with His Presence, & saying—If I had told thee to do a hard thing for Me, in order to be admitted to so Divine a Feast, thou shouldst have done it gladly & generously, to gain so great a Blessing; but what do I ask of thee? Nothing but thy love. My Love for Souls calls into life their love for Me, & makes them anxious to do My Will. I love, in order to be loved; I ask the Soul for nothing else but her love, because I know it makes her happy to possess Me.

Prostrate thyself at thy Divine LORD's Feet, & say to Him—O my GOD, Whose Love is infinite, my GOD, my Strength, my Refuge, my Deliverer, the Food of my Soul, shall I not love Thee? Yea, I will love Thee, O LORD my GOD!

If thou desirest to know GOD, & to serve Him continually, love Him; for a man who loves not, would give himself in vain to the study of GOD's Word, to Prayer & Meditation. He would take infinite pains, & yet would work fruitlessly; he would soon

soon get weary, while he who loves GOD does not think about his trouble.

Resolve once for all to despise the promises, the threats, the attractions of the world, for the Love of the LORD JESUS, Whom thou hast seen, & loved, & known in Holy Communion: for the Love of GOD, in Whom thou hast believed, & Who has kindled the flame of His Love in thy heart.

II. Behold with the eye of Faith our LORD JESUS CHRIST, Who having come into thy heart, says to thee—I wish Mine Elect would think Me less severe, & believe that I accept even the least sacrifice which they make for Me, as acceptable unto Me. Thus it would be an acceptable Offering to Me, if a Soul found no pleasure in fulfilling her Acts of Devotion, & would, notwithstanding this dryness, strive unweariedly to offer up her Prayers & Meditations & other Acts of Worship, hoping that GOD in His infinite Mercy would condescend to accept these Acts of devotion. Prostrate thyself at thy Divine LORD's Feet, & say—O LORD JESU, where could an earthly master be found, who could accept as a benefit a service due to him, especially a service rendered unwillingly? How easy is it to satisfy Thee, if only we could understand Thy infinite Love & Bounty!

Fear is a feeling belonging to slaves; confidence belongs to friends; love to children. Think of the name which our LORD JESUS CHRIST deigns to take with regard to thee, & act towards Him accordingly.

Nothing is so careful as Love, when it is afraid of losing the object of its desire. You may fear, but let your fear be full of Love, & it will lose all that is faulty, & will become pleasing unto thy Divine Master.

Tuesday.

Tuesday.

I. Behold with the eye of Faith our Lord Jesus Christ, Who having come into thy heart, offers thee His Own, saying—In this world friends give presents to each other, as tokens of their love, because they can give their hearts to one another only in desire, but are unable to give it in reality. I have made My Omnipotence servant to My Love, in order to enable Me to offer thee My Heart truly & really in this Sacrament of My Love; & that not only once, but as often as thou wilt receive Me. And do thou, O my Soul, lying prostrate at thy Blessed Lord's Feet, thus answer Him—O my God, is Thy Heart a present of trifling value, because Thou offerest it to so unworthy a creature as I am? My Lord, my Love has yet another power passing that of all earthly love. Thou canst make those worthy of Thy Love, on whom Thou wilt bestow it. I beseech Thee, Lord Jesu, make me holy, since Thou hast condescended to love me.

Jesus Christ, the same yesterday, to-day, and for ever. His Designs of Love & Mercy are immutable; all the ingratitude of thy heart has not been able to make Him renounce thee. Pray for deepened Contrition while thou recallest to mind thy changeableness, the inconstancy of thy heart, thy want of resolution, thy faithlessness & lukewarmness in His Service.

Nothing is more grateful than to live with a faithful friend, to whom one can open one's heart wholly. Live so with our Lord Jesus Christ. Return to Him, if thou art far from Him; never leave Him, & thou wilt become perfect.

II. Be-

II. Behold with the eye of Faith our LORD JESUS CHRIST in the very depth of thy heart, Who offers thee His bleeding Hand, pierced with cruel Nail, & saying—To-day I have taken thy Soul to be My Bride. I am from henceforth thy Husband, thou must serve Me & live to My Glory, & I will watch over thy life & thine honour. Cast thyself, O my Soul, at His sacred Feet, & answer Him thus—My LORD, how canst Thou so forget Thy Glory as to form such a bond between Thyself, & a miserable creature such as I am? Thou indeed wilt be true to it; but alas! what shall I do, not to fall away? Teach Thou me to do the thing that pleaseth Thee, for Thou art my GOD. Let Thy Loving SPIRIT lead me forth in the paths of Righteousness.

In the very Presence of thy LORD thank Him for all the Graces with which He has endowed thy Soul, & tell Him that thou lovest Him still more than His Gifts. Be not afraid of the risings of self-love, while thou acknowledgest these Divine Gifts. He Who has bestowed them upon thee, will add yet another, that of rendering to Him alone Glory & Honour & Praise.

Whenever thou art lifted up by vain-glory or cast down by humiliation, say in the spirit of self-sacrifice—My glory is nothing, & my shame is nothing. If only GOD be honoured & glorified, I am content.

Wednesday.

I. Contemplate with the eye of Faith our LORD JESUS CHRIST, Who abiding in the depth of thy Soul says to thee—The exceeding greatness of My Love & Mercy does not find an answer in thy Soul. If thou knowest the Gift, if thou knowest the Treasure hidden in in the Holy Eucharist, if thou knowest Who it is, that speaks to thee under the Vail of these sacred Elements, Who it is, that says to thee—Give Me to drink, satisfy the parching thirst for Souls which consumes Me in this Sacrament, where so few hearts beat in answer to My Heart, thou wouldest have asked of Him, to satisfy the cravings of thy heart, & He would have given thee Living Water springing up into Everlasting Life. O my Soul, thus answer Him, lying prostrate at His Feet—O LORD JESUS, how is it, that Thou, being GOD, askest drink of me who am only a poor & miserable creature? How is it, that Thou condescendest to speak to me as to Thine equal, Thou, the King of kings, the Almighty GOD Who madest Thy people to tremble at the foot of Mount Sinai. Thou knowest my poverty! Alas, LORD, give me, I beseech Thee to-day, give me every day, give me unceasingly this Living Water which Thou biddest me ask of Thee, give me this Water, that I thirst not, neither come hither to draw.

Adore the GOD of Love, Who has made Himself thy Food in this Blessed Sacrament, & Who is still speaking to thee in the depth of thy Soul where He dwells—I am this long expected MESSIAH Whose Almighty Word has renewed the world, and Who is even now giving thee a new heart, I that speak unto thee am He.

There can be no Communion without union of thy will with the Will of GOD. Without this Union, thou wilt lose the most precious Fruits of this Divine Sacrament. Pray then most fervently, that all that is within thee, every thought, every feeling, every impulse may be brought into absolute subjection to the

adora-

adorable Will of GOD, so that thou mayest be enabled to say in truth—My Meat art Thou, O LORD JESU, my Meat is to do Thy Will, which I long to fulfil, even as Thou didst fulfil the Will of Thy FATHER.

II. Behold with the eye of Faith our LORD JESUS CHRIST, Who having come into the very depth of thy Soul, offers thee His own sacred Heart saying—Behold this Heart, Which has loved thee so unspeakably, Which has not spared Itself, Which has consumed Itself, & spent Itself for Love of thee, & as a reward thou givest Me only ingratitude, irreverence, contempt & coldness in this Sacrament of My Love. O my Soul, cast thyself at His Feet covered with shame & confusion & implore His Pardon, saying—LORD, chasten me, as Thou wilt, only let me remain close to Thee, uphold me still with Thy Hand, let me never go far from Thee, grant me Grace ever to remain beside Thee, O Blessed LORD, remember Thou, that Love never is tired of pardoning offences, & pardon me, I beseech Thee.

Desire that henceforth all thy prayers, all thy works, that every moment of thy life may be dedicated to the Love of GOD, & given up to works of Love & Mercy in order to make amends for thy past negligences.

Ask thy LORD to give thee a deep & loving contrition which would make thee zealous in serving Him & punishing thyself.

Thursday.

I. Behold with the eye of Faith our LORD JESUS CHRIST in the depth of thy Soul Who says to thee— My Son, give Me thine heart, & I will give thee Mine, heart for Heart. While thou receivest this glorious Gift, prostrate

prostrate thyself before Him & say with deepest reverence—O my Lord, what an exchange! Thy Heart for mine! And I know that Thou givest Thyself unreservedly & for ever; but, alas, how changeable, how faithless am I. How often have I not given Thee this heart, which again I venture to offer Thee this day, how often given it & as often taken it back! Teach me, O Lord, I beseech Thee, to give it up to Thee wholly & for ever. Say with a holy Man in the confusion & bitterness of thy Soul—Immensity loves us; Love which passes all knowledge loves us; Eternity loves us; & yet we measure our love.

Pray for that Divine Wisdom for which Solomon prayed, that It may be with thee, & act in thee, that in all things thou mayest be enabled to discern what would be most pleasing to God Who loves thee, & Whom thou desirest to love. Give me Wisdom that sitteth by Thy Throne; & reject me not from among Thy Children. O send her out of Thy holy Heavens, & from the Throne of Thy Glory, that being present, she may labour with me, that I may know what is pleasing unto Thee.

II. Behold with the eye of Faith our Lord Jesus Christ, Who says to thee—Love Me, for I have loved thee. I have loved thee from Eternity, I have loved thee in time, I have lived & died for thee; I love thee still, I have invented this Mystery of self-abasement & love for thee, in which I share thine exile; & if thou wilt I will love thee through all Eternity. Love Me, for I have loved thee. O my Soul, do thou answer Him with feelings of deepest reverence & love—What have I done, what have I suffered for Thee, my Lord? I beseech Thee write Thy Law of Love deep into my Soul.

Conferences. 315

Soul. Teach me, O Lord, the Way of Thy Statutes, & I shall keep it unto the end. Who could teach me Thy Law except Thyself, Blessed Lord? My desires, my tears, my cries have been powerless. O Thou with Whom all things are possible, say to my heart—*GOD is Love.*

Thou art surprised that after so many Communions thou art still the same as before; remember that earthly love hinders the union of thy heart with the Heart of our Lord Jesus Christ, & see how many are the ties by which thou art still bound to creatures, to thyself; to the love of honour & esteem; think how sensitive thou art still to blame, to contempt, to slight, to neglect, how many plans thou formest out of God; how little thou hast learnt to moderate the restless activity of thy mind.

Long to be enabled to say truthfully with a Saint of old—If I knew a single fibre in my heart which is not God's I would tear it out. When thou hast learnt to do this God will give thee His Grace without measure.

Friday.

I. Behold with the eye of Faith our Lord Jesu Christ in the depth of thy heart offering thee His sacred Heart, & saying—The Love for thy Soul which glows in My Heart is so fervent that it rises up unceasingly in an ever-blazing flame; so humble, that it shrinks from no self-abasement; so strong & generous, that it triumphs over all torments & over death itself; so liberal, that it gives all, even itself: what dost thou offer Me in return? And do thou, O my Soul, lying prostrate at His Feet answer Him thus—O Blessed Lord, kindle in my Soul one spark of the Love which glows

glows in Thine, & I shall in the strength of that Love be enabled to go joyfully through all shame & suffering, & toil, & peril, & temptation for Thy Name's sake; & at last, when I have sacrificed all, even my very life, I shall still know that I have done nothing worthy of Thy Love.

Remember that our LORD JESUS CHRIST does not only give Himself to thee, to fill thy Soul with the sweetness of Divine Consolation, but in order that thou shouldest become more energetic in thy actions, stronger in temptation, more generous in the practice of holiness, more careful in fulfilling all thy duties, more perfect in thy ordinary actions.

Pray our LORD that the remembrance of the sufferings which He endured to win thy Soul may teach thee to bear for Him all sorrow.

II. Behold with the eye of Faith our LORD JESUS CHRIST in the depth of thy heart, Who says to thee—Desirest thou to give Me thy heart as a resting-place for My suffering Love, which the world despiseth? If this is thy desire, thy motto must be—Love & Suffering; one Heart, one Love, one GOD. O my Soul, make answer to thy LORD, prostrating thyself before Him, & thanking Him for bestowing upon thee the privilege of associating thee with His Sufferings, & saying to Him—Can the Bride rejoice, when the Bridegroom is sorrowful? The day will come, when she shall rejoice, indeed, the day when He shall appear in Power & great Glory, & then wonder shall take her joy from her.

Remember that this world has nothing for thee, but the Cross; but thy Cross is the Cross of JESUS, the Cross for the Love of JESUS, the Cross in the Heart of JESUS.

Love

Love & Suffering! The one is inseparable from the other; the one is the sweetness of the other. The Heart which loved more than any other heart, the Heart of Jesus, has also suffered more than any other. Behold whether there be any sorrow like unto My Sorrow? This thought makes suffering precious to all who love our Lord. Thou art afraid of it, thou shrinkest from it, thou dost not love Him much.

Saturday.

I. Behold with the eye of Faith our Lord Jesus Christ, the Spouse of thy Soul, Who saith to thee— Thou shalt make My wounded Heart thy continual & abiding Home. From henceforth thou shalt live only in Me, thou art dead, & thy life is hid with Me in God. Thou must think no more of thy body than if it had already ceased to exist; all thy powers, all thy senses must be buried in Me. Thou must be dumb, deaf, blind to all earthly objects of desire. Thou must have no desire, no affection of thy own, no will but Mine, thou must surrender thy judgment to Me, thou must seek nothing out of Me, for I will be All in All to thee.

Cast thyself, O my Soul, at His sacred Feet, & answer Him—Alas, my Lord, Thou proposest me the way of perfection! Canst Thou indeed count me among Thy Faithful; alas, if all Thine Elect were like me, how poor, how imperfect would be Thy Court, O my King.

Rejoice to think that there are not only in Heaven, but on earth many Souls who make up, as it were their love for thy coldness, thy cowardice, thine inconstancy,

ftancy, & whofe life is fo completely united with that of our LORD, fo loft in His, that they can indeed fay with the holy Apoftle—*I live, yet not I, but CHRIST liveth in me.*

II. Behold with the eye of Faith in the very depth of thy heart our LORD JESUS CHRIST, Who comes to thee from Edom, with Raiment dyed in Blood, to remind thee of the Price which He paid for thy Redemption, & who invites thee to enlift again in the army of the Heavenly King, with thefe Almighty Words, which have won fo many hearts—Come & follow Me. *Who is this, that cometh from Edom, with dyed garments from Bozrah? This, that is glorious in His Apparel, travelling in the greatnefs of His Strength? I, that speak in Righteoufnefs, Mighty to fave.* O my Soul, proftrate thyfelf before Him, put thy hands into His pierced Hands, & renew all thy vows, which bind thee to Him; thy promifes made for thee at thy Baptifm, & all other acts of felf-dedication, by which thou haft bound thyfelf to belong to Him alone.

Mourn in the bitternefs of thy Soul the lofs of that precious Robe of Baptifmal purity, with which thou wert clothed at thy Baptifm, & which made thee fo precious in the eyes of GOD, of the holy Angels, & of all the Saints of the LORD.

Pray fervently for Grace to live wholly to the Glory of GOD, & to defend it againft His enemies with the facred zeal with which a loving fon would defend the honour of his father.

Aspirations

AFTER THE BLESSED SACRAMENT.

Sunday.

O mighty Love of God, how different is thine influence from that of this world's love. This desires no company, fearing to lose what it possesses; but the Love of God, the more numerous its lovers, the greater it becomes; & thus its joys are diminished by seeing that all do not enjoy that good. O my Good, thus it happens, that in the highest pleasures & delights that are enjoyed with Thee, we are pained by the remembrance of the many who desire not Thy Joys, & of those who will for ever lose them.. Therefore the Soul seeks to find companions, & willingly departs from her own joy with the hope of doing somewhat to lead others unto it.

But, O my Heavenly Father, would it not be better to leave such wishes for times when the Soul is less filled with Thy pleasures, & now to occupy myself only in enjoying Thee?

O my Jesus, how great is the Love Thou hast for the children of men, since the greatest service they can render Thee is, for Thy Love to leave all others for Thee, & then art Thou most entirely possessed. For though the joy of the will satisfies not greatly, yet the Soul rejoices that she is pleasing unto Thee, & sees that our joys on earth (though given by Thee) are uncertain, unless accompanied by love to our neighbour. Who loves not him, loves not Thee, my Lord; since

by

by Thy BLOOD so freely shed, we see how great Love Thou hast for the sons of men.

Monday.

O my Hope, my Father, my Creator, my true LORD & Brother, when I consider how Thou sayest that Thy Delights are with the sons of men, my Soul rejoices greatly. O LORD of Heaven & earth, what words are these? They are such that no sinner need distrust Thee. Hast Thou none, O LORD, with whom to delight Thyself, that Thou seekest such a worm as I am? Thy Voice was heard at the Baptism, saying —*This is My Beloved SON, in Whom I am well pleased.* Are we then, LORD, to be equal with Him? Oh, what most great compassion, what favour so undeserved, & yet we altogether forget all this. Remember, my GOD, our so great misery; behold our infirmity, for Thou knowest all things.

O my Soul, consider the great Delight that the FATHER hath in knowing the SON, & the SON in knowing the FATHER, & the Fervour with which the HOLY SPIRIT is united with Them, and how neither separates Himself from this Love & Knowledge, for they are ONE. These Sovereign Persons know, love, & delight one Another. What need then is there of my love? Why dost Thou desire it, O my GOD? or what dost Thou gain? Oh, blessed be Thou, blessed be Thou for ever. Let all things praise Thee, O LORD, without end; since there can be no end in Thee. Be glad, O my Soul, that there is Who can love GOD as He deserves. Be glad that there is Who knows His Goodness & Worthiness. Give Him thanks that He gave us on earth One Who knows Him, even His Own Son.

With such an aid thou canst approach & pray, that since His Divine Majesty delights itself with thee, all worldly things may be unable to draw thee away from delighting thyself & rejoicing in the Greatness of GOD, & in His Worthiness to be loved & praised; & that He would help thee, so that thou mayest have some little portion in blessing His holy Name; & mayest be able to say in truth—My Soul doth magnify & praise the LORD.

Tuesday.

O LORD my GOD, what Words of Life Thou hast, wherein all mortals might find what they desired if they would but seek. But what marvel, dear LORD, that we forget Thy Words through the madness & infirmity caused by our evil deeds?

O my GOD, my GOD, Creator of all, & what is all creation if Thou, LORD, shouldst will to create yet more? for Thou art Almighty, & Thy Works are past finding out.

Grant then, LORD, that Thy Words may not depart from my mind. Thou sayest—*Come unto Me, all ye that are weary & heavy laden, & I will give you rest.* What more, LORD, do we need? What do we ask? Why do men lose themselves in this world but to seek rest? O LORD, my LORD, what unhappiness, what blindness is this, that we seek where it is impossible to find. Pity, O Creator, these Thy creatures. Behold how we neither understand ourselves, nor know what we want, nor attain what we seek.

LORD,

Lord, give us light; for more needful is it than to him who was born blind, since he desired to see the light & could not; but now, Lord, men will not see. Oh, incurable evil! Here, Lord, show Thy Power, show Thy Mercy. And yet how hard a thing, my God, do I ask of Thee, that Thou wouldest love those who love not Thee; that Thou wouldest open to those that do not knock; that Thou wouldest give health to those who love sickness & seek it. Thou sayest, Lord, that Thou art come to seek sinners. These are the true sinners. Look not, my God, on our blindness; but on the Precious Blood, which Thy Son shed for us. Lord, we are Thy Work; let Thy Goodness & Mercy help us.

Wednesday.

O Merciful & Loving Lord of my life, Thou sayest —*Let him that is athirst come, & I will give him drink.* O Life, Who givest life to all, deny me not this most precious Water, which Thou promisest to those who desire it. Lord, I desire it; I ask for it; I come to Thee. Hide not Thyself, Lord, from me, for Thou knowest my necessity, and what is the true healing for the Soul which Thou hast wounded.

O Lord, how many are the fires of this world. Some consume the Soul; others purify it, that it may live, ever rejoicing in Thee. O living Fountains of the Wounds of my God, how will ye ever flow abundantly for our support. And how safely will he pass through this miserable life, who seeks to be sustained by this Divine Drink.

Thursday.

Thursday.

O JESU, how long is the life of man, though it be called brief. Brief, O my GOD, to gain therein Life everlasting; but very long for the Soul which yearns to be present with GOD. What remedy dost Thou give for this suffering? There is none; save that we are suffering for Thee.

Since then, O my GOD, we must live, let us live for Thee. Away with all our own desires, & interests. What greater gain than to please Thee, O my Happiness? O my GOD, what shall I do to please Thee? Worthless indeed are my services, even should I do many for my GOD. Why then must I abide in this misery? To do the Will of GOD, what can be greater gain?

Wait, my Soul, wait; for thou knowest not the day nor the hour. Watch with care; for all passes briefly; although thy longing makes the certain appear uncertain, & the brief time to appear long. Behold, the more thou fightest, the more thou wilt show thy love for GOD; & the more thou wilt enjoy thy Beloved with a joy & delight which can never end.

Friday.

O my GOD & my Wisdom, Infinite, & Perfect above & beyond all understanding angelic or human. O Love, who lovest me more than I can love myself or can understand. Why, LORD, should I desire more than Thou willest to give me? Why should I weary myself in asking, since of all things which my understanding devises & my desires long for, Thou knowest already

ready the end & final result, while I understand not what is for my own profit? The very thing which my Soul expects to turn out for her gain, may be my loss. For if I ask Thee to deliver me from some labour, & that should have for its end my mortification, what is it, LORD, that I ask? If I ask Thee to lay it on me, perchance it suits not my endurance which is yet weak & cannot bear so great a trial. Or if I pass through it, & be not strong in humility, perhaps I shall think that I have done somewhat, whilst Thou, my GOD, hast done it all.

How miserable is the wisdom of mortal men, how uncertain their foresight. Do Thou, by Thy Wisdom & Foresight, order the necessary means whereby my Soul may serve Thee more than its own pleasure. Chastise me not, by giving that which I seek or desire, if Thou desire it not. Let self die in me, & let Another live in me, Who is greater than self & for me better than self. Let Him reign & let me be His captive, since my Soul desires no other liberty. How shall that be free which is apart from the Supreme? What more miserable slavery, than for the Soul to be loosed from the Hand of its Creator?

Saturday.

How long, O LORD, is my banishment from Thee? O my Soul, when will be that happy day when thou shalt find thyself swallowed up in the infinite ocean of Supreme Truth; whence thou shalt no longer be free to wander; nor wilt desire to be so, for thou shalt be secure from all misery; incorporated into the Life of thy GOD. He is Blessed, because He knows & loves & joys in Himself, with no possibility of being otherwise.

wise. And then, my Soul, wilt thou enter into thy rest when thou art interpenetrated by this Supreme Good, understandest what He understandeth, lovest what He loveth, enjoyest what He enjoyeth, & losest thine own changeable will. Then, then will there be no more change, since the Grace of GOD hath had power to make thee partaker of the Divine Nature, with such perfection that thou wilt never be able or desire to be able to forget the Chief Good, nor cease to enjoy Him with His Love.

Blessed are they who are written in this book of life. Rather would I live & die, seeking & hoping for this Life eternal, than to possess all creatures & all goods that have an end. Forsake me not, O LORD, for in Thee is my hope. Let me ever serve Thee, & make me what Thou willest.

Affections:

ON THE SACRAMENT OF LOVE.

Sunday.

My delights were with the sons of men.

The LORD is in this place. Love drew Him from Heaven to die for us on earth. Love still constrains Him to abide with us, beneath the Sacramental Veil: for, My delights, saith He, were with the sons of men. How shall we sin against a GOD Who so loveth us? Have we no delight in Him? we, above all men, who have been admitted to dwell in His Courts? Greatly is that slave honoured, whom the King welcomes to his

his palace. This is the Palace of the True King; the abode where we dwell with Jesus. Let us learn how to render Him thanks for His great Mercy, & how to profit by these precious moments. Behold, O Lord my God, I kneel before that Altar where, for my sake, Thou art present. Thou art the Fountain of all Blessing, the Healer of all sickness, the Treasure of all the poor. Look in pity upon me, most poor, most frail, most sinful: I cast myself before Thy Feet: have mercy upon me. I own my misery, & yet I come to Thee in faith, believing, that Thou hast been pleased to come down from Heaven for very love of me. I praise Thee, I thank Thee, I love Thee, dearest Lord: & if Thou wilt that I ask an alms of Thee, this thing I ask; O hear Thou my petition—I desire to sin no more against Thee, & I pray that Thou wouldst give me Light & Grace to love Thee with all my might. Lord, I love Thee with all my Soul, & all my powers. Grant that I may say this truly, & for ever.

Monday.

Where your treasure is, there will your heart be also.

So that the hearts of the Saints, & all their love, are wrapt up in the Holy Sacrament, because they love & delight in none save Jesus. O Lord most dear, most marvellously veiled beneath Sacramental Forms, Who, for love of me, art present on Thine Altar, draw my heart, I pray Thee, to Thyself, that it may think of none, may love, may seek, may hope in none save Thee. Do this, O Lord, for Thine own Passion's sake, wherein my trust is fixed.

My Hidden Saviour, how tender are the devices of
that

that Love whereby Thou wouldſt win Souls to Thee. O Eternal Word made Man, Thou wert not content to die for us; Thou haſt moreover given us this Sacrament to be our companion, our ſupport, & the earneſt of Paradiſe. Thou appeareſt among us, now as a Child laid in a manger, now as a poor Man in a workſhop, now as a criminal upon a Croſs, now as Bread upon an Altar. Couldſt Thou deviſe aught more to gain our love? O worthy of infinite love, when ſhall I truly begin to correſpond to ſuch ineffable tenderneſs? Lord, I deſire to live only to Thy Love. What ſhall my life profit me, except I ſpend it all in loving & ſerving Thee, my Deareſt Saviour, Who didſt ſpend all Thy Life for me? And what have I to love, ſave Thee, Who art all Beauty, all Tenderneſs, all Gentleneſs, all Love, all Lovelineſs? Let my Soul live only to love Thee, let it melt at the very remembrance of Thy Love, & let the ſlighteſt mention of the Manger, of the Croſs, or of the Sacrament kindle within me the deſire to do great things for Thee, O Jesu, Who haſt done ſo great things for me.

Tuesday.

Lo! I am with you alway, even unto the end of the world.

The loving Shepherd, Who gave His Life for us His Sheep, would not part from us, even in death. Behold, beloved, ſaith He, I am ever with you: for your ſakes I abide in the Holy Sacrament: here ye ſhall find Me whenever ye deſire the ſtrength & comfort of My Preſence; I will never leave you nor forſake you.

O Lord moſt ſweet, O Saviour moſt tender, I come indeed

indeed before Thy Presence now, but oh, how far beyond my love for Thee is that wherewith Thou on Thy part comest unto me when Thou dost enter into my Soul at the moment of Communion. Then, Thou art not only present with me, but Thou dost give Thyself to me for food: Thou dost wholly unite & join Thyself to me, so that in good truth I can say: O LORD Beloved, Thou art mine. If then Thou dost wholly give Thyself to me, it is meet that I wholly give myself to Thee. I am a worm, Thou art GOD, O GOD of Love! O Love of my Soul! when, when shall I be truly Thine, not in name only, but in very deed? Thou, LORD, canst make me wholly Thine: O increase my trust in the merits of Thy Blood, that I may obtain of Thee this one Grace, to be entirely Thine before I die. Thou knowest, O LORD, the desires of all hearts; shut not Thy merciful ears to the prayer of a Soul which truly yearns to love Thee. I desire to love Thee with all my might, & to obey Thy Will in all things, without self-seeking, consolation, or reward. I desire to serve Thee for love, for no other end save that of pleasing Thee, Who dost so inexpressibly love me. The love of Thee will be my reward. O beloved SON of the Eternal FATHER, take my liberty, my life, my will, take all I have, take my whole self, & give Thyself to me. I love Thee, seek Thee, long for Thee; yea, with desire do I desire Thee.

Wednesday.

This shall be My rest for ever: here will I dwell, for I have a delight therein.

If this be so, O LORD, if love thus constrained Thee to abide among us, & to find Thy rest upon our Altars,

it

it is fitting that our hearts should likewise abide with Thee, & in Thee find all rest & all delight. Blessed are ye, O loving Souls, who know no rest so sweet as that ye find in the most Blessed Eucharist. And blessed were I, if, from this day forth, I know no greater joy than to be ever in Thy Presence, or at the least to bear the thought of Thee within my heart, as Thou, Lord, dost will ever to be with me, & ever to bear me on Thy Heart.

Lord, I bewail from my heart the time past of my life, wherein I loved Thee not. Blessed be the Patience of my God, Who hath borne my want of love with such long-suffering. And yet, Thou waitest to be gracious: whence is this to me, O God? because Thou wouldest win my heart, even mine, by Thine unspeakable Love & Mercy. Amen, O Lord: be it unto me according to Thy Will: I yield myself to Thee, my life, whether long or short, is a little thing to offer Thee: yet, Lord, accept it of Thy Mercy: put away my ingratitude & all my sin, & help me to be wholly Thine. In Thee I trust, O Jesu, Who didst so tenderly love & care for me while I fled from Thee, & despised Thee: wilt Thou not much more bless me when I seek Thee & long to love Thee? Grant me this Grace, O Thou Who art infinitely worthy of all Love. I love Thee with all my heart, beyond all things created; I love Thee more than myself, more than my life. O infinite Goodness, I do repent me of my sins past; forgive me, I beseech Thee, & with Thy pardon grant me Grace earnestly to love Thee till death in this life, & to all eternity in the next. O God most Mighty, show forth, I pray Thee, Thy Power, & turn my ingratitude into burning love. Do this, O Jesu, for
Thine

Thine own Merit's fake. Thus I defire, thus I will henceforth to live: Thou haft given me the will, give me alfo ftrength to perform it.

Thursday.

In that day there fhall be a Fountain opened to the houfe of David & to the inhabitants of Jerufalem for fin & for uncleannefs.

The Fountain foretold by the Prophet, is the Bleffed Sacrament, whither whofo will, may come, to wafh away every ftain of fin. Where elfe fhould we turn, when through frailty we have fallen? Yea, LORD JESU, I will alway thus come to Thee; I know that thefe bleffed Waters not only purify my Soul, but give it light, & ftrength, & love. I know Thou waiteft for me here, that Thou mayeft give me all thefe Bleffings. Even fo, deareft LORD; wafh me, I befeech Thee, from all the fins which I have this day committed, for, behold I grieve from my heart that I have thereby offended Thee: Grant me ftrength that I may fall no more, & that I may cheerfully fuffer for Thy Sake, & O kindle Thou the fire of Thy Love in my heart.

O LORD, my glorious Portion, & my only Good, I fee that Thou didft therefore inftitute this Sacrament, & art prefent on this Altar, becaufe Thou wouldft be loved by me: therefore didft Thou give me a heart capable of Thy Love. But why is it, alas, fo cold & dead? Thy Love at leaft deferves return. It were a fmall thing that I fhould fpend myfelf for Thee Who diedft for me, yea, Who doft daily offer Thyfelf for me. Thou art GOD Almighty & Infinite; I am a miferable worm. I do defire to love Thee with that

perfect

perfect love which is Thy due. Help me, O JESU, help me to love Thee, & so to fulfil all Thy Will.

Friday.

Cry out & shout, thou inhabitant of Zion: for great is the Holy ONE of Israel in the midst of thee.

O LORD, what then should be our joy, our hope & love, when we know that in the midst of us abides the Holiest of the Holy, Very GOD of Very GOD, He Whose Presence is the bliss of Saints in Paradise, He Who is Love itself. This Sacrament is not only the Sacrament of Love: it is Love, it is GOD Himself, Who for the marvellous Love He bears His creatures, names Himself, & is very Love. Yet, O JESU, I hear Thee complain that Thou camest, for our sakes to be our guests, & that we received Thee not. Alas, LORD, it is too true: I, even I, am among those who have neglected Thee, & not even cared to come before Thy Presence. Chastise me as Thou wilt: yet not as I deserve, by the withdrawal of Thy Presence: nay, for I will strive to make amends for my irreverence & neglect. From this day forth I will draw nigh to Thee as often, & abide in Thy Presence as long, as shall be possible to me. O most Pitiful SAVIOUR, grant that I may be faithful unto Thee, & that my fervour may kindle the love of others. Behold, I hear the Words of the Eternal FATHER, saying—*This is My Beloved SON, in Whom I am well pleased.* GOD delighteth in Thee: to whom else then should I seek, who am but dust & ashes; with whom else then should I dwell in this vale of tears? O consuming Fire, destroy in me all love of things created, lest they wean my my heart from Thee. *LORD, if Thou wilt, Thou canst make me clean.* So much Thou hast done for me: do this thing likewise; drive from my heart all love that tendeth not to Thee. Behold, I give myself to Thee: this day I consecrate my life to the love of the most Holy Sacrament. Thou, O JESU, shalt be my comfort & my love in life & death, & Thou shalt lead me unto Bliss eternal.

Saturday.

Behold, I stand at the door & knock.

O most tender Shepherd, Who for love of Thy sheep wast not content to die upon the Altar of the Cross, but didst moreover deign to hide Thyself in this Divine Sacrament, that so Thou mightest knock at the door of our hearts, & we might open unto Thee. O that I could taste the sweetness of Thy Presence, like Thy holy Bride in the Canticles, saying—*I sat down under His shadow with great delight.* Oh, if I loved Thee, if I loved Thee truly, sweetest SAVIOUR, I should fain abide before Thine Altar day & night. Here, kneeling before Thy veiled Majesty, I should feel the joy & happiness which thrill the hearts that beat for Thee alone. Draw me by the fragrance of Thy Beauty & of the matchless Love which Thou dost here display. Yea, LORD, then shall I leave all creatures & all earthly pleasures, to run after Thee, O JESU. All manner of pleasant fruits are laid up for their Beloved by those happy Souls whose hearts are laid upon His Altar. But I, O LORD, blush to come before Thee. I miserable, poor, & naked. None shall appear before Me empty—thus Thou speakest; what then do I here?

What shall I do? Must I come no more into Thy Presence? Nay, Lord, I know that such is not Thy will, & therefore, I will come, poor as I am, beseeching Thee to grant me the Gifts which Thou desirest at my hands. Therefore, O Jesu, dost Thou abide in this Sacrament, not only to be the Reward of loving Souls, but also to supply the poor out of Thy boundless Treasures.

O let Thy gracious Work begin. I adore Thee, O Thou Lover of men. O true Shepherd of the sheep: I approach Thy threshold, but I have nought to offer Thee save this miserable heart. I consecrate it to Thy Love & resign it to Thy good pleasure. O draw it & bind it to Thyself according to Thy will, so that I may henceforth say joyfully with Thine Apostle that I am bound with the chain of Thy Love. O Lord, unite me wholly to Thyself: make me even forget myself, so that I may at last gladly lose all things, & my own self also, in order to find Thee & love Thee alone & for ever. Lord Jesu, I love Thee, I cling to Thee: O let me never lose Thee; fill me with Thy Love & never more depart from me.

Acts of Contrition.

Prayer before Confession.

To Thee, most Gentle Jesu, my Refuge & Consolation, I come mourning & sorrowful as I review before Thee in the littleness of my Soul, my years & my sins. To Thee I pour forth words of sorrow, beseeching Thy Mercy, that Thou wouldest do Thy work, which is to have mercy & to forgive, taking away my my sins that are my greatest grief. Despise not Thou the prayers & the sighings of a lost sheep, a prodigal son, returning to Thy tender compassion from a far country; for Thou hast no pleasure in the death of him that dieth, Who didst deign to suffer death that I might not die; I, a worm of earth have returned Thee evil for good, & what evil & grievous sins for gifts so great & rich. And yet Thou wilt speak to Thy Spouse, even my erring Soul, after she hath committed adultery with many lovers, that she may return to Thee. And do Thou sustain her, for Thy mercy is over all Thy works, & Thy lovingkindness is greater than mine iniquity: therefore I arise & come to Thee with a broken & contrite heart. I come for cleansing, O Fountain of eternal Life, for Whom I thirst as the hart for the water brooks. I come that I may be enlightened & love Thee, O my Light. I acknowledge my injustice against myself. Send forth Thy Light & Thy Truth & enlighten my understanding that I may clearly know all the evils which I have done, & the good which I have left undone, & may humbly confess my faults. And do Thou Who hast compassion upon all men, & hatest nothing that Thou hast made, suffer me not to become corrupt in mine uncleanness. Make me to leave my evil habits & to occupy myself in the works that please Thee, that where sin hath abounded Thy Grace may yet more abound. And whereas I have felt that I was wandering from Thee, may I, being turned again, seek Thee with tenfold earnestness. Most merciful Jesus, I grieve for my sins one & all, & abhor them above all evils, not with my barren & imperfect heart alone, but also with the heart & feeling of all true penitents,

from

from a willing love for Thee, for Thou art GOD, most worthy of infinite love: & I firmly resolve rather to undergo any evils than again to consent unto sin. Moreover I would most thoroughly confess & make entire restitution to Thee & to my neighbour, & henceforth avoid all occasion of sin. Whatsoever is wanting in me may Thy Death, Thy Blood, & Thy exceeding Merits supply; trusting wherein, I hope to obtain pardon, & grace to amend my ways, & to continue steadfast in that which is good unto the end. And now, LORD, Who hast granted unto me to know my sins, do Thou perfect my contrition. Make me to burn with the fire of Thy love, & keep far from me all that is displeasing to Thy Majesty. Purify in me all that is pleasing unto Thee, that I may live unto Thee & not unto myself, & may die in Thee and for Thee, my SAVIOUR, Who livest & reignest for ever & ever. Amen.

Acts of Contrition.

I. O LORD GOD Almighty, covered with shame & confusion of face I appear before Thee, loaded with the intolerable burden of my many sins by which, by thought, word, & deed I have so often offended against Thy Divine Majesty, & have so greatly injured my own immortal Soul. Alas, O my GOD, with what confidence shall I appear in Thy Presence; or how shall I presume to lift up my eyes to Thee, weighed down as I am with so many sins, & sullied with the stains of so many transgressions? Ah, my Good & Gracious Master, if Thou shalt enter into judgment with Thy servant, how shall I be able to stand before Thee? But Thou hast revealed Thyself as a GOD of

Pity & Compassion, willing to forgive the sins of those that truly repent, & that with contrition, confession, & satisfaction turn unto Thee for pardon. Wherefore, O my LORD, I return unto Thee, full of grief & sorrow for having offended Thee. And because I have nothing of my own wherewith to atone for my numberless sins, behold, O Sovereign Judge, I offer unto Thee this most adorable Sacrifice of the very BODY, BLOOD, SOUL, & DIVINITY of Thine only SON JESUS CHRIST, as a one, full, perfect, & sufficient Sacrifice, Oblation, & Satisfaction for the sins of the whole world, & especially for those I have myself committed against Thee, O most Mighty GOD, through the merits of this Spotless VICTIM, & of the Bloody Sacrifice which He offered on the Cross; I pray, I beg, I beseech, I implore Thee to be appeased with me, Thy unworthy Servant, & with all true penitents, & to grant unto me, & to all Thy faithful ones, perfect contrition & a hearty penitence, which may produce a repentance not to be repented of. Hear, O Merciful FATHER, I most humbly beseech Thee; hearken unto the Sacred BLOOD of JESUS, which cries unto Thee continually, not for vengeance but for pardon, mercy, & peace. Grant me, Dear LORD, pardon through the Precious BLOOD; forgive me all that is past, & think no more of it; give me Grace to amend my life, & never more to offend Thee in time to come; give me strength to persevere in Thy holy Service, in all Good Works; & grant that I may set forth Thy Glory to the end of my life, & may hereafter for ever sing the praises of Thy Mercy in the Congregation of the Saints.

II. O Only SON of GOD, JESUS, my LORD & my Redeemer,

Redeemer, how great & ineffable are the Blessings I have received from Thee. Thou hast framed me from the dust of the earth; Thou hast created my Soul out of nothing, according to Thy Image & Likeness, enduing me with understanding, memory, & will; Thou hast given me a free will, together with all my members & senses, in order that I might know & love Thee; Thou hast covered me in my mother's womb, to the end I might not die without the saving Water of Holy Baptism. After so many sins as I have multiplied against Thee, Thou hast had long Patience with me, even unto this hour, whilst many others, less guilty than myself, whom Thou hast not so long expected to Repentance, are now in torment. Besides this, O my LORD, Thou hast vouchsafed to make Thyself MAN, & to converse amongst men for my sake. For me Thou wouldest suffer grievous Afflictions, a bitter Agony, Sorrow of Soul, & a Bloody Sweat. Thou wouldest be apprehended, bound, buffeted, spit upon, struck, injured, & blasphemed. Thou wouldest be also clad, at one time in a white Robe, & at another in a Purple Garment in mockery. For me Thou wouldest be beaten, scourged, crowned with thorns, struck with a reed upon Thy sacred Head; Thou wouldest be blindfolded, condemned to Death & led to the place of execution with a heavy Cross upon Thy Shoulders, to which Thou wouldest be fastened with most sharp & cruel nails. Thou wouldest be placed between two thieves, & numbered amongst the wicked. Thou wouldest have gall & vinegar presented to Thee for Thy last draught; & finally, Thou wouldst lose Thy Life by a most shameful Death. In this manner, O my LORD, & with these Sufferings hast Thou redeemed

deemed me; & yet, LORD JESUS, I, most ungrateful for so great Benefits, have many times crucified Thee afresh by my sins.

Moreover, what shall I say of the fearful manner in which I have abused Thy Holy Sacraments, those Blessed Remedies for sin which Thou hast purchased for me with Thy most Precious BLOOD? Thou hast washed & redeemed me in Holy Baptism, as one belonging to Thyself. There hast Thou consecrated me as Thy Holy Temple; Thou hast anointed me as a Priest, as a King, as a Soldier who ought incessantly to fight against Thy enemies; there Thou hast espoused my Soul to Thyself, & hast adorned her with all the Ornaments needful to so high a Dignity. What have I done with all these Jewels? What care have I taken to preserve such priceless Riches? Thou hast adopted me as a Son; & I have sold myself a slave to sin. Thou hast consecrated me Thy Temple; & I have made myself a very den of Devils. Thou hast armed me as a soldier; & I have taken part with Thy enemies. Thou hast anointed me a King; & I have employed the power Thou hast given me in rebelling against Thee. Thou hast espoused my Soul to Thyself in perpetual charity; & I have loved vanity more than Truth, & have preferred the creature before the Creator.

It is now time, O my LORD & my GOD, that he who hath committed all these sins should repent of them. And this is what Thou hast expected of me, ever since Thou hast given me life. For this Thou hast so often called me, & so long borne with me. For this Thou hast sometimes chastised me, at others comforted me; Thy infinite Goodness having used all
possible

possible means to draw me unto Thee. Thou hast patiently awaited me; & I have abused Thy Patience. Thou hast called me; & I have shut my ears against Thy Divine Voice. Thou hast given me time to repent; & I have employed it in pride & vanity. Thou hast smitten me; & I have been insensible to Thy Strokes. Thou hast chastised me; & I have rejected Thy Discipline. Thou hast laboured & striven to purify me; yet neither Thy merciful Sufferings on the one side, nor Thy just Chastisements on the other, have been able to quench my love for sin. Nevertheless, LORD JESU, since Thou hast suffered so much for me, & hast commanded me never to lose confidence in Thee, I return with my whole heart to Thy boundless Mercy, beseeching Thee to give me Grace for amendment, in order that for the time to come I may love & serve Thee in such manner that I may never be separated from Thee, world without end.

Prayer after Confession.

I render Thee thanks, O LORD, my FATHER, & the Ruler of my life, because Thou hast not dealt with me after my sins, but hast made Mercy to rejoice against Judgment, & hast cast all my sins into the depth of the sea. O my GOD, that I could excite within me such true Contrition as that which the man after Thine own Heart, David, felt; or as that which S. Peter, S. Mary Magdalene, & other Penitents have felt for their sins. How earnestly I would that my head were waters, & my eyes a fountain of tears, until my sins were washed away, & Thou dost graciously show me the Light of Thy Countenance. But my Soul has become in Thy sight as a land where no water is; my strength is dried up like a potsherd. And since my strength has departed from me, this only have I left, to lift up mine eyes to my Redeemer, & to offer unto Thee His Tears, which He poured out so abundantly for me; that appeased thereby, Thou mayest open to me the doors of Thy Mercy, & receive me graciously when I flee unto Thee from mine enemies. Look on me, & have mercy on me, O Patient & Merciful LORD; speak to my stony heart; strike it with the rod of Thy Power, that the streams of compunction may flow, those healing waters, by which my Soul shall be cleansed. Strengthen within me, I beseech Thee, whatever Thou hast wrought in me; & may my Confession be pleasing & acceptable unto Thee, Thy Goodness & Mercy supplying all its deficiencies. I ask for pardon & absolution, O my GOD, with a full determination, Thy Grace assisting me, to sin again no more for ever; & to apply myself to good works. O Thou that never failest them that seek Thee, suffer me no longer to wander after the vanities of this life; for day after day & year after year pass by, & I advance not in holiness. Turn Thou then, & have mercy upon me, Thy most unworthy servant; & be not so mindful of my wickedness as to be unmindful of Thy Goodness; for if I have committed that for which Thou canst condemn me, Thou hast not left undone that by which Thou wilt save me, & receive me into Thy Favour, O my GOD, Who livest & reignest for ever & ever.

Commemoration of the Passion.

I. Most merciful FATHER, I will recall to mind, & my Soul shall languish within me; I will recall with
sighs

sighs & tears all the Agony & Passion & most bitter Death of Thy Son, my Lord Jesus Christ, because He, my Salvation & my Life, hath hung upon the Tree before mine eyes, offering Himself to Thee as a Sacrifice, for my Salvation & that of all the world. This lively Oblation which Thou in much pity didst send to be offered upon the altar of the Cross for us, this same I now offer to Thee, celebrating & representing His Passion & Death, as He Himself commanded when He said that we should do the same in remembrance of Him. Be mindful therefore of His Humility, Patience, Love, Gentleness, & Obedience. Consider His pains, His fastings, His being rejected, reviled, bound, scourged, & unjustly condemned. Look upon the Face of Thine Anointed, & behold Him more beautiful than the sons of men, so marred by dishonour, by injuries, by stripes, by bruisings, by smitings, that there is no form nor comeliness in Him. See that most noble Head furrowed with the piercings of the thorns & bruised by blows. See that most modest Face defiled by spittings, wounded by buffetings, stained with blood. See those most loving Eyes suffused with tears, & blindfolded that they might mock Him. See that most sweet Mouth parched with most burning thirst, & given gall & vinegar to drink. See that Back lacerated by the stripes, & the Shoulders bending beneath the weight of the Cross. See those most adorable Arms bound with cords, & cruelly extended on the Cross. See those most innocent Hands, pierced with the hardest nails. See those delicate Feet wearied with so many journeyings, & at length fastened to the Cross. See that much to be revered Body suspended on the Cross for us, wounded, dead, & buried. See that

that most precious Blood mercifully poured out, even to the last drop, for our Salvation. For I offer & represent these things unto Thee with all the fervour of devotion of which I am capable, humbly praying that the same love with which Thou didst yield up Thy SON for us may constrain Thee to have mercy upon all for whom He, being made obedient unto death, did deign to undergo the Cross. Amen.

II. O LORD GOD Almighty, I am covered with shame & confusion of face; I am filled with fear & trembling at Thy Presence. For who am I to appear before Thee? & what is Thy servant that he should worship before Thy Holy Altar? Conscious, O my GOD, of my great unworthiness, I prostrate myself before Thy Divine Majesty, to cry for mercy through the Precious BLOOD of JESUS, here mystically & most truly shed before Thee. With all the affection of my Soul, O LORD, I offer up to Thee this adorable Sacrifice, in union with that Divine Intention with which my Blessed SAVIOUR offered it up to Thee, when He instituted It, before His Passion, in the Upper Chamber; & when, after His Agony, He consummated It on the shameful, yet most glorious Cross. What He did then & there, O my GOD, is done now & here; & for the selfsame end for which He did It, I offer up this Holy Oblation, by the hands of Thy Priest, to Thy Divine Majesty, with the special Intention of Thy Honour & greater Glory. I offer It up also, O Heavenly FATHER, in union with that sacred Intention, with which Thy Beloved SON, the Holy CHILD JESUS, offers Himself to Thee, this day, upon the Altar of the Church. I sincerely, heartily, & with the greatest possible feelings of reverence

ence & devotion, join my sinful Soul with the Spotless SOUL of JESUS; I unite my frail body with the Sacred BODY of JESUS; I mingle my impure blood with the Cleansing & Lifegiving BLOOD of JESUS. With the Senses, Thoughts, Words, & Works of the Blessed JESUS, I make one my works, & words, & thoughts, & senses. I make my memory His Memory; my understanding His Understanding; my will His Wishes; my desires His Inclination. All that I am or have I unite with all that He has or is. I dedicate myself wholly to Thee, O Heavenly FATHER, in union with Thy JESUS. I give up myself entirely to Thee along with JESUS. I beseech Thee, by Thy Adorable Self, to accept of me in Mercy for the sake of Thy JESUS. And I pray Thee, grant me Thy Grace, that I may be constantly employed in doing Thy Blessed Will, & in advancing Thy greater Glory.

Finally, I offer up to Thee this most Holy Sacrifice, in commemoration of all the painful Sufferings & bitter Passion of Thy Well-beloved SON. Behold Him, O my GOD, in the Garden of Gethsemane, in His Agony & Bloody Sweat. See Him in the House of Annas, in the Palace of Caiaphas, blindfolded, buffeted, spit upon, smitten with impious hands, with every indignity offered to His Sacred Person. See Him bound to the Pillar, & scourged in a most cruel & ignominious way. See Him crowned with a Crown of Thorns; holding a Reed as a sceptre; clothed in White & Purple; & insulted & mocked as a pretended King. Behold, Him, O FATHER Almighty, laden with the heavy Cross. Behold Him nailed thereto; stripped to the gaze of all; raised between Heaven & earth, & hanging there three livelong hours, in agony of pain, abandoned by men,

forsaken

forsaken even of Thee; until, of His own free-will, & crying with a loud & supernatural Voice, He yielded up the Ghost. O LORD my GOD, I offer up to Thee this most Holy Victim, Present upon the Altar, in commemoration of all these dreadful Sufferings & afflictions of my JESUS: of His Passion, Agony, & Death; & of His glorious Resurrection & Ascension. And in union with all, I offer up to Thee my Soul & body; & I dedicate myself & all that I have, or am, or shall be, to Thy Service, to be continually employed therein, to do, to suffer, & to undergo whatsoever seems good unto Thee.

Eucharistic Prayers.

I. Most Merciful FATHER, look down from Thy Sanctuary, the Heaven of heavens, & behold this spotless Victim which our great High Priest, Thy SON JESUS CHRIST, the SAVIOUR of the world offers to Thee for the sins of His brethren, & be merciful to our numberless iniquities; for the voice of the BLOOD of our LORD calleth to Thee from the Cross. This is my justification, & sanctification, & propitiation. Turn away Thy Face from my sins, & look upon the Face of Thine Anointed; for I offer to Thee His merits, & I have all my confidence centred in Him. And forasmuch as Thou hast willed me, unworthy though I am, to be a partaker of this great Feast, Thou wilt not of Thy Love reject me coming to Thee with Thy most Divine gifts, so that not presumptuously drawing nigh to Thy Glory, I who wait for Thee may be worthy of the protection of Thine Only-begotten SON, & the
Illumi-

Illumination of Thy HOLY SPIRIT, & praying for all, may be heard for all, Thou being my helper, O my GOD, the FATHER of Mercies, Who with the same Thy SON, in the Unity of the same HOLY SPIRIT, livest & reignest world without end.

II. Almighty & Everlasting GOD, Preserver of Souls, & Redeemer of the world, most graciously behold me Thy servant, prostrate before Thy Majesty; & most graciously look on the Sacrifice which I have joined in offering to the honour of Thy Name, for the Salvation of the Faithful, both living & departed, & for my sins & offences. Take away Thine Anger far from me, & give me Thy Grace & Mercy. Open to me the gates of Paradise, mightily deliver me from all evils, & in Thy Clemency pardon whatsoever I have committed by my offences, & so make me to persevere in this life in Thy Commandments, that I may become worthy to be united to the band of the Elect by Thy Goodness, O my GOD, Whose blessed Name, Honour, & Kingdom remaineth for ever & ever.

III. O LORD, Who blessest those who bless Thee, & sanctifiest all who put their trust in Thee, save Thy People, & bless Thine Inheritance, & guard & protect Thy Spouse the Church. Sanctify those who love the beauty of Thy House. Grant them glory by Thy Divine Power, & forsake not those who hope in Thee, O GOD. Give aid, health, & consolation to the sick. Give peace to those who are travelling. Rule the weather. Bless the fruits of the earth. Keep in peace the world, churches, kings, priests, & all Thy people. Grant rest to the faithful departed, & remember those who have offered gifts, & those for whom they have been offered. Save those who are in

any

any trouble & diſtreſs, & grant us Thy Grace evermore.

IV. I give Thee thanks, O LORD JESUS CHRIST, for Thine ineffable Love which led Thee when about to depart out of this world unto the FATHER, to prepare a Table for me in Thy Sweetneſs, a Table truly royal, containing within itſelf every delight; the moſt precious Table of Thy BODY & BLOOD, to repleniſh my Soul with marrow & fatneſs, & to ſtrengthen my weakneſs with the ſecret infuſion of Thy Suſtenance. And whence is this to me, moſt glorious SON of GOD, that Thou ſhouldeſt permit me to come to Thee, & to feaſt with others who come to Thy Table? And would that free from every fault, cleanſed from every ſtain, purged from every vice, & purified from all inordinate affections, I might be perfectly without blemiſh, & ſo be able to approach to this moſt Heavenly Feaſt, burning with love, ſnow-white with innocence, & adorned with the beauty of Holineſs. But foraſmuch as I am moſt miſerable, devoid of all graces, I beſeech Thee, moſt Bountiful SAVIOUR, Whoſe Love is boundleſs, & Whoſe Goodneſs is infinite, to waſh my Soul in Thy BLOOD, & to make it whiter than ſnow, to clothe it with Thy Righteouſneſs, & to warm it with that fire of moſt ardent Love which conſtrained Thee when about to depart from us to inſtitute this life-giving Feaſt. And foraſmuch as I am a partaker with all them that fear Thee, I offer to Thee the devotion & purity of all the Prieſts & of all the faithful who, on this day, celebrate & communicate. I offer the graces & the holy deſires of all the righteous from the beginning to the end of the world, to Thee, moſt Sweet JESUS, Preſent in the Holy Sacrament, namely, the

Grace

Grace of the most strong faith & lively appreciation of those things which are to be believed concerning this greatest Mystery; the Grace of most perfect charity & closest communion with Thee; of hunger & vehement desire for receiving Thee, Who art All-goodness; of child-like confidence & hope in Thy Mercy set forth in so wondrous a manner; of zeal for the glory of GOD, & love of one's neighbour, for whose Salvation this Sacrifice is offered; of wonderment at so great condescension & so deep humility; of joy & gladness in Thee & for Thee; of praise, gratitude, adoration, & devotion. These & other graces I offer to Thee, to make up for my own insufficiency, & I will do this with the fullest purpose of promoting Thy Honour & Glory, for Thou art worthy. Accept, O LORD, this my desire, & do not Thou reject me from Thy Table, until satiated with this Food, & renewed with this Drink, I may have life, & have it more abundantly, here & for ever.

V. I adore Thee, & give Thee thanks, O most Kind LORD JESU CHRIST, Who hast deigned to admit me, a sinner, to the life-giving Banquet of Thy Holy Table. Alas, woe to me, that I have so unworthily joined in offering up this Holy Sacrifice. Have mercy on me, & pardon me. I commend what I have done to Thy Divine HEART, to be amended & corrected. Accept, I beseech Thee, these Sacred Mysteries of Thy BODY & BLOOD which I have offered to the eternal Glory of Thy Name, & to my salvation & that of all the faithful, living & departed. Receive this most Holy Sacrament as a full Satisfaction for all my sins & negligences, & for the sins of the whole world. By It, O my GOD, sanctify Thy Church, & take from it all scandals & divisions, that it may become one Fold under one Shepherd. By It pour out Thy Mercy on all nations which know Thee not, & enlighten their hearts, that they may know & love Thee. By It bring to nought the counsels of the wicked, that they harm not Thy Kingdom, nor the furtherance of Thy Glory. Grant to Bishops, Priests, & Deacons Thy Divine Love, that they may duly perform their duties; to Kings, Princes, & all Magistrates, wisdom, that they may faithfully administer justice & follow after peace; & to all Thy people give Thy Blessing. Grant to those in the agony of death true contrition & love for Thee; to my enemies, Thy Love & Sweetness; to my friends, benefactors, & relations, Thy Love; & direct us & all our doings, that Thy Worship may ever & everywhere flourish & increase; to the Souls of the faithful departed, those chiefly which need our prayers, or for whom I am bound to pray, grant eternal Rest, a merciful Judgment, & a blessed Enjoyment of Thee.

VI. Come, LORD JESUS, the only Salvation of my Soul, & pour into my bosom the abundance of Thy Sweetness, that I may love nothing, desire nothing beside Thee. Come, my Joy & Gladness; come, my Hope & Strength, for with Thee are riches & glory. Thou art my Life & Consolation, Thou art a Paradise of Delight. And would that by Thy Coming to me all the sweets of the world might be turned into bitterness, that united to Thee in this Heavenly Banquet, I may never be separated from Thee through all Eternity. In vain might I spend my money for that which is not bread, & my labour for that which satisfieth not, although I might provide myself with all the dainties of Egypt, if this Bread were wanting, which affords sweetness to Kings, & I were destitute of Thy Wine,

whose

whose richness far surpasses all the good things of this world. And whence is this so great good to me, that I should be thought worthy to feast with Thee, O King of terrible majesty, I, Thy most unworthy servant, who daily sin, & wretched that I am, persist in evil? But infinitely greater is Thy Mercy than my vileness, & Thou, my most sweet Refreshment, transformest me into another man, & by the Word of Thy Power healest all mine infirmities. To Thee therefore do I come, confiding in Thy Love, & trusting in Thee I shall never be confounded. Stablish the Soul of Thy servant, & supply what Thou seest to be wanting in me. O most Loving SAVIOUR, Who hast deigned to call all men unto Thee, saying—*Come unto Me, all that travail & are heavy laden, & I will refresh you.* Refresh me with Thyself, for in Thee are all the delights of Heaven, which flow forth from the full river of the gladness of GOD in so great abundance that all who worthily draw nigh to Thee may be fulfilled with joy unspeakable. Knit my Soul closely to Thyself, & make me worthy to sit down at Thy most Heavenly Table, in the garment of holiness required by Thee, & may enjoy the fruition of Thy Present GODHEAD.

VII. O most Patient LORD JESU, Who art wounded in Thy Sacrament with such countless insults, I detest & abhor from all my heart all those injuries inflicted on Thee by sinners. I beseech Thee by the ineffable Love of Thy most Sacred Heart, that Thou mayest be a Propitiation for them before Thine Almighty FATHER. Kindle in me, O JESU, by the presence of Thy BODY, a burning zeal, that I may be able to bewail the sacrileges committed against Thee, & by Thy Goodness avert those about to be committed.

VIII. O

VIII. O Lord God Almighty, Father of our Lord Jesus Christ, Thy Blessed Son, Who heareth all who rightly pray to Thee, Who knowest the prayers also of those who are silent; we give Thee thanks that Thou hast counted us worthy to partake of these Thy sacred Mysteries, Which Thou hast given to us, that we may be fully persuaded of those things which we have well known, because the Name of Christ has been called over us. O Thou Who hast separated us from the council of the ungodly, make us one with those who have been consecrated to Thee; confirm us in the truth by the Coming of Thy Holy Spirit; reveal what we are ignorant of, supply what is lacking in us, assure us of what we know. Preserve Thy Priests blameless in Thy Worship; preserve Kings in peace, Magistrates in justice, the weather in serenity, fruits in abundance, the world by Thine Almighty Providence; quiet the people who delight in war, convert the erring, sanctify Thy people, preserve virgins, keep the married in their faith; strengthen the chaste, strengthen the weak, give sight to the blind, & gather us all into the Kingdom of Heaven in Christ Jesus our Lord.

From Ancient Sources.

Edited by the Rev. Orby Shipley, M.A.

Second Thousand, small 8vo.   Price 2s. 6d. Cloth.

The Divine Liturgy: *A Manual of Devotions for the Sacrament of the Altar; for daily use.*

Contents:—Office in Preparation, with Hymns: the Divine Liturgy, or the Order of Offering the Sacrifice and Administering the Sacrament of the Altar, according to the Use of the English Church; with Devotions for those who Communicate, and for those who Worship without Communicating; including Meditation, Acts of Christian Virtue, Prayers for the Invocation, Colloquies, Considerations, Acts of Oblation, Reparation, Adoration, and Intercession; Conferences, Contemplations, Hymns, Thanksgivings and Devotions after Holy Communion: Office in Thanksgiving, with Hymns: Eucharistic Litanies: Eucharistic Hymns.

Second Thousand, small 8vo.   Price 2s. 6d. Cloth.

The Daily Sacrifice: *A Manual of Spiritual Communion; for daily use.*

Contents:—Office in Preparation; Direction of the Intention; Acts of Contrition, Faith, Hope, Love, and Humility; Prayer for Grace; Memorial of the Passion; and Hymn; for every day in the week: Meditations, Conferences, Soliloquies, Sentiments, and Affections for daily use; and Collects for the Seasons.

Royal 18mo.   Toned paper and plate.   Price 2s. Cloth.

Rodriguez: *A Treatise of the Virtue of Humility.* Abridged from the Spanish. Part I.

Contents:—Of the Excellency of the Virtue of Humility, and in what it consists; Of the First Degree of Humility; Of the Second Degree of Humility; and of the means by which Humility is acquired, and the Benefits of it.

Part II. in preparation.

Royal 18mo. Toned paper and plate. Price 3s. Cloth.

LUIS DE GRANADA: *CONSIDERATIONS ON MYSTERIES OF THE FAITH.* Newly translated and abridged from the original Spanish.

Containing Meditations on Self-Knowledge; Life; Death; Judgment; Hell; Heaven; and the Divine Blessings.

Royal 18mo. Toned paper and plate. Price 2s. Cloth.

DAILY MEDITATIONS FOR A MONTH: *On some of the more moving Truths of Christianity, in order to determine the Soul to be in earnest in the Love and Service of her GOD.*

Contents:—Of our first Beginning and last End; Redemption and Holy Baptism; Sin, Repentance, Confession and Absolution; Death, Judgment, Hell, and Heaven; Divine Love, and Love to our Neighbour; &c.

Small 8vo. Toned paper and plates. Price 3s. 6d. Cloth.

DAILY MEDITATIONS FOR THE SEASONS: *Advent to Trinity.*

Containing Short Meditations for every day for the Seasons of Advent, Christmas, Epiphany, Septuagesima, Lent, Easter, Ascension, Whitsun-tide, and Trinity Sunday, on the Incarnation, Nativity, Infancy, Ministry, Passion, Resurrection, and Ascension, &c. of our Blessed Lord.

Small 8vo. Price 2s. 6d. Cloth.

EUCHARISTIC LITANIES.

Containing, amongst others, Litanies from the Paris Missal, the Mozarabic Liturgy, the Sarum Offices, a Copto-Arabic MS., the Armenian, an Ethiopic MS., Sacramentary of S. Gregory, the Eucharistic Month, the Imitation, the Paradise, the Cœleste Palmetum, &c.

8vo. Price 4d.

LUIS DE GRANADA: *THE RESURRECTION: An Easter Sermon.* Translated from the Spanish.

LONDON: MASTERS, ALDERSGATE STREET,
AND 78, NEW BOND STREET.

www.ingramcontent.com/pod-product-compliance
Lightning Source LLC
Chambersburg PA
CBHW020334240426
43673CB00039B/937